Transcendentalism in New England

Pennsylvania Paperbacks

Pennsylvania Paperbacks continued

TRANSCENDENTALISM

IN NEW ENGLAND

A HISTORY

Octavius Brooks Frothingham

Introduction by Sydney E. Ahlstrom
Yale University

UNIVERSITY OF PENNSYLVANIA PRESS

PHILADELPHIA

M73

Introduction © Copyright 1959 by Sydney E. Ahlstrom
First published in 1876 by G. P. Putnam's Sons, New York
Library of Congress catalog card number: 59–10346

First PENNSYLVANIA PAPERBACK edition 1972

ISBN: 0–8122–1038–7

Printed in the United States of America

CONTENTS

VIII.

INTRODUCTION

BY SYDNEY E. AHLSTROM

Octavius Brooks Frothingham's history of *Transcendentalism in New England* deserves to have again the wide audiences it enjoyed before its long retreat into scholarly sanctuaries and out-of-the-way secondhand bookstores. Instead of merely being honored through repeated citation as "indispensable on its subject," the book may now be read by the students and general readers for whom it was intended. One does not even have to speak with delicate concern of issuing *another* such volume. The remarkable fact of the matter is that aside from Perry Miller, whose massive anthology *The Transcendentalists* is invaluable, Frothingham is the only discerning, sensitive, and critical writer who has turned his hand to writing an integrated account of the Transcendental movement as a whole: its philosophical background and place in the history of thought, its central message, its practical accomplishments, and its major leaders. There have, of course, been innumerable biographies and studies on Emerson alone, not to mention Thoreau, Alcott, Brownson, Parker, and many of the others. Individually and collectively the writings of these prolific reformers have been anthologized over and over again. Specialized monographs have considered the movement from many angles. In greater or lesser detail, in the popular vein or the academic, the movement has also been covered in countless literary, religious, philosophical, and general histories, some of which (notably those of Parrington and Van Wyck Brooks) have almost become American institutions. The terrain of Transcendentalism, we may say, has been microscopically analyzed as well as aerially photographed; but only very rarely has it been viewed, as in this volume, at intermediate range where both detail and larger context could be examined.

The place of Frothingham's *Transcendentalism in New England* is securely fixed, however, by still other considerations. First published in 1876, it is the only serious historical effort written by a man deeply involved in the movement who yet lived long enough beyond its golden season to view matters with circumspection and a degree of objectivity. Frothingham produced an unduplicable account that speaks from within the Transcendental impulse. He expresses its central concerns as one who had felt them. He catches the fervor of its reforming spirit. He realizes its essentially religious character and shares its deep dissatisfaction with the old order in the churches. To a remarkable extent, he presents the movement's own estimate of its significance and place in the complex currents of philosophy, social reform, Christian theology, and New England Puritanism. After the passing of his generation the opportunity for writing such a work was gone forever.

Octavius Brooks Frothingham was born in 1822 into the benign luminescence of Boston's most respected parsonage. His father, Nathaniel Langdon Frothingham (1793–

1870), was a sensitive, scholarly man who, like the First
Church to which he ministered, had moved into Unitarianism gradually and peaceably. Though living during tumultuous years, he had performed his pastoral duties in a
quiet, devoted way and avoided theological controversy.
His deepest pleasures were in communing on literary and
humane topics with his ministerial brethren, with choice
spirits among his distinguished parishioners, or with such
leading literary lights of the city as George Ticknor and
William Hickling Prescott. The meditation and translation
of Rome's classic poetry was a favorite avocation—one
which he memorialized in the "Christian" name of his
distinguished son. He married the daughter of the prominent Boston merchant, Peter Chardon Brooks, and with
her provided their five children with a home in which personal virtue was encouraged, intellectual and artistic sensibility cultivated, and native ability allowed to flower.

Octavius, the second child, was prepared for college at
the Boston Latin School and graduated from Harvard College with high honors in 1843. He entered the Harvard
Divinity School as a matter of course and completed the
broad and uncontroversial course of studies conducted by
Professors George Rapall Noyes and Convers Francis at
a time when student life there was still "half-monastic"
and when "a tone of old-fashioned piety" pervaded the
institution.[1]

His first pastorate was in the handsome North Church
in Salem, but at a time (1847–55) when the old splendor
of the city had departed. "Derby Street was deserted, the
great warehouses were tenements for laborers . . . . the

commerce, owing mainly to the shallowness of the water in the harbor, had gone to Boston and New York." Yet opportunities for cultured conversation abounded. He was happily married to Caroline Curtis of Boston. "There were long hours for studying; the parish work was not hard"; and a peaceful ministry was in prospect.

Peace and complacency were soon shattered, however, by the accumulating force of the antislavery impulse: "Garrison, the incarnate conscience, was enunciating the moral law . . . the intrepid Phillips was throwing the light of history on politics . . . Parker was proclaiming the absolute justice. . . ." Perhaps most decisively of all, "the spiritual philosophy [of Transcendentalism] was in the air; its ideas were unconsciously absorbed by the enthusiastic spirits. They constituted the life of the period; they were a light to such as dwelt in darkness or sat under the shadow of death"—or to restless men like Frothingham who were not born to dispense platitudes in a quiet backwater. A minor parochial duty brought him into personal contact with Theodore Parker whose Boston ministry was then at its height; and Parker's passionate witness swept the young minister into discipleship. "Then, if ever, we ascended the Mount of Vision. I was brought into close communion with living men, the most living of the time. . . . It was a great experience; not only was religion brought face to face with ethics, but it was identified with ethics."

Confronted by these exciting forces, Frothingham's conservative Unitarianism yielded to radical Transcendentalism. The traditional message, offices, and ordinances of the instituted Church lost their appeal. Moreover, because Parker and the slavery question had brought about his conversion—rather than Emerson's Divinity School Address of a decade before—the stimulus had been intensely moral, not spiritual. The response, in turn, was activistic rather than mystical. But the immediate effect was the same. His relatives and friends on Beacon Street—as Henry Adams reported—were distressed and scandalized. So were his parishioners; and soon the young man was looking for a new church.

Change of location came through a call to a Unitarian Society being organized in Jersey City by a small group of New York businessmen who lived in that quiet and substantially rural town of twenty thousand people. Again "there was wealth [and] culture" in his congregation, but more important for him was their "interest in social matters." They built a meetinghouse and gave their minister complete freedom to express his radicalism. To the great ease of Frothingham's conscience, they also allowed him to forego observance of the Lord's Supper. "[The church] was scarcely Unitarian, not even Christian in a technical sense or in any other but a broad moral signification. It was Theism founded on the Transcendental philosophy, a substitute for the authority of Romanism and of Protestantism."

But Jersey City was likewise too isolated a place for an ambitious reformer. It was valuable, perhaps, as a place to reform his churchmanship and theology, but no final theater of activity. The opportunity for a larger work was soon provided in New York, to which he moved in 1859, having been invited and encouraged to form a Third (and uptown) Unitarian Society there. He had no more than arrived when John Brown raided Harpers Ferry; then came the War, the tumult of the "conscription riots," and the long task of upholding the moral basis of a moral war. "Full justice has never been done," he would say much later, "to those who were obliged to stay at home and uphold this feature."

During the first years the new Society met in a rented hall, but in 1863 a church building was erected on 40th Street. Frothingham had occasion to taste the fruits of radicalism when not one of his brethren in the New York and Brooklyn Unitarian ministry appeared for the dedication. He persevered, however, and his congregation of civic-minded and rationalistically inclined men and women grew in strength—and radicalism. By 1869 his views and the character of the Society had so far changed that the church building was sold. Lyric Hall, a dance hall on 6th Avenue between 40th and 41st Streets, became the new seat of his Independent Liberal Church. For the man who was increasingly regarded as the inheritor of Parker's mantle, the location must have aroused many memories of Parker's lectures in the Boston Melodeon and Music Hall. Nor was Frothingham much less successful. Over six hundred people, many of them prominent in the city's public, business, and cultural affairs, attended his weekly lectures. In 1875 the Society moved again, to the more spacious elegance of the new Masonic Hall on 6th Avenue and 23rd Street. Here he addressed the largest Sunday audience in the city with an oratorical power unequaled in a Unitarian pulpit since his uncle Edward Everett, had retired from the ministry. But Frothingham ended his New York labors four years later, in the spring of 1879, after which the Society was disbanded and its membership dispersed.

He had, of course, been involved in other less localized institutions, most notably the Free Religious Association, a loose federation of religious radicals, most of them Unitarians who in 1865 had been virtually excluded from the National Unitarian Conference. Their purpose was to promote the free and scientific discussion of religion through public meetings and the printed word. Frothingham was president of the Association from its founding in 1867 until 1878, by which time it had lost its springtime fervor and was foundering on the rocks of excessive individualism.

Whether he was preaching at Lyric Hall or addressing a Boston conclave of the Free Religious Association, Frothingham's religious and ethical message was positive, confident, and evocatively expressed. Neither his cultivated manner and aristocratic bearing nor his preference for traditional ways of life nor his fundamental disinclination for drastic action was set aside; yet the mark of Darwin and Spencer was upon him. Repeatedly and with increasing force he documented his transition from Transcendentalism to what he called Rationalism: "the scientific view . . . succeeded to the transcendental, and I began to walk by knowledge, steadily and surely, but not buoyantly any more." He stated his views most systematically in *The Religion of Humanity,* first published in 1872 but kept in

print through successive editions and widely read for
several decades. The volume revealed a positivistic but
undogmatic "scientific theism" wherein the transcendental
intuitions were seen as remnants of authoritarianism.
Man's faith, he insisted, should be in "essential human
nature." Christ was the symbol of the "Messiah cradled in
the bosom of every man." In this Messiah he rested hopes
that could hardly be said to lack buoyancy:

> There will be no more intellectual superciliousness or
> spiritual contempt, no more assumption of infallibility. . . .
> With mingled pride and humility, earnest minds will address
> themselves to their task of enlightening themselves and man-
> kind. . . . The great prayer will be for the Spirit of Truth,
> that shall lead them a little way further towards all truth.
> (*The Religion of Humanity,* pp. 338–39)

New York, however, was not destined to be the scene of
Frothingham's last efforts to lead men "further towards all
truth." That city was still alien ground for a Bostonian and
especially alien to a born traditionalist whose most cherished associations were rooted in the sacred precincts of
Boston, Cambridge, and Concord. Frothingham had in fact
already made a vicarious return to these haunts and to his
earlier enthusiasms with biographies of Parker (1874) and
Gerrit Smith (1877) and the history of *Transcendentalism
in New England* (1876). What remained was the final act
of homage: the return to his native city and a life of retro-
spective literary endeavor.

According to Frothingham's own explanation, his retirement from active work for the free religious cause was
"due entirely to my ill health." Easily detected, however,

are his recoil from the baffling problems of urbanism and inchoate doubts about the "clerical profession" itself. As he confided to Francis E. Abbot, his ally in many radical battles, he longed for "the quiet ways of culture." On returning to Boston, therefore, he gave rein to his conservative tendencies and, to the irritation of old comrades, even resumed his place at First Church on Sunday mornings. Most importantly he devoted his attention to the primary components of his own intellectual and moral heritage. His mind had always been immensely absorptive, his reading vast and endless, his didactic impulse very strong. Given his sentimental temperament, it was almost inevitable that he would turn his very considerable powers for lucid, felicitous expression toward "filiopietistic" tasks. To the volumes written during his later New York years he added a biography of *George Ripley* for the American Men of Letters Series (1882), a long *Memoir of William Henry Channing* (1886), a nostalgic but discerning account of *Boston Unitarianism* (1890) into which he wove the life of his father, several biographical memoirs for the Massachusetts Historical Society, and finally his autobiographical *Reflections and Impressions* (1891). He died in 1895.

Frothingham's mature philosophical position gave him a conception of historical reality highly conducive to a durable interpretation of intellectual movements. Never lost to his mind was the spiritual dimension of human history which the post-Kantian idealists had so profoundly stressed. (His warm appreciation for their efforts can be seen in the first five chapters of the present volume.) He was likewise a legatee of the historical renaissance which sprang from this same general movement. Beyond a lively interest in historical narrative, moreover, Frothingham, like almost any philosophically inclined American in the later nineteenth century, had also absorbed much Hegelian influence. (See pp. 43 ff. below.) History, to him, was of the essence of things: the prime category was not Being, but Becoming. Historical Reason was a throned monarch: Ferdinand Christian Baur, David Friedrich Strauss, Victor Cousin, and Ernest Renan were his heroes. (See pp. 186, 61.) Finally he belonged to the generation that felt the influence of William Graham Sumner and the new science of sociology. "Social Darwinism" accentuated his historical emphasis. Continuity, process, struggle, environment, and the evolutionary concept of social progress became tools of interpretation.

Frothingham announced his primary principle of analysis and told the spirit of his approach to history in the opening paragraph of *The Religion of Humanity:*

It is admitted truth now, that the thought of a period represents the life of the period, and affects that life by its reaction on it; and therefore he who would move strongly straightforward must move with its providential current. It is not ours to remould the age, to recast it, to regenerate it, to cross it or struggle with it, but *to penetrate its meaning, enter into its temper, sympathize with its hopes, blend with its endeavors, helping it by helping its development and saving it by fostering the best elements of its growth.* The interior spirit of any age is the spirit of God; and no faith can be living that has that spirit against it; no Church can be strong except in that alliance. The life of the time appoints the creed of the time and modifies the establishment of the time. [Italics added.]

The doctrinaire elements in such a statement stand out clearly. But in the last instance Frothingham knew that every philosophical system, every *Weltanschauung,* every "admitted truth," would pass away. Historicism had him in its firm grip; and whether or not it provided a viable philosophy of life, we are deeply indebted to it for the zest and method it gave to his historical endeavor. The italicized phrases in the quotation above suggest the spirit of his approach to Transcendentalism, and explain his success.

Needless to say, much new primary material has become available during the fourscore years since Frothingham wrote. An immense amount of detailed research has been done, and new critical perspectives have been brought to bear on the Transcendentalist literature and activity—indeed, since then "American literature," "American intellectual history," and "American Studies" have come into existence as departments of academic concern. Partly because of these developments, Frothingham's attitude toward the early Unitarians may now seem unduly condescending, his critique of Transcendental philosophy somewhat presumptuous, and his slighting of Thoreau ill-considered. Yet these are all illuminating and representative qualities that accentuate the book's importance. A continuous historical process had in fact alienated his entire intellectual community from both catholic and protestant orthodoxy, including the "Christian Unitarianism" of his father's generation. The positivistic phase in philosophy, stemming from Comte, Mill, and Spencer, and appropriated by Frothingham, was notoriously blind to the noninductive and "unscientific" modes of apprehending reality which Transcendentalists often championed. As for the ignoring of Thoreau, it was probably the common tendency until more modern criticism began to impose its values on the Transcendental movement. The text of the present volume, therefore, has been left precisely as it was published, even to including the full text of Emerson's Lord's Supper sermon of 1832 which Frothingham placed within his final chapter. It would be sheer pedantry to renovate his treatise with a network of "corrective" footnotes and editorial interpolations.[2]

What an editor and admirer of this work has most to lament is the lapse of Frothingham's highly developed dramatic sense which allowed him to open the book with several pages of metaphysical discussion seemingly designed to frighten away unphilosophic readers, and to close it without adequate summation or final estimate. Yet the interested reader can easily transcend the former deficiency and after reading the book he will be challenged to amend the latter for himself. In the process he will probably discover that even Frothingham's uncertainty about the movement's lasting significance illustrates the difficulties created for all latter-day Transcendentalists by evolutionary naturalism, the continued advance of science, and the rise of urban industrial civilization. The peculiarly inconclusive final chapter which Frothingham provided for this, his most significant literary achievement, becomes a symbol of the Transcendental crisis and a major commentary on his state of mind. He could see the spiritual unity of the Unitarianism of his father and the advocacy of Emerson; he could also appreciate the tensions between them. But he was far less capable of drawing the lines down into his own epoch. In this sense his experience parallels *The Education of Henry Adams:* "The two-thousand-years' failure of Christianity roared upward from Broadway, and no Constantine the Great was in sight." Given a little more candor, he might have admitted with his cousin "that nine-tenths of his acquired education was useless, and the other tenth harmful," that he would have to "begin again from the beginning." [3] By the same token *Transcendentalism in New England* bears a certain resemblance to Adams' *Mont-Saint-Michel and Chartres.* In both works the milieu under inspection is conceived as splendidly creative—integrated, vital, and wonderful in itself—but in neither case is its relation to subsequent developments, above all to the present, seen as anything but ambiguous and problematic.

This book is, nevertheless, a virtual demonstration of how exciting ideas and the history of ideas can be; and not only for an individual mind, but for a region, a country, and a civilization. The study of both the Lockean and the Kantian traditions has been immeasurably deepened since 1876, but nobody has done better than Frothingham in presenting the dramatic and dynamic consequences of Kant's "Copernican revolution." The same could be said of our concrete knowledge of Herder, Schleiermacher, Carlyle, and Coleridge; yet here again Frothingham performs an immense service by exhibiting the historical significance and the peculiar power of the religious and ethical revolution embodied in their new conceptions of the spiritual life and the theological task. The whole matter is lifted out of the realm of academic distinctions, metaphysical debating, and doctrinal fine-points.

Transcendental ideas and transvaluations would, in the course of the century, win many victories far beyond the Concord-Boston coterie here dealt with: the universities and seminaries, nearly all religious movements (Protestant, Catholic, and Jewish), the very ideals and behavior of the American people—all would be altered, enlivened, and directed toward new channels of interest. Yet many of these later developments would be staid and formal, or gradual and covert; their significance would often be veiled. With the Transcendentalists, on the other hand, the veil was for a time enthusiastically cast off. The full potential impact of the century's great intellectual revolution stood revealed; and Frothingham's history is a monument to the earnestness and vitality of that collective performance. In fact, what Frothingham did and what his whole life prepared him to do, was to leave an account of Transcendentalism which would itself be a kind of sunset classic of the movement.

Yale University

[1] My quotations in this Introduction, unless otherwise identified, are from Frothingham's *Recollections and Impressions, 1822–1890* (New York: Putnam's, 1891). On his life see also the following brief memoirs: G. H. Genzmer in the *Dictionary of American Biography* (1932); P. R. Frothingham in *Heralds of a Liberal Faith*, 3 vols., S. A. Eliot, ed. (Boston: Amer. Unitarian Assn., 1910), III, 120–27; and J. P. Quincy in *Proceedings of the Mass. Historical Soc.*, 2nd Series, X (1895–96), 507–39. On his intellectual background see Stow Persons, *Free Religion, An American Faith* (New Haven: Yale University Press, 1947); Richard Hofstadter, *Social Darwinism in American Thought, 1860–1915* (Philadelphia: University of Pennsylvania Press, 1944; Ralph H. Gabriel, *The Course of American Democratic Thought*, 2nd ed. (New York: Ronald Press, 1956); Frank H. Foster, *The Modern Movement in American Theology* (New York: Fleming H. Revell, 1939); and Howard B. Radest, *Toward Common Ground: The Story of the Ethical Socialists in the United States* (New York: Frederick Ungar, 1969).

[2] For further reading on the Unitarian background of Frothingham and of New England Transcendentalism, see Conrad Wright, *The Beginnings of Unitarianism in America* (Boston: Beacon Press, 1955); Daniel W. Howe, *The Unitarian Conscience: Harvard Moral Philosophy, 1805–1861* (Cambridge: Harvard University Press, 1970); John W. Chadwick, *Old and New Unitarian Belief* (Boston, 1894), and two biographies that complement Frothingham's account of his own father: William C. Gannett, *Ezra Stiles Gannett* (Boston, 1875) and William Henry Channing, *William Ellery Channing* (Boston, 1880).

As introductions and bibliographical guides to the vast literature on the Transcendental movement see the following: Perry Miller, *The Transcendentalists: An Anthology* (Cambridge: Harvard University Press, 1950); George Hochfield, ed., *Selected Writings of the American Transcendentalists* (New York: New American Library Signet Classic, 1966); William R. Hutchison, *The Transcendentalist Ministers: Church Reform in the New England Renaissance* (New Haven: Yale University Press, 1959); F. O. Matthiessen, *American Renaissance: Art and Expression in the Age of Emerson and Whitman* (New York: Oxford University Press, 1941); Kenneth W. Cameron, *The Transcendental Climate* (Hartford: Transcendental Books, 1963), and Robert E. Spiller *et al., Literary History of the United States*, 3 vols. (New York: Macmillan Co., 1948), especially the bibliography edited by T. C. Johnson; and Harry H. Clark, ed., *Transitions in American Literary History* (Durham, N.C.: Duke University Press, 1954).

On the European background and the larger Romantic movement, which Frothingham properly emphasizes, see the following, several of which serve excellently as guides to the larger literature: John

B. Halsted, ed., *Romanticism: Definition, Explanation, and Evaluation* (Boston: D. C. Heath Co., 1965) ; John B. Halsted, ed., *Romanticism* (New York: Harper & Row Torchbook, 1969), an anthology of primary writings ; Lilian R. Furst, *Romanticism in Perspective: A Comparative Study of the Romantic Movements in England, France and Germany* (London: Macmillan Co., 1969) ; Harald Höffding, *History of Modern Philosophy* (New York: Macmillan Co., 1900) ; Wilhelm Windelband, *A History of Philosophy* (New York: Macmillan Co., 1901) ; Josiah Royce, *The Spirit of Modern Philosophy* (Boston: Houghton Mifflin Co., 1893) ; Henry D. Aiken, ed., *The Age of Ideology* (Boston: Houghton Mifflin Co., 1956) ; H. R. Mackintosh, *Types of Modern Theology* (London: Nisbet, 1937) ; E. C. Moore, *History of Christian Thought since Kant* (New York: Scribners, 1912) ; Arthur C. McGiffert, *The Rise of Modern Religious Ideas* (New York: Macmillan Co., 1915) ; Karl Barth, *Protestant Thought: from Rousseau to Ritschl* (New York: Harper & Row, 1959) ; and *Studies in Romanticism,* a quarterly journal published by the Graduate School, Boston University.

The following works suggest the nature and importance of European and American interrelationships, in New England and elsewhere: Henry A. Pochmann, *German Culture in America: Philosophical and Literary Influences, 1600–1900* (Madison: University of Wisconsin Press, 1957) ; Stanley M. Vogel, *German Literary Influences on the American Transcendentalists* (New Haven: Yale University Press, 1955) ; Walter L. Leighton, *French Philosophers and New England Transcendentalism* (Charlottesville: University of Virginia Press, 1908) ; Loyd D. Easton, *Hegel's First American Followers: The Ohio Hegelians* (Athens: Ohio University Press, 1966) ; James H. Nichols, *Romanticism in American Theology: Nevin and Schaff at Mercersberg* (Chicago: University of Chicago Press, 1961) ; Jurgen Herbst, *The German Historical School in American Scholarship* (Ithaca: Cornell University Press, 1965) ; and Jerry W. Brown, *The Rise of Biblical Criticism in America, 1800–1870:* The New England Scholars (Middletown, Conn.: Wesleyan University Press, 1969).

Autobiographies, journals, and biographies are essential to an understanding of this time of spiritual stress and intellectual transition. New works or editions in this area, as well as topical monographs, continue to provide bibliographical guidance to recent scholarship on both general and specific matters.

A great many of the works listed above have been published in paper or new reprint editions, often by a different publishing company ; and still others are constantly appearing. The reader, therefore, is referred to catalogues of paperbacks and other books in print, available at any good bookseller.

[3] *The Education of Henry Adams* (Boston: Houghton Mifflin, 1918), pp. 253, 499–500.

PREFACE.

WHILE we are gathering up for exhibition before other nations, the results of a century of American life, with a purpose to show the issues thus far of our experiment in free institutions, it is fitting that some report should be made of the influences that have shaped the national mind, and determined in any important degree or respect its intellectual and moral character. A well-considered account of these influences would be of very great value to the student of history, the statesman and philosopher, not merely as throwing light on our own social problem, but as illustrating the general law of human progress. This book is offered as a modest contribution to that knowledge.

Transcendentalism, as it is called, the transcendental movement, was an important factor in American life. Though local in activity, limited in scope, brief in duration, engaging but a comparatively small number of individuals, and passing over the upper regions of the mind, it left a broad and deep trace on ideas and institutions. It affected thinkers, swayed politicians, guided moralists, inspired philanthropists, created reformers. The moral enthusiasm of the last generation, which broke out with such prodigious power in the holy war against slavery; which uttered such earnest protests against capital punishment, and the wrongs inflicted on women; which made such passionate pleading in behalf of the weak, the injured, the disfranchised of every race and condition; which exalted humanity above institutions, and proclaimed the inherent worth of man,—owed, in larger measure than is suspected, its glow and force to the Transcendentalists. This, as a fact of history, must be admitted, as well by those who judge the movement unfavorably, as by its friends. In the view of history, which is concerned with causes and effects in their large human relations, individual opinions on them are of small moment. It was once the fashion—and still in some quarters it is the fashion—to laugh at Transcendentalism as an incomprehensible folly, and to call Transcendentalists visionaries. To admit that they were, would not alter the fact that they exerted an influence on their generation. It is usual with critics of a cold, unsympathetic, cynical cast, to speak of Transcendentalism as a form of sentimentality, and of Transcendentalists as sentimentalists; to decry enthusiasm, and deprecate the mischievous effects of feeling on the discussion of social questions. But their disapproval, however just and wholesome, does not abolish the trace which moral enthusiasm, under whatever name these judges may please to put upon it, has left on the social life of the people. Whether the impression was for evil or for good, it is there, and equally significant for warning or for commendation.

As a form of mental philosophy Transcendentalism may have had its day; at any rate, it is no longer in the ascendant, and at present is manifestly on the decline, being suppressed by the philosophy of experience, which, under different names, is taking possession of the speculative world. But neither has this consideration weight in deciding its value as an element in progress. An unsound system requires as accurate a description and as severe an analysis as a sound one; and no speculative prejudice should interfere with the most candid acknowledgment of its importance. Error is not disarmed or disenchanted by caricature or neglect.

To those who may object that the writer has too freely indulged his own prejudices in favor of Transcendentalism and the Transcendentalists, and has transgressed his own rules by writing a eulogy instead of a history, he would reply, that in his belief every system is best understood when studied sympathetically, and is most fairly interpreted from the inside. We can know its purposes only from its friends, and we can do justice to its friends only when we accept their own account of their beliefs and aims. Rénan somewhere says, that in order to judge a faith one must have confessed it and abandoned it. Such a rule supposes sincerity in the confession and honesty in the withdrawal; but with this qualification its reasonableness is easily admitted. If the result of such a verdict prove more favorable than the polemic would give, and more cordial than the critic approves, it may not be the less just for that.

The writer was once a pure Transcendentalist, a warm sympathizer with transcendental aspirations, and an ardent admirer of transcendental teachers. His ardor may have cooled ; his faith may have been modified ; later studies and meditations may have commended to him other ideas and methods ; but he still retains enough of his former faith to enable him to do it justice. His purpose has been to write a history ; not a critical or philosophical history, but simply a history ; to present his subject with the smallest possible admixture of discussion, either in defence or opposition. He has, therefore, avoided the metaphysics of his theme, by presenting cardinal ideas in the simplest statement he could command, and omitting the details that would only cumber a narrative. Sufficient references are given for the direction of students who may wish to become more intimately acquainted with the transcendental philosophy, but an exhaustive survey of the speculative field has not been attempted. This book has but one purpose—to define the fundamental ideas of the philosophy, to trace them to their historical and speculative sources, and to show whither they tended. If he has done this inadequately, it will be disclosed ; he has done it honestly, and as well as he could. In a little while it will be difficult to do it at all ; for the disciples, one by one, are falling asleep ; the literary remains are becoming few and scarce ; the materials are disappearing beneath the rapid accumulations of thought ; the new order is thrusting the old into the background ; and in the course of a few years, even they who can tell the story feelingly will have passed away. The author, whose task was gladly accepted, though not voluntarily chosen, ventures to hope, that if it has not been done as well as another might have done it, it has not been done so ill that others will wish he had left it untouched.

O. B. F.

New York, April 12, 1876.

TRANSCENDENTALISM

I.

BEGINNINGS IN GERMANY

To make intelligible the Transcendental Philosophy of the last generation in New England it is not necessary to go far back into the history of thought. Ancient idealism, whether Eastern or Western, may be left undisturbed. Platonism and neo-Platonism may be excused from further tortures on the witness stand. The speculations of the mystics, Romanist or Protestant, need not be re-examined. The idealism of Gale, More, Pordage, of Cudworth and the later Berkeley, in England, do not immediately concern us. We need not even submit John Locke to fresh cross-examination, or describe the effect of his writings on the thinkers who came after him.

The Transcendental Philosophy, so-called, had a distinct origin in Immanuel Kant, whose "Critique of Pure Reason" was published in 1781, and opened a new epoch in metaphysical thought. By this it is not meant that Kant started a new movement of the human mind, proposed original problems, or projected issues never contemplated before. The questions he discussed had been discussed from the earliest times, and with an acumen that had searched out the nicest points of definition. In the controversy between the Nominalists, who maintained that the terms used to describe abstract and universal ideas were mere names, designating no real objects and corresponding to no actually existing things, and the Realists, who contended that such terms were not figments of language, but described realities, solid though incorporeal, actual existences, not to be confounded with visible and transient things, but the essential types of such,—the scholastics of either school discussed after their manner, with astonishing fulness and subtlety, the matters which later metaphysicians introduced. The modern Germans revived in substance the doctrines held by the Realists. But the scholastic method, which was borrowed from the Greeks, lost its authority when the power of Aristotle's name declined, and the scholastic discussions, turning, as they signally did, on theological questions, ceased to be interesting when the spell of theology was broken.

Between the schools of Sensationalism and Idealism, since John Locke, the same matters were in debate. The Scotch as well as the English metaphysicians dealt with them according to their genius and ability. The different writers, as they succeeded one another, took up the points that were presented in their day, exercised on them such ingenuity as they possessed, and in good faith made their several contributions to the general fund of thought, but neglected to sink their shafts deep enough below the surface to strike new springs of water.

Locke's Essay on the Human Understanding was an event that made an epoch in philosophy, because its author, not satisfied to take up questions where his predecessors had left them, undertook an independent examination of the Human Mind, in order to ascertain what were the conditions of its knowledge. The ability with which this attempt was made, the entire sincerity of it, the patient watch of the mental operations, the sagacity that followed the trail of lurking thoughts, surprised them in their retreats, and extracted from them the secret of their combinations, fairly earned for him the title of " Father of Modern Psychology." The intellectual history of the race shows very few such examples of single-minded fidelity combined with rugged vigor and unaffected simplicity. With what honest directness he announced his purpose ! His book grew out of a warm discussion among friends, the fruitlessness whereof convinced him that both sides had taken a wrong course ; that before men set themselves upon inquiries into the deep matters of philosophy " it was necessary to examine our own abilities, and see what objects our understandings were or were not fitted to deal with." To do this was his purpose.

" First," he said, " I shall inquire into the original of those ideas, notions, or whatever else you please to call them, which a man observes and is conscious to himself he has in his mind ; and the ways whereby the understanding comes to be furnished with them.

" Secondly, I shall endeavor to show what knowledge the understanding hath by those ideas, and the certainty, evidence and extent of it.

" Thirdly, I shall make some inquiry into the nature and grounds of faith or opinion ; whereby I mean that assent which we give to any proposition as true, of whose truth we have yet no certain knowledge ; and we shall have occasion to examine the reasons and degrees of assent."

Locke did his work well: how well is attested by the excitement it caused in the intellectual world, the impulse it gave to speculation in England and on the continent of Europe, the controversies over the author's opinions, the struggle of opposing schools to secure for their doctrines his authority, the appreciation on one side, the depreciation on the other, the disposition of one period to exalt him as the greatest discoverer in the philosophic realm, and the disposition of another period to challenge his title to the name of philosopher. The " Essay " is a small book, written in a homely, business-like style, without affectation of depth or pretence of learning, but it is charged with original mental force. Exhaustive it was not ; exhaustive it could not have been. The England of the seventeenth century was not favorable to original researches in that field. The " Essay " was planned in 1670, completed after considerable interruptions in 1687, and published in 1690. To one acquainted with the phases through which England was passing at that period, these dates will tell of untoward influences that might account for graver deficiencies than characterize Locke's work. The scholastic philosophy, from which Locke broke contemptuously away at Oxford, seems to have left no mark on his mind ; but the contemptuous revulsion, and the naked self-reliance in which the sagacious but not generously cultivated man found refuge, probably roughened his speculative sensibility, and made it impossible for him to handle with perfect nicety the more delicate facts of his science. It can hardly be claimed that Locke was endowed by nature with philosophical genius of the highest order. While at Oxford he abandoned philosophy, in disgust, for medicine, and distinguished himself there by judgment and penetration. Subsequently his attention was turned to politics, another pursuit even less congenial with introspective genius. These may not be the reasons for the " incompleteness " which so glowing a eulogist as Mr. George H. Lewes admits in the " Essay ; " but at all events, whatever the reasons may have been, the incompleteness was felt ; the debate over the author's meaning was an open proclamation of it ; at the close of a century it was apparent to at least one mind that Locke's attempt must be repeated, and his work done over again more carefully

The man who came to this conclusion and was moved to act on it was IMMANUEL KANT, born at Königsberg, in Prussia, April 22d, 1724 ; died there February 12th, 1804. His was a life rigorously devoted to philosophy. He inherited from his parents a love of truth, a respect for moral worth, and an intellectual integrity which his precursor in England did not more than match. He was a master in the sciences, a proficient in languages, a man cultivated in literature, a severe student, of the German type, whose long, calm, peaceful years were spent in meditation, lecturing and writing. He was dis· tinguished as a mathematician before he was heard of as a philosopher, having predicted the existence of the planet Uranus before Herschel discovered it. He was forty-five years old when these trained powers were brought to bear on the study of the human mind : he was sixty-seven when the meditation was ended. His book, the " Critique of Pure Reason," was the result of twelve years of such thinking as his genius and training made him capable of. In what spirit and with what hope he went about his task, appears in the Introduction and the Prefaces to the editions of 1781 and 1787. In these he frankly opens his mind in regard to the condition of philosophical speculation. That condition he describes as one of saddest indifference. The throne of Metaphysics was vacant, and its former occupant was a wanderer, cast off by the meanest of his subjects. Locke had started a flight of hypotheses, which had frittered his force away and made his effort barren of definite result. Theories had been suggested and abandoned ; the straw had been thrashed till only dust remained ; and unless a new method could be hit on, the days of mental philosophy might be considered as numbered. The physical sciences would take advantage of the time, enter the deserted house, secure possession, and set up their idols in the ancient shrine.

These sciences, it was admitted, command and deserve unqualified respect. To discover the secret of their success Kant passed in review their different systems, examined them in respect to their principles and conditions of progress, with a purpose to know what, if any, essential difference there might be between them and the metaphysics which had from of old claimed to be, and had the name of being, a science. Logic, mathematics, physics, are sciences : by virtue of what inherent peculiarity do they claim superior right to that high appellation? Intellectual philosophy has always been given over to conflicting parties. Its history is a history of controversies, and of controversies that resulted in no triumph for either side, established no doctrine, and reclaimed no portion of truth. Material philosophy has made steady advances from the beginning ; its disputes have ended in demonstrations, its contests have resulted in the establishment of legitimate authority : if its progress has been slow it has been continuous ; it has never receded ; and its variations from a straight course are insignificant when surveyed from a position that commands its whole career.

Since Aristotle, logic has, without serious impediment or check, matured its rules and methods. Holding the same cardinal positions as in Aristotle's time, it has simply made them stronger, the rules being but interpretations of rational principles, the methods following precisely the indications of the human mind, which from the nature of the case remain always the same.

The mathematics, again, have had their periods of uncertainty and conjecture. But since the discovery of the essential properties of the triangle, the career has been uninterrupted. The persistent study of constant properties, which were not natural data, but mental conceptions formed by the elimination of variable quantities, led to results which had not to be abandoned.

It was the same with physics. The physics of the ancients were heaps of conjecture. The predecessors of Galileo abandoned conjecture, put themselves face to face with Nature, observed and classified phenomena, but possessed no method by which their labors could be made productive of cumulative results. But after Galileo had experimented with balls of a given weight on an inclined plane, and Torricelli had pushed upward a weight equal to a known column of water, and Stahl had reduced metals to lime and transformed lime back again into metal, by the addition and subtraction of certain parts, the naturalists carried a torch that illumined their path. They perceived that reason lays her own plans, takes the initiative with her own principles, and must compel nature to answer her questions, instead of obsequiously following its leading-string. It was discovered that scattered observations, made in obedience to no fixed plan, and associated with no necessary law, could not be brought into systematic form. The discovery of such a law is a necessity of reason. Reason presents herself before nature, holding in one hand the principles which alone have power to bring into order and harmony the phenomena of nature ; in the other hand grasping the results of experiment conducted according to those principles. Reason demands knowledge of nature, not as a docile pupil who receives implicitly the master's word, but as a judge who constrains witnesses to reply to questions put to them by the court. To this attitude are due the happy achievements in physics; reason seeking—not fancying—in nature, by conformity with her own rules, what nature ought to teach, and what of herself she could not learn. Thus physics became established upon the solid basis of a science, after centuries of error and groping.

Wherefore now, asks Kant, are metaphysics so far behind logic, mathematics, and physics? Wherefore these heaps of conjecture, these vain attempts at solution? Wherefore these futile lives of great men, these abortive flights of genius? The study of the mind is not an arbitrary pursuit, suggested by vanity and conducted by caprice, to be taken up idly and relinquished at a moment's notice. The human mind cannot acquiesce in a judgment that condemns it to barrenness and indifference in respect to such questions as God, the Soul, the World, the Life to Come; it is perpetually revising and reversing the decrees pronounced against itself. It must accept the conditions of its being.

From a review of the progress of the sciences it appeared to Kant that their advance was owing to the elimination of the variable elements, and the steady contemplation of the elements that are invariable and constant, the most essential of which is the contribution made by the human mind. The laws that are the basis of logic, of the mathematics, and of the higher physics, and that give certitude to these sciences, are simply the laws of the human mind itself. Strictly speaking, then, it is in the constitution of the human mind, irrespective of outward objects and the application of principles to them, that we must seek the principle of certitude. Thus far in the history of philosophy the human mind had not been fairly considered. Thinkers had concerned themselves with the objects of knowledge, not with the mind that knows. They had collected facts ; they had constructed systems ; they had traced connections ; they had drawn conclusions. Few had defined the relations of knowledge to the human mind. Yet to do that seemed the only way to arrive at certainty, and raise metaphysics to the established rank of physics, mathematics, and logic.

Struck with this idea, Kant undertook to transfer contemplation from the objects that engaged the mind to the mind itself, and thus start philosophy on a new career. He meditated a fresh departure, and proposed to effect in metaphysics a revolution parallel with that which Copernicus effected in astronomy. As Copernicus, finding it impossible to explain the movements of the heavenly bodies on the supposition of their turning round the globe as a centre, bethought him to posit the sun as a centre, round which the earth with other heavenly bodies turned—so Kant, perceiving the confusion that resulted from making man a satellite of the external world, resolved to try the effect of placing him in the position of central sway. Whether this pretension was justifiable or not, is not a subject of inquiry here. They may be right who sneer at it as a fallacy ; they may be right who ridicule it as a conceit. We are historians, not critics

That Kant's position was as has been described, admits of no question. That he built great expectations on his method is certain. He anticipated from it the overthrow of hypotheses which, having no legitimate title to authority, erected themselves to the dignity of dogmas, and assumed supreme rank in the realm of speculation. That it would be the destruction of famous demonstrations, and would reduce renowned arguments to naught, might be foreseen ; but in the place of pretended demonstrations, he was confident that solid ones would be established, and arguments that were merely specious would give room to arguments that were profound. Schools might be broken up, but the interests of the human race would be secured. At first it might appear as if cardinal beliefs of mankind must be menaced with extinction as the ancient supports one after another fell ; but as soon as the new foundations were disclosed it was anticipated that faith would revive, and the great convictions would stand more securely than ever. Whatever of truth the older systems had contained would receive fresh and trustworthy authentication ; the false would be expelled ; and a method laid down by which new discoveries in the intellectual sphere might be confidently predicted.

In this spirit the author of the transcendental philosophy began, continued, and finished his work.

The word " transcendental " was not new in philosophy. The Schoolmen had used it to describe whatever could not be comprehended in or classified under the so-called categories of Aristotle, who was the recognized prince of the intellectual world. These categories were ten in number : Quantity, Quality, Relation, Action, Passion, The Where, The When, Position in Space, Possession, Substance. Four things were regarded by the Schoolmen as transcending these mental forms—namely, Being, Truth, Unity, Goodness. It is hardly necessary to say that the Transcendentalism of modern times owed very little to these distinctions, if it owed anything to them. Its origin was not from thence ; its method was so dissimilar as to seem sharply opposed.

The word "transcendental" has become domesticated in science. Transcendental anatomy inquires into the idea, the original conception or model on which the organic frame of animals is built, the unity of plan discernible throughout multitudinous genera and orders. Transcendental curves are curves that cannot be defined by algebraic equations. Transcendental equations express relations between transcendental qualities. Transcendental physiology treats of the laws of development and function, which apply, not to particular kinds or classes of organisms, but to all organisms. In the terminology of Kant the term "transcendent" was employed to designate qualities that lie outside of all "experience," that cannot be brought within the recognized formularies of thought, cannot be reached either by observation or reflection, or explained as the consequences of any discoverable antecedents. The term "transcendental" designated the fundamental conceptions, the universal and necessary judgments, which transcend the sphere of experience, and at the same time impose the conditions that make experience trib·

utary to knowledge. The transcendental philosophy is the philosophy that is built on these necessary and universal principles, these primary laws of mind, which are the ground of absolute truth. The supremacy given to these and the authority given to the truths that result from them entitle the philosophy to its name. "I term all cognition transcendental which concerns itself not so much with objects, as with our mode of cognition of objects so far as this may be possible à priori. A system of such conceptions would be called Transcendental Philosophy."

II.

TRANSCENDENTALISM IN GERMANY.

KANT.

THERE is no call to discuss here the system of Kant, or even to describe it in detail. The means of studying the system are within easy reach of English readers.* Our concern is to know the method which Kant employed, and the use he made of it, the ground he took and the positions he held, so far as this can be indicated within reasonable compass, and without becoming involved in the complexity of the author's metaphysics. The Critique of Pure Reason is precisely what the title imports—a searching analysis of the human mind ; an attempt to get at the ultimate grounds of thought, to discover the à priori principles. "Reason is the faculty which furnishes the principles of cognition à priori. Therefore pure reason is that which contains the principles of knowing something, absolutely à priori. An organon of pure reason would be a summary of

---

* See Kant's Critique of Pure Reason, London, 1838 ; Morell's History of Modern Philosophy ; Chalybäus' Historical Development of Speculative Philosophy from Kant to Hegel ; Lewes' Biographical History of Philosophy ; Cousin's Leçons, Œuvres, 1ere série, vol. 5, give a clear account of Kant's philosophy.

these principles, according to which all pure cognition à priori can be obtained, and really accomplished. The extended application of such an organon would furnish a system of pure reason."

The problem of modern philosophy may be thus stated : *Have we or have we not ideas that are true of necessity, and absolutely ? Are there ideas that can fairly be pronounced independent in their origin of experience, and out of the reach of experience by their nature ?* One party contended that all knowledge was derived from experience ; that there was nothing in the intellect that had not previously been in the senses : the opposite party maintained that a portion, at least, of knowledge came from the mind itself ; that the intellect contained powers of its own, and impressed its forms upon the phenomena of sense. The extreme doctrine of the two schools was represented, on the one side by the materialists, on the other by the mystics. Between these two extremes various degrees of compromise were offered.

The doctrine of innate ideas, ascribed to Descartes,— though he abandoned it as untenable in its crude form, —affirmed that certain cardinal ideas, such as causality, infinity, substance, eternity, were native to the mind, born in it as part of its organic constitution, wholly independent therefore of experience. Locke claimed for the mind merely a power of reflection by which it was able to modify and alter the material given by the senses, thus exploding the doctrine of innate ideas.

Leibnitz, anxious to escape the danger into which

Descartes fell, of making the outward world purely
phenomenal, an expression of unalterable thought, and
also to escape the consequences of Locke's position
that all knowledge originates in the senses, suggested
that the understanding itself was independent of experience, that though it did not contain ideas like a vessel,
it was entitled to be called a power of forming ideas,
which have, as in mathematics, a character of necessary
truths.   These necessary laws of the understanding,
which experience had no hand in creating, are, according to Leibnitz, the primordial conditions of human
knowledge.

Hume, taking Locke at his word, that all knowledge
came from experience, that the mind was a passive
recipient of impressions, with no independent intellectual substratum, reasoned that mind was a fiction ; and
taking Berkeley at his word that the outward world had
no material existence, and no *apparent* existence except
to our perception, he reasoned that matter was a fiction.
Mind and matter both being fictions, there could be no
certain knowledge ; truth was unattainable ; ideas were
illusions.   The opposing schools of philosophers annihilated each other, and the result was scepticism.

Hume started Kant on his long and severe course of
investigation, the result of which was, that neither of the
antagonist parties could sustain itself : that Descartes
was wrong in asserting that such abstract ideas as causality, infinity, substance, time, space, are independent of
experience, since without experience they would not
exist, and experience takes from them form only ; that

Locke was wrong in asserting that all ideas originated in experience, and were resolvable into it, since the ideas of causality, substance, infinity and others certainly did not so originate, and were not thus resolvable. It is idle to dispute whether knowledge comes from one source or another—from without through sensation, or from within through intuition; the everlasting battle between idealism and realism, spiritualism and materialism, can never result in victory to either side. Mind and universe, intelligence and experience, suppose each other; neither alone is operative to produce knowledge. Knowledge is the product of their mutual co-operation. Mind does not originate ideas, neither does sensation impart them. Object and subject, sterile by themselves, become fruitful by conjunction. There are not two sources of knowledge, but one only, and that one is produced by the union of the two apparent opposites. Truth is the crystallization, so to speak, that results from the combined elements.

Let us follow the initial steps of Kant's analysis. Mind and Universe—Subject and Object—Ego and Non-ego, stand opposite one another, front to front. Mind is conscious only of its own operations: the subject alone considers. The first fact noted is, that the subject is sensitive to impressions made by outward things, and is receptive of them. Dwelling on this fact, we discover that while the impressions are many in number and of great variety, they all, whatever their character, fall within certain inflexible and unalterable conditions—those of space and time—which must, therefore, be regarded as pre-established forms of sensibility. " Time is no empirical conception which can be deduced from experience. Time is a necessary representation which lies at the foundation of all intuitions. Time is given à priori. In it alone is any reality of phenomena possible. These disappear, but it cannot be annihilated." So of space. " Space is an intuition, met with in us à priori, antecedent to any perception of objects, a pure, not an empirical intuition." These two forms of sensibility, inherent and invariable, to which all experiences are subject, are primeval facts of consciousness. Kant's argument on the point whether or no space and time have an existence apart from the mind, is interesting, but need not detain us.

The materials furnished by sensibility are taken up by the understanding, which classifies, interprets, judges, compares, reduces to unity, eliminates, converts, and thus fashions sensations into conceptions, transmutes impressions into thoughts. Here fresh processes of analysis are employed in classifying judgments, and determining their conditions. All judgments, it is found, must conform to one of four invariable conditions. I. Quantity, which may be subdivided into unity, plurality, and totality : the one, the many, the whole. II. Quality, which is divisible as reality, negation, and limitation : something, nothing, and the more or less. III. Relation, which also comprises three heads : substance and accident, cause and effect, reciprocity, or action and reaction. IV. Modality, which embraces the possible and the impossible, the existent and the non-existent, the necessary and the contingent. These categories, as they were called, after the terminology of Aristotle, were supposed to exhaust the forms of conception.

Having thus arrived at conceptions, thoughts, judgments, another faculty comes in to classify the conceptions, link the thoughts together, reduce the judgments to general laws, draw inferences, fix conclusions, proceed from the particular to the general, recede from the general to the particular, mount from the conditioned to the unconditioned, till it arrives at ultimate principles. This faculty is reason,—the supreme faculty, above sensibility, above understanding. Reason gives the final generalization, the idea of a universe comprehending the infinitude of details presented by the senses, and the worlds of knowledge shaped by the understanding; the idea of a personality embracing the infinite complexities of feeling, and gathering under one dominion the realms of consciousness; the idea of a supreme unity combining in itself both the other ideas; the absolute perfection, the infinite and eternal One, which men describe by the word God.

Here the thinker rested. His search could be carried no further. He had, as he believed, established the independent dominion of the mind, had mapped out its confines, had surveyed its surface; he had confronted the idealist with the reality of an external world; he had confronted the sceptic with laws of mind that were independent of experience; and, having done so much, he was satisfied, and refused to move an inch beyond the ground he occupied. To those who applied to him

for a system of positive doctrines, or for ground on
which a system of positive doctrines could be erected,
he declined to give aid. The mind, he said, cannot go
out of itself, cannot transgress its own limits. It has
no faculty by which it can perceive things *as they are ;*
no vision to behold objects corresponding to its ideas ;
no power to bridge over the gulf between its own consciousness and a world of realities existing apart from
it. Whether there be a spiritual universe answering to
our conception, a Being justifying reason's idea of supreme unity, a soul that can exist in an eternal, supersensible world, are questions the philosopher declined
to discuss. The contents of his own mind were revealed
to him, no more. Kant laid the foundations, he built no
structure. He would not put one stone upon another ;
he declared it to be beyond the power of man to put
one stone upon another. The attempts which his
earnest disciples—Fichte, for example—made to erect
a temple on his foundation he repudiated. As the
existence of an external world, though a necessary
postulate, could not be demonstrated, but only logically affirmed ; so the existence of a spiritual world
of substantial entities corresponding to our conceptions, though a necessary inference, could only be
logically affirmed, not demonstrated. Our idea of
God is no proof that God exists. That there is a
God may be an irresistible persuasion, but it can be
nothing more ; it cannot be knowledge. Of the facts
of consciousness, the reality of the ideas in the mind,
we may be certain ; our belief in them is clear and

solid ; but from *belief* in them there is no bridge to *them*.

Kant asserted the veracity of consciousness, and demanded an absolute acknowledgment of that veracity. The fidelity of the mind to itself was a first principle with him. Having these ideas, of the soul, of God, of a moral law ; being certain that they neither originated in experience, nor depended on experience for their validity, that they transcended experience altogether—man was committed to an unswerving and uncompromising loyalty to himself. His prime duty consisted in deference to the integrity of his own mind. The laws of his intellectual and moral nature were inviolable. Whether there was or was not a God ; whether there was or was not a substantial world of experience where the idea of rectitude could be realized, the dictate of duty justified, the soul's affirmation of good ratified by actual felicity,— rectitude was none the less incumbent on the rational mind ; the law of duty was none the less imperative ; the vision of good none the less glorious and inspiring. Virtue had its principle in the constitution of the mind itself. Every virtue had there its seat. There was no sweetness of purity, no heroism of faith, that had not an abiding-place in this impregnable fortress.

Thus, while on the speculative side Kant came out a sceptic in regard to the dogmatic beliefs of mankind, on the practical side he remained the fast friend of intellectual truth and moral sanctity. Practical ethics never had a more stanch supporter than Immanuel Kant. If a man cannot pass beyond the confines of his own mind, he has, at all events, within his own mind a temple, a citadel, a home.

The " Critique of Pure Reason " made no impression on its first appearance. But no sooner was its significance apprehended, than a storm of controversy betrayed the fact that even the friends of the new teacher were less content than he was to be shut up in their own minds. The calm, passionless, imperturbable man smoked his pipe in the peace of meditation ; eager thinkers, desirous of getting more out of the system than its author did, were impatient at his backwardness, and made the intellectual world ring with their calls to improve upon and complete his task.

The publication of Kant's great work did not put an end to the wars of philosophy. On the contrary, they raged about it more furiously than ever. As the two schools found in Locke fresh occasion for renewing their strife under the cover of that great name, so here again the latent elements of discord were discovered and speedily brought to the surface. The sceptics seized on the sceptical bearings of the new analysis, and proceeded to build their castle from the materials it furnished ; the idealists took advantage of the positions gained by the last champion, and pushed their lines forward in the direction of transcendental conquest. We are not called on to follow the sceptics, however legitimate their course, and we shall but indicate the progress made by the idealists, giving their cardinal principles, as we have done those of their master.

JACOBI.

The first important step in the direction of pure transcendentalism was taken by Frederick Henry Jacobi, who was born at Düsseldorf, January 25, 1743. He was a man well educated in philosophy, with a keen interest in the study of it, though not a philosopher by profession, or a systematic writer on metaphysical subjects. His position was that of a civilian who devoted the larger part of his time to the duties of a public office under the government. His writings consist mainly of letters, treatises on special points of metaphysical inquiry, and articles in the philosophical journals. His official position gave repute to the productions of his pen, and the circumstance of his being, not an amateur precisely, but a devotee of philosophy for the love of it and not as a professional business, imparted to his speculation the freshness of personal feeling. His ardent temperament, averse to scepticism, and touched with a mystical enthusiasm, rebelled against the formal and deadly precision of the analytical method, and sought a way out from the intellectual bleakness of the Kantean metaphysics into the sunshine and air of a living spiritual world. The critics busied themselves with mining and sapping the foundations of consciousness as laid by the philosopher of Königsberg, who, they complained, had been too easy in conceding the necessity of an outward world. Jacobi accepted with gratitude the intellectual basis afforded, and proceeded to erect thereupon his observatory for studying the heavens. Though not the originator of the

" Faith Philosophy," as it was called, he became the finisher and the best known expositor of it. " Since the time of Aristotle," he said, " it has been the effort of philosophical schools to rank direct and immediate knowledge below mediate and indirect ; to subordinate the capacity for original perception to the capacity for reflection on abstract ideas ; to make intuition secondary to understanding, the sense of essential things to definitions. Nothing is accepted that does not admit of being proved by formal and logical process, so that, at last, the result is looked for there, and there only. The validity of intuition is disallowed."

Jacobi's polemics were directed therefore against the systems of Spinoza, Leibnitz, Wolf—in a word against all systems that led to scepticism and dogmatism ; and his positive efforts were employed in constructing a system of Faith. His key-word was " Faith," by which he meant intuition, the power of gazing immediately on essential truth ; an intellectual faculty which he finally called Reason, by which supersensual objects become visible, as material objects become visible to the physical eye ; an inward sense, a spiritual eye, that " gives evidence of things not seen and substance to things hoped for ; " a faculty of vision to which truths respecting God, Providence, Immortality, Freedom, the Moral Law, are palpably disclosed. Kant had pronounced it impossible to prove that the transcendental idea had a corresponding reality as objective being. Jacobi declared that no such proof was needed ; that the reality was necessarily assumed. Kant had denied the existence of any faculty that could guarantee the existence of either a sensual or a supersensual world.   Jacobi was above all else certain that such a faculty there was, that it was altogether trustworthy, and that it actually furnished material for religious hope and spiritual life : the only possible material, he went on to say ; for without this capacity of intuition, philosophy could be in his judgment nothing but an insubstantial fabric, a castle in the air, a thing of definitions and terminologies, a shifting body of hot and cold vapor.

This, it will be observed, seemed a legitimate consequence of Kant's method.   Kant had admitted the subjective reality of sensible impressions, and had claimed a similar reality for our mental images of supersensible things. He allowed the validity *as conceptions*, the practical validity, of the ideas of God, Duty, Immortality.   Jacobi contended that having gone so far, it was lawful if not compulsory to go farther ; that the subjective reality implied an objective reality ; that the practical inference was as valid as any logical inference could be ; and that through the intuition of reason the mind was placed again in a living universe of divine realities.

Chalybäus says of Jacobi : '' With deep penetration he traced the mystic fountain of desire after the highest and best, to the point where it discloses itself as an immediate feeling in consciousness ; that this presentiment was nothing more than Kant said it was—a faint mark made by the compressing chain of logic, he would not allow ; he described it rather as the special endowment and secret treasure of the human mind, which he that

would not lose it must guard against the touch of evil-
minded curiosity ; for whoever ventures into this sanctuary with the torch of science, will fare as did the youth
before the veiled image at Sais." And again : " This
point, that a self-subsisting truth must correspond to the
conscious idea, that the subject must have an object
which is personal like itself, is the ore that Jacobi was
intent on extracting from the layers of consciousness :
he disclosed it only in part, but unsatisfactory as his exposition was to the stern inquisition of science, his purpose was so strong, his aim so single, we cannot wonder
that, in spite of the outcry and the scorn against his
' Faith or Feeling Philosophy,' his thought survived,
and even entered on a new career in later times. It
must, however, be confessed that instead of following up
his clue, speculative fashion, he laid down his undevel-
oped theorem as an essential truth, above speculation,
declaring that speculation must end in absolute idealism,
which was but another name for nihilism and fatalism.
Jacobi made his own private consciousness a measure
for the human mind." At the close of his chapter,
Chalybäus quotes Hegel's verdict, expressed in these
words : " Jacobi resembles a solitary thinker, who, in
his life's morning, finds an ancient riddle hewn in the
primeval rock ; he believes that the riddle contains a
truth, but he tries in vain to discover it. The day long
he carries it about with him ; entices weighty suggestions
from it ; displays it in shapes of teaching and imagery
that fascinate listeners, inspiring noblest wishes and anticipations : but the interpretation eludes him, and at

evening he lays him down in the hope that a celestial dream or the next morning's waking will make articulate the word he longs for and has believed in."

FICHTE.

The transcendental philosophy received from Jacobi an impulse toward mysticism. From another master it received an impulse toward heroism. This master was Johann Gottlieb Fichte, born at Rammenau, in Upper Lusatia, on the 19th of May, 1762. A short memoir of him by William Smith, published in 1845, with a translation of the "Nature of the Scholar," and reprinted in Boston, excited a deep interest among people who had neither sympathy with his philosophy nor intelligence to comprehend it. He was a great mind, and a greater character—sensitive, proud, brave, determined, enthusiastic, imperious, aspiring ; a mighty soul ; " a cold, colossal, adamantine spirit, standing erect and clear, like a Cato Major among degenerate men ; fit to have been the teacher of the Stoa, and to have discoursed of beauty and virtue in the groves of Academe ! So robust an intellect, a soul so calm, so lofty, massive, and immovable, has not mingled in philosophical discussion since the time of Luther. For the man rises before us amid contradiction and debate like a granite mountain amid clouds and winds. As a man approved by action and suffering, in his life and in his death, he ranks with a class of men who were common only in better ages than ours."

Thus wrote Thomas Carlyle of him more than a generation ago.

The direction given to philosophy by such a man could not but be decided and bold. His short treatises, all marked by intellectual power, some by glowing eloquence, carried his thoughts beyond the philosophical circle and spread his leading principles far beyond the usual speculative lines. " The Destination of Man," " The Vocation of the Scholar," " The Nature of the Scholar," " The Vocation of Man," " The Characteristics of the Present Age," " The Way towards the Blessed Life," were translated into English, published in the " Catholic Series " of John Chapman, and extensively read. The English reviewers helped to make the author and his ideas known to many readers.

The contribution that Fichte made to the transcendental philosophy may be described without using many words. He became acquainted with Kant's system in Leipsic, where he was teaching, in 1790. The effect it had on him is described in letters to his friends. To one he wrote : " The last four or five months which I have passed in Leipsic have been the happiest of my life ; and the most satisfactory part of it is, that I have to thank no man for the smallest ingredient in its pleasures. When I came to Leipsic my brain swarmed with great plans. All were wrecked ; and of so many soap-bubbles there now remains not even the light froth that composed them. This disturbed a little my peace of mind, and half in despair I joined a party to which I should long ere this have belonged. Since I could not alter my outward condition, I resolved on internal change. I threw myself into philosophy, and, as you know, the Kantean. Here I found the remedy for my ills, and joy enough to boot. The influence of this philosophy, the moral part of it in particular (which, however, is unintelligible without previous study of the ' Critique of Pure Reason '), on the whole spiritual life, and especially the revolution it has caused in my own mode of thought, is indescribable." To another he wrote in similar strain : " I have lived in a new world since reading the ' Critique of Pure Reason.' Principles I believed irrefragable are refuted; things I thought could never be proved—the idea of absolute freedom, of duty, for example—are demonstrated ; and I am so much the happier. It is indescribable what respect for humanity, what power this system gives us. What a blessing to an age in which morality was torn up by the roots, and the word duty blotted out of the dictionary!" To Johanna Rahn he expresses himself in still heartier terms : " My scheming mind has found rest at last, and I thank Providence that shortly before all my hopes were frustrated I was placed in a position which enabled me to bear the disappointment with cheerfulness. A circumstance that seemed the result of mere chance induced me to devote myself entirely to the study of the Kantean philosophy—a philosophy that restrains the imagination, always too strong with me, gives reason sway, and raises the soul to an unspeakable height above all earthly concerns. I have accepted a nobler morality, and instead of busying myself with outward things, I concern myself more with my own being. It has given me a peace such as I never before experienced ; amid uncertain worldly prospects I have passed my happiest days. It is difficult beyond all conception, and stands greatly in need of simplification. . . . The first elements are hard speculations, that have no direct bearing on human life, but their conclusions are most important for an age whose morality is corrupted at the fountain head ; and to set these consequences before the world would, I believe, be doing it a good service. I am now thoroughly convinced that the human will is free, and that to be happy is not the purpose of our being, but to deserve happiness." So great was Fichte's admiration of Kant's system, that he became at once an expositor of its principles, in the hope that he might render it intelligible and attractive to minds of ordinary culture.

Fichte considered himself a pure Kantean, perhaps the only absolutely consistent one there was ; and that he did so is not surprising ; for, in mending the master's positions, he seemed to be strengthening them against assault. He did not, like Jacobi, draw inferences which Kant had laboriously, and, as it seemed, effectually cut off ; he merely entrenched himself within the lines the philosopher of Königsberg had drawn. Kant had, so his critics charged, taken for granted the reality of our perceptions of outward things. This was the weak point in his system, of which his adversaries took advantage. On this side he allowed empiricism to construct his wall, and left incautiously an opening which the keen-sighted foe perceived at once. Fichte bethought him to fortify that point, and thus make the philosophy unassailable ; to take it, in fact, out of the category of a philosophical system, and give it the character of a science. To this end, with infinite pains and incredible labor, he tested the foundations to discover the fundamental and final facts which rested on the solid rock. The ultimate facts of consciousness were in question.

Fichte accepted without hesitation the confinement within the limits of consciousness against which Jacobi rebelled, and proceeded to make the prison worthy of such an occupant. The facts of consciousness, he admitted, are all we have. The states and activities of the mind, perceptions, ideas, judgments, sentiments, or by whatever other name they may be called, constitute, by his admission, all our knowledge, and beyond them we cannot go. They are, however, solid and substantial. Of the outward world he knew nothing and had nothing to say ; he was not concerned with that. The mind is the man ; the history of the mind is the man's history; the processes of the mind report the whole of experience ; the phenomena of the external universe are mere phenomena, reflections, so far as we know, of our thought ; the mountains, woods, stars, are facts of consciousness, to which we attach these names. To infer that they exist because we have ideas of them, is illegitimate in philosophy. The ideas stand by themselves, and are sufficient of themselves.

The mind is first, foremost, creative and supreme. It takes the initiative in all processes. He that assumes the existence of an external world does so on the author-

ity of consciousness.   If he says that consciousness compels us to assume the existence of such a world, that it
is so constituted as to imply the realization of its conception, still we have simply the fact of consciousness ;
power to verify the relation between this inner fact and
a corresponding physical representation, there is none.
Analyze the facts of consciousness as much as we may,
revise them, compare them, we are still within their
circle and cannot pass beyond its limit.   Is it urged that
the existence of an external world is a *necessary* postulate ?   The same reply avails, namely, that the idea of necessity is but one of our ideas, a conception of the mind,
an inner notion or impression which legitimates itself
alone.   Does the objector further insist, in a tone of ex-
asperation caused by what seems to him quibbling, that
in this case consciousness plays us false, makes a promise to the ear which it breaks to the hope—lies, in short ?
The imperturbable philosopher sets aside the insinua-
tion as an impertinence.   The fact of consciousness, he
maintains, stands and testifies for itself.   It is not answerable for anything out of its sphere.   In saying what
it does it speaks the truth ; the whole truth, so far as
we can determine.   Whether or no it is absolutely the
whole truth, the truth as it lies in a mind otherwise constituted, is no concern of ours.

The reasoning by which Fichte cut off the certainty of
a material world outside of the mind, told with equal
force against the objective existence of a spiritual world.
The mental vision being bounded by the mental sphere,
its objects being there and only there, with them we

must be content. The soul has its domain, untrodden forests to explore, silent and trackless ways to follow, mystery to rest in, light to walk by, fountains and floods of living water, starry firmaments of thought, continents of reason, zones of law, and with this domain it must be satisfied. God is one of its ideas; immortality is another; that they are anything more than ideas, cannot be known.

That the charge of atheism should be brought against so uncompromising a thinker, is a less grave imputation upon the discernment of his contemporaries than ordinarily it is. That he should have been obliged, in consequence of it, to leave Jena, and seek an asylum in Prussia, need not excite indignation, at least in those who remember his unwillingness or inability to modify his view, or explain the sense in which he called himself a believer. To " charge " a man with atheism, as if atheism were guilt, is a folly to be ashamed of; but to " class " a man among atheists who *in no sense* accepts the doctrine of an intelligent, creative Cause, is just, while language has meaning. And this is Fichte's position. In his philosophy there was no place for assurance of a Being corresponding to the mental conception. The word " God " with him expressed the category of the Ideal. The world being but the incarnation of our sense of duty, the reflection of the mind, the creator of it is the mind. God, being a reflection of the soul in its own atmosphere, is one of the soul's creations, a shadow on the surface of a pool. The soul creates; deity is created. This is not even ideal atheism, like that of Etienne

Vacherot ; it may be much nobler and more inspiring than the recognized forms of theism ; it is dogmatic or speculative atheism only : but that it is, and that it should confess itself. It was natural that Fichte, being perfect master of his thought, should disclaim and resent an imputation which in spirit he felt was undeserved. It was natural that people who were not masters of his thought, and would not have appreciated it if they had been, should judge him by the only definitions they had. Berkeley and Fichte stood at opposite extremes in their Idealism. Berkeley, starting from the theological conception of God, maintained that the outward world had a real existence in the supreme mind, being phenomenal only to the human. Fichte, starting from the human mind, contended that it was *altogether* phenomenal, the supreme mind itself being phantasmal.

How came it, some will naturally ask, that such a man escaped the deadly consequences of such resolute introspection ? Where was there the indispensable basis for action and reaction ? Life is conditioned by limitation ; the shore gives character to the sea ; the outward world gives character to the man, excites his energy, defines his aim, trains his perception, educates his will, offers a horizon to his hope. The outward world being removed, dissipated, resolved into impalpable thought, what substitute for it can be devised ? Must not the man sink into a visionary, and waste his life in dream ?

That Fichte was practically no dreamer, has already been said. The man who closed a severe, stately, and glowing lecture on duty with the announcement — it

was in 1813, when the French drums were rattling in the
street, at times drowning the speaker's voice—that the
course would be suspended till the close of the campaign,
and would be resumed, if resumed at all, in a free country, and thereupon, with a German patriot's enthusiasm,
rushed himself into the field—this man was no visionary,
lost in dreams. The internal world was with him a living world ; the mind was a living energy ; ideas were
things ; principles were verities ; the laws of thought
were laws of being. So intense was his feeling of the
substantial nature of these invisible entities, that the obverse side of them, the negation of them, had all the *vis
inertia*, all the objective validity of external things. He
spoke of "absolute limitations," "inexplicable limitations," against which the mind pressed as against palpa-
ble obstacles, and in pressing against which it acquired
tension and vigor. Passing from the realm of speculation into that of practice, the obstacles assumed the
attributes of powers, the impediments became foes,
to be resisted as strenuously as ever soldier opposed
soldier in battle. From the strength of this conviction
he was enabled to say : " I am well convinced that
this life is not a scene of enjoyment, but of labor and
toil, and that every joy is granted but to strengthen
us for further exertion ; that the control of our fate is
not required of us, but only our self-culture. I give
myself no concern about external things ; I endeavor to
be, not to *seem ;* I am no man's master, and no man's
slave."

Fichte was a sublime egoist. In his view, the mind

was sovereign and absolute, capable of spontaneous, self-determined, originating action, having power to propose its own end and pursue its own freely-chosen course ; a live intelligence, eagerly striving after self-development, to fulfil all the possibilities of its nature. Of one thing he was certain—the reality of the rational soul, and in that certainty lay the ground of his tremendous weight of assertion. His professional chair was a throne ; his discourses were prophecies ; his tone was the tone of an oracle. It made the blood burn to hear him ; it makes the blood burn at this distance to read his printed words. To cite a few sentences from his writings in illustration of the man's way of dealing with the great problems of life, is almost a necessity. The following often-quoted but pregnant passage is from " The Destination of Man : " " I understand thee now, spirit sublime ! I have found the organ by which to apprehend this reality, and probably all other. It is not knowledge, for knowledge can only demonstrate and establish itself ; every kind of knowledge supposes some higher knowledge upon which it is founded ; and of this ascent there is no end. It is faith, that voluntary repose in the ideas that naturally come to us, because through these only we can fulfil our destiny ; which sets its seal on knowledge, and raises to conviction, to certainty, what, without it, might be sheer delusion. It is not knowledge, but a resolve to commit one's self to knowledge. No merely verbal distinction this, but a true and deep one, charged with momentous consequences to the whole character. All conviction is of faith, and proceeds from the heart, not from the understanding. Knowing this, I will enter into no controversy, for I foresee that in this way nothing can be gained. I will not endeavor, by reasoning, to press my conviction on others, nor will I be discouraged if such an attempt should fail. My mode of thinking I have adopted for myself, not for others, and to myself only need I justify it. Whoever has the same upright intention will also attain the same or a similar conviction, and without it that is impossible. Now that I know this, I know also from what point all culture of myself and others must proceed ; from the will, and not from the understanding. Let but the first be steadily directed toward the good, the last will of itself apprehend the true. Should the last be exercised and developed, while the first remains neglected, nothing can result but a facility in vain and endless refinements of sophistry. In faith I possess the test of all truth and all conviction ; truth originates in the conscience, and what contradicts its authority, or makes us unwilling or incapable of rendering obedience to it, is most certainly false, even should I be unable to discover the fallacies through which it is reached. . . . . What unity, what completeness and dignity, our human nature receives from this view ! Our thought is not based on itself, independently of our instincts and inclinations. Man does not consist of two beings running parallel to each other ; he is absolutely one. Our entire system of thought is founded on intuition ; as is the heart of the individual, so is his knowledge."

" The everlasting world now rises before me more brightly, and the fundamental laws of its order are more clearly revealed to my mental vision. The will alone, lying hid from mortal eyes in the obscurest depths of the soul, is the first link in a chain of consequences that stretches through the invisible realm of spirit, as, in this terrestrial world, the action itself, a certain movement communicated to matter, is the first link in a material chain that encircles the whole system. The will is the effective cause, the living principle of the world of spirit, as motion is of the world of sense. The will is in itself a constituent part of the transcendental world. By my free determination I change and set in motion something in this transcendental world, and my energy gives birth to an effect that is new, permanent, and imperishable. Let this will find expression in a practical deed, and this deed belongs to the world of sense and produces effects according to the virtue it contains."

This is the stoical aspect of the doctrine. The softer side of it appears throughout the book that is entitled " The Way towards the Blessed Life." We quote a few passages from the many the eloquence whereof does no more than justice to the depth of sentiment :

" Full surely there is a blessedness beyond the grave for those who have already entered on it here, and in no other form than that wherein they know it here, at any moment. By mere burial man arrives not at bliss ; and in the future life, throughout its whole infinite range, they will seek for happiness as vainly as they sought it here, who seek it in aught else than that which so closely surrounds them here—the Infinite."

"Religion consists herein, that man in his own person, with his own spiritual eye, immediately beholds and possesses God. This, however, is possible through pure independent thought alone; for only through this does man assume real personality, and this alone is the eye to which God becomes visible. Pure thought is itself the divine existence; and conversely, the divine existence, in its immediate essence, is nothing else than pure thought."

"The truly religious man conceives of his world as action, which, because it is his world, he alone creates, in which alone he can live and find satisfaction. This action he does not will for the sake of results in the world of sense; he is in no respect anxious in regard to results, for he lives in action simply as action; he wills it because it is the will of God in him, and his own peculiar portion in being."

"As to those in whom the will of God is not inwardly accomplished,—because there is no inward life in them, for they are altogether outward,—upon them the will of God is wrought as alone it can be; appearing at first sight bitter and ungracious, though in reality merciful and loving in the highest degree. To those who do not love God, all things must work together immediately for pain and torment, until, by means of the tribulation, they are led to salvation at last."

Language like this from less earnest lips might be deceptive; but from the lips of a teacher like Fichte it tells of the solid grandeurs that faithful men possess in the ideal creations of their souls ; the habitableness of air-castles.

The chief sources from which the transcendental philosophy came from Germany to America have been indicated.   The traces of Jacobi and Fichte are broad and distinct on the mind of the New World.   Of Schelling little need be said, for his works were not translated into English, and the French translation of the " Transcendental Idealism " was not announced till 1850, when the movement in New England was subsiding.   His system was too abstract and technical in form to interest any but his countrymen.   Coleridge was fascinated by it, and yielded to the fascination so far as to allow the thoughts of the German metaphysician to take possession of his mind ; but for Coleridge, indeed, few English-speaking men would have known what the system was.   Transcendentalism in New England was rather spiritual and practical than metaphysical.   Jacobi and Fichte were both ; it can scarcely be said that Schelling was either.   His books were hard ; his ideas underwent continual changes in detail ; his speculative system was developed gradually in a long course of years.   But for certain grandiose conceptions which had a charm for the imagination and fascinated the religious sentiment, his name need not be mentioned in this little incidental record at all.   There was, however, in Schelling something that recalled the ideal side of Plato, more that suggested Plotinus, the neo-Platonists and Alexandrines, a mystical pantheistic quality that mingled well with the general elements of Idealism, and gave atmosphere, as it were, to the tender feeling of Jacobi and the heroic will of Fichte.

Schelling was Fichte's disciple, filled his vacant chair in Jena in 1798, and took his philosophical departure from certain of his positions. Fichte had shut the man up close in himself, had limited the conception of the world by the boundaries of consciousness, had reduced the inner universe to a full-orbed creation, made its facts substantial and its fancies solid, peopled it with living forces, and found room in it for the exercise of a complete moral and spiritual life. In his system the soul was creator. The outer universe had its being in human thought. Subject and object were one, and that one was the subject.

Schelling restored the external world to its place as an objective reality, no fiction, no projection from the human mind. Subject and object, in his view, were one, but in the ABSOLUTE, the universal soul, the infinite and eternal mind. His original fire mist was the unorganized intelligence of which the universe was the expression. Finite minds are but phases of manifestation of the infinite mind, inlets into which it flows, some deeper, wider, longer than others. Spirit and matter are reverse aspects of being. Spirit is invisible nature, nature invisible spirit. Starting from nature, we may work our way into intelligence ; starting from intelligence, we may work our way out to nature. Thought and existence

having the same ground, ideal and real being one,
the work of philosophy is twofold—from nature to arrive at spirit, from spirit to arrive at nature.   They who
wish to know how Schelling did it must consult the
histories of philosophy ; the most popular of them will
satisfy all but the experts.   It is easy to conjecture into
what mysterious ways the clue might lead, and in what
wilderness of thickets the reader might be lost ; how in
mind we are to see nature struggling upward into consciousness, and in nature mind seeking endless forms of
finite expression.   To unfold both processes, in uniform
and balanced movement, avoiding pantheism on one
side, and materialism on the other, was the endeavor we
shall not attempt, even in the most cursory manner, to
describe.   God becomes conscious in man, the philosophic man, the man of reason, in whom the absolute being recognizes himself.   The reason gazes immediately
on the eternal realities, by virtue of what was called
" intellectual intuition," which beholds both subject and
object as united in a single thought.   Reason was impersonal, no attribute of the finite intelligence, no fact
of the individual consciousness, but a faculty, if that be
the word for it, that transcended all finite experience,
commanded a point superior to consciousness, was, in
fact, the all-seeing eye confronting itself.   What room here
for intellectual rovers !   What mystic groves for ecstatic
souls to lose themselves in !   What intricate mazes for
those who are fond of hunting phantoms !   Flashes of dim
glory from this tremendous speculation are seen in the
writings of Emerson, Parker, Alcott, and other seers,

probably caught by reflection, or struck out, as they were by Schelling himself, by minds moving on the same level. In Germany the lines of speculation were carried out in labyrinthine detail, as, fortunately, they were not elsewhere.

Of Hegel, the successor in thought of Schelling, there is no call here to speak at all. His speculation, though influential in America, as influential as that of either of his predecessors, was scarcely known thirty-five years ago, and if it had been, would have possessed little charm for idealists of the New England stamp. That system has borne fruits of a very different quality, being adopted largely by churchmen, whom it has justified and fortified in their ecclesiastical forms, doctrinal and sacramental, and by teachers of moderately progressive tendencies. The duty of unfolding his ideas has devolved upon students of German, as no other language has given them anything like adequate expression. Hegel, too, was more formidable than Schelling ; the latter was brilliant, dashing, imaginative, glowing ; his ideas shone in the air, and were caught with little toil by enthusiastic minds. To comprehend or even to apprehend Hegel requires more philosophical culture than was found in New England half a century ago, more than is by any means common to-day. Modern speculative philosophy is, as a rule, Hegelian. Its spirit is conservative, and it scarcely at all lends countenance to movements so revolutionary as those that shook New England.

Long before the time we are dealing with—as early as

1824—the philosophy of Hegel had struck hands with church and state in Prussia ; Hegel was at once prophet, priest, and prince. In the fulness of his powers, ripe in ability and in fame, he sat in the chair that Fichte had occupied, and gave laws to the intellectual world. He would " teach philosophy to talk German, as Luther had taught the Bible to do." A crowd of enthusiasts thronged about him. The scientific and literary celebrities of Berlin sat at his feet ; state officials attended his lectures and professed themselves his disciples. The government provided liberally for his salary, and paid the travelling expenses of this great ambassador of the mind. The old story of disciple become master was told again. The philosopher was the friend of those that befriended him ; the servant, some say, of those that lavished on him honors. Then the new philosophy that was to reconstruct the mental world learned to accept the actual world as it existed, and lent its powerful aid to the order of things it promised to reconstruct. Throwing out the aphorism, " The rational is the actual, the actual is the rational," Hegel declared that natural right, morality, and even religion are properly subordinated to authority. The despotic Prussian system welcomed the great philosopher as its defender. The Prussian Government was not tardy in showing appreciation of its advocate's eminent services.

The church, taking the hint, put in its claim to patronage. It needed protection against the rationalism that was coming up ; and such protection the majesty of Hegel vouchsafed to offer. Faith and philosophy formed a new alliance. Orthodox professors gave in their loyalty to the man who taught that " God was in process of becoming," and the man who taught that "God was in process of becoming" welcomed the orthodox professors to the circle of his disciples. He was more orthodox than the orthodox ; he gave the theologians new explanations of their own dogmas, and supplied them with arguments against their own foes. Trinity, incarnation, atonement, redemption, were all interpreted and justified, to the complete satisfaction of the ecclesiastical powers.

This being the influence of the master, and of philosophy as he explained it, the formation of a new school by the earnest, liberal men who drew very different conclusions from the master's first principles, was to be expected. But the " New Hegelians," as they were called, became disbelievers in religion and in spiritual things altogether, and either lapsed, like Strauss, into intellectual scepticism, or, like Feuerbach, became aggressive materialists. The ideal elements in Hegel's system were appropriated by Christianity, and were employed against liberty and progress. Spiritualists, whether in the old world or the new, had little interest in a philosophy that so readily favored two opposite tendencies, both of which they abhorred. To them the spiritual philosophy was represented by Hegel's predecessors. The disciples of sentiment accepted Jacobi ; the loyalists of conscience followed Fichte ; the severe metaphysicians, of whom there were a few, adhered to Kant ; the soaring speculators and imaginative theosophists spread their " sheeny vans," and soared into the regions of the absolute with Schelling.   The idealists of New England were largest debtors to Jacobi and Fichte.

III

TRANSCENDENTALISM IN THEOLOGY AND LITERATURE.

ONE of the earliest students of the German language in Boston was Dr. N. L. Frothingham, Unitarian minister of the First Church. Among the professional books that interested him was one by Herder, " Letters to a Young Theologian," chapters from which he translated for the " Christian Disciple," the precursor of the " Christian Examiner." Of Herder, George Bancroft wrote an account in the " North American Review," and George Ripley in the " Christian Examiner." The second number of " The Dial " contains a letter from Mr. Ripley to a theological student, in which this particular book of Herder is warmly commended, as being worth the trouble of learning German to read. The volume was remarkable for earnest enlightenment, its discernment of the spirit beneath the letter, its generous interpretations, and its suggestions of a better future for the philosophy of religion. Herder was one of the illuminated minds ; though not professedly a disciple, he had felt the influence of Kant, and was cordially in sympathy with the men who were trying to break the spell of form and tradition. With Lessing more especially, Herder's " Spirit of Hebrew Poetry," of which a translation by Dr. James Marsh was published in 1833, found its

way to New England, and helped to confirm the disposition to seek the springs of inspiration in the human
mind, whence all poetry proceeded. The writer of the
book, by applying to Hebrew poetry the rules of critical
appreciation by which all poetic creations are judged,
abolished so far the distinction between sacred and secular, and transferred to the credit of human genius the
products commonly ascribed to divine. In the persons
of the great bards of Israel all bards were glorified ; the
soul's creative power was recognized, and with it the
heart of the transcendental faith.

The influence of Schleiermacher was even more distinct than that of Herder. One book of his, in particular,
made a deep impression,—the " Reden über Religion,"
published in 1799. The book is thus described by Mr.
George Ripley, in a controversial letter to Mr. Andrews
Norton, who had assailed Schleiermacher as an atheist.
" The ' Discourses on Religion ' were not intended to
present a system of theology. They are highly rhe-
torical in manner, filled with bursts of impassioned eloquence, always intense, and sometimes extravagant ;
addressed to the feelings, not to speculation ; and ex-
pressly disclaiming all pretensions to an exposition of
doctrine. They were published at a time when hostility
to religion, and especially to Christianity as a divine revelation, was deemed a proof of talent and refinement.
The influence of the church was nearly exhausted ; the
highest efforts of thought were of a destructive character ; a frivolous spirit pervaded society ; religion was
deprived of its supremacy ; and a 'starveling theology '

was exalted in place of the living word. Schleiermacher could not contemplate the wretched meagreness and degradation of his age without being moved as by 'a heavenly impulse.' His spirit was stirred within him as he saw men turning from the true God to base idols. He felt himself impelled to go forth with the power of a fresh and youthful enthusiasm, for the restoration of religion; to present it in its most sublime aspect, free from its perversions, disentangled from human speculation, as founded in the essential nature of man, and indispensable to the complete unfolding of his inward being. In order to recognize everything which is really religious among men, and to admit even the lowest degree of it into the idea of religion, he wishes to make this as broad and comprehensive in its character as possible." In illustration of this purpose Mr. Ripley quotes the author as follows : " I maintain that piety is the necessary and spontaneous product of the depths of every elevated nature; that it possesses a rightful claim to a peculiar province in the soul, over which it may exercise an unlimited sovereignty; that it is worthy, by its intrinsic power, to be a source of life to the most noble and exalted minds ; and that from its essential character it deserves to be known and received by them. These are the points which I defend, and which I would fain establish."

From this it will appear that Schleiermacher gave countenance to the spiritual aspect of transcendentalism, and co-operated with the general movement it represented. His position that religion was not a system of

dogmas, but an inward experience ; that it was not a
speculation, but a feeling ; that its primal verities rested
not on miracle or tradition, not on the Bible letter or on
ecclesiastical institution, but on the soul's own sense of
things divine ; that this sense belonged by nature to the
human race, and gave to all forms of religion such genuineness as they had ; that all affirmation was partial,
and all definition deceptive ; proved to be practically
the same with that taken by Jacobi, and was so received
by the disciples of the new philosophy.

But Schleiermacher was an Evangelical Lutheran, a
believer in supernatural religion, in Christ, in Christianity as a special dispensation, in the miracles of the
New Testament. So far from being a " rationalist,"
he was the most formidable opponent that " rationalism " had ; for his efforts were directed against the
critical and theological method, and in support of the
spiritual method of dealing with religious truths. In
explaining religion as being in its primitive character
a sense of divine things in the soul, and as having its
seat, not in knowledge, nor yet in action, neither
in theology nor in morality, but in feeling, in aspiration, longing, love, veneration, conscious dependence,
filial trust, he deprived " rationalism " of its strength.
Hence his attraction for liberal orthodox believers in
America. Schleiermacher had as many disciples among
the Congregationalists as among their antagonists of
the opposite school. Professors Edwards and Park
included thoughts of his in their " Selections from
German Literature." The pulpit transcendentalists

acknowledged their indebtedness to him, and the debt they acknowledged was sentimental rather than intellectual. They thanked him for the spirit of fervent piety, deep, cordial, human, unlimited in generosity, untrammelled by logical distinctions, rather than for new light on philosophical problems. His bursts of eloquent enthusiasm over men whom the church outlawed—Spinoza for example—made amends with them for the absence of doctrinal exactness. A warm sympathy with those who detached religion from dogma, and recognized the religious sentiment under its most diverse forms, was characteristic of the new spirit that burned in New England. Schleiermacher was one of the first and foremost to encourage such sympathy : he based it on the idea that man was by nature religious, endowed with spiritual faculties, and that was welcome tidings ; and though he retained the essence of the evangelical system, he retained it in a form that could be dropped without injury to the principle by which it was justified. Thus Schleiermacher strengthened the very positions he assailed, and gave aid and comfort to the enemy he would overthrow. The transcendentalists, it is true, employed against the " rationalists " the weapons that he put into their hands. At the same time they left as unimportant the theological system which his weapons were manufactured to support.

But it was through the literature of Germany that the transcendental philosophy chiefly communicated itself. Goethe, Richter and Novalis were more persuasive teachers than Kant, Jacobi or Fichte. To those who could not read German these authors were interpreted by Thomas Carlyle, who took up the cause of German philosophy and literature, and wrote about them with passionate power in the English reviews; not contenting himself with giving surface accounts of them, but plunging boldly into the depths, and carrying his readers with him through discussions that, but for his persuasive eloquence, would have had little charm to ordinary minds. Goethe and Richter were his heroes : their methods and opinions are of the greatest account with him ; and he leaves nothing unexplained of the intellectual foundations on which they builded. Consequently, in the remarkable papers that Carlyle wrote about them and their books, full report is given of the place held by the Kantean philosophy in their culture. The article on Novalis, in the " Foreign Review " of 1829, No. 7, presents with a master hand the peculiarities of the new metaphysics that were regenerating the German mind. Regenerating is not too strong a word for the influence that he ascribes to it. Thus in 1827 he wrote in the " Edinburgh Review : "

" The critical philosophy has been regarded by persons of approved judgment, and nowise directly implicated in the furthering of it, as distinctly the greatest intellectual achievement of the century in which it came to light. August Wilhelm Schlegel has stated in plain terms his belief that in respect of its probable influence on the moral culture of Europe, it stands on a line with the Reformation. We mention Schlegel as a man whose opinion has a known value among ourselves. But the worth of Kant's philosophy is not to be gathered from votes alone. The noble system of morality, the purer theology, the lofty views of man's nature derived from it ; nay, perhaps the very discussion of such matters, to which it gave so strong an impetus, have told with remarkable and beneficial influence on the whole spiritual character of Germany. No writer of any importance in that country, be he acquainted or not with the critical philosophy, but breathes a spirit of devoutness and elevation more or less directly drawn from it. Such men as Goethe and Schiller cannot exist without effect in any literature or any century ; but if one circumstance more than another has contributed to forward their endeavors and introduce that higher tone into the literature of Germany, it has been this philosophical system, to which, in wisely believing its results, or even in wisely denying them, all that was lofty and pure in the genius of poetry or the reason of man so readily allied itself."

After quoting from " Meister's Apprenticeship " a noble passage on the spiritual function of art, Carlyle comments thus : " To adopt such sentiments into his sober practical persuasion ; in any measure to feel and believe that such was still and must always be, the high vocation of the poet ; on this ground of universal humanity, of ancient and now almost forgotten nobleness, to take his stand, even in these trivial, jeering, withered, unbelieving days, and through all their complex, dispiriting, mean, yet tumultuous influences, to make his light shine before men that it might beautify even our rag-

gathering age with some beams of that mild divine splendor which had long left us, the very possibility of which
was denied ; heartily and in earnest to meditate all this
was no common proceeding ; to bring it into practice,
especially in such a life as his has been, was among the
highest and hardest enterprises which any man whatever
could engage in."

From Schiller's correspondence with Goethe, Carlyle
quotes the following tribute to the Kantean philosophy :
" From the opponents of the new philosophy I expect
not that tolerance which is shown to every other system
no better seen into than this ; for Kant's philosophy
itself, in its leading points, practises no tolerance, and
bears much too rigorous a character to leave any room
for accommodation.   But in my eyes this does it honor,
proving how little it can endure to have truth tampered
with.   Such a philosophy will not be shaken to pieces
by a mere shake of the head.   In the open, clear, accessible field of inquiry it builds up its system, seeks no
shade, makes no reservation, but even as it treats its
neighbors, so it requires to be treated, and may be for-
given for lightly esteeming everything but proofs.   Nor
am I terrified to think that the law of change, from
which no human and no divine work finds grace, will
operate on this philosophy as on every other, and one
day its form will be destroyed, but its foundations will not
have this fate to fear, for ever since mankind has existed,
and any reason among mankind, these same first principles have been admitted, and on the whole, acted on."

Of Richter he writes : " Richter's philosophy, a matter of no ordinary interest, both as it agrees with the common philosophy of Germany, and disagrees with it, must not be touched on for the present. One only observation we shall make : it is not mechanical or sceptical; it springs not from the forum or the laboratory, but from the depths of the human spirit, and yields as its fairest product a noble system of morality, and the firmest conviction of religion. An intense and continual faith in man's immortality and native grandeur accompanies him ; from amid the vortices of life he looks up to a heavenly loadstar; the solution of what is visible and transient, he finds in what is invisible and eternal. He has doubted, he denies, yet he believes."

Of Novalis, scarcely more than a name to Americans, the same oracle speaks thus : " The aim of Novalis' whole philosophy is to preach and establish the majesty of reason, in the strict philosophical sense ; to conquer for it all provinces of human thought, and everywhere resolve its vassal understanding into fealty, the right and only useful relation for it. How deeply these and the like principles (those of the Kantean philosophy) had impressed themselves on Novalis, we see more and more the further we study his writings. Naturally a deep, religious, contemplative spirit, purified also by harsh affliction, and familiar in the ' Sanctuary of Sorrow,' he comes before us as the most ideal of all idealists. For him the material creation is but an appearance, a typical shadow in which the Deity manifests himself to man. Not only has the unseen world a reality, but the only reality; the rest being not metaphorically, but liter-

ally and in scientific strictness, ' a show ; ' in the words of
the poet :

' Sound and smoke overclouding the splendor of heaven ! '

The invisible world is near us ; or rather, it is here, in us
and about us ; were the fleshly coil removed from our
soul, the glories of the unseen were even now around
us, as the ancients fabled of the spheral music.   Thus,
not in word only, but in truth and sober belief he feels
himself encompassed by the Godhead ; feels in every
thought that ' in Him he lives, moves, and has his
being.' "

These declarations from a man who was becoming
prominent in the world of literature, and whose papers
were widely and enthusiastically read, had great weight
with people to whom the German was an unknown
tongue.   But it was not an unknown tongue to all, and
they who had mastered it were active communicators of
its treasures.   Carlyle's efforts at interesting English
readers through his remarkable translation of Wilhelm
Meister, and the " Specimens of German Romance,"
which contained pieces by Tieck, Jean Paul, Hoffmann,
and Musæus, published in 1827, were seconded here
by F. H. Hedge, C. T. Brooks, J. S. Dwight, and
others, who made familiar to the American public the
choicest poems of the most famous German bards.
Richter became well known by his " Autobiography,"
" Quintus Fixlein," " Flower, Fruit, and Thorn Pieces,"
" Hesperus," " Titan," " The Campaner Thal," the
writings and versions of Madame de Staël.   The third

volume of the " Dial," July, 1841, opened with a remarkable paper on Goethe, by Margaret Fuller. The
pages of the " Dial " abounded in references to Goethe's
ideas and writings. No author occupied the cultivated
New England mind as much as he did. None of these
writers taught formally the doctrines of the transcendental philosophy, but they reflected one or another aspect
of it. They assumed its cardinal principles in historical
and literary criticism, in dramatic art, in poetry and
romance. They conveyed its spirit of aspiration after
ideal standards of perfection. They caught from it their
judgments on society and religion. They communicated
its aroma, and so imparted the quickening breath of its
soul to people who would have started back in alarm
from its doctrines.

The influence of the transcendental philosophy on German literature was fully conceded by Menzel, who, however, found little trace of it in Goethe. Of the author
of the philosophy he wrote : " Kant was very far from
assenting to French infidelity and its immoral consequences. He directed man to himself, to the moral law
in his own bosom ; and the fresh breath of life of the old
Grecian dignity of man penetrates the whole of his luminous philosophy." Of Goethe he wrote : " If he ever
acknowledged allegiance to a good spirit, to great ideas,
to virtue, he did it only because they had become
the order of the day, for, on the other hand, he has,
again, served every weakness, vanity and folly, if they
were but looked on with favor at the time ; in short, like
a good player, he has gone through all the parts."

Menzel's book was translated by a man who had no sympathy with Transcendentalism—Prof. C. C. Felton; was admired by people of his own school, and was sharply criticised, especially in the portions relating to Goethe, by the transcendentalists, who accepted Carlyle's view. He and they put the most generous interpretations on the masterpieces of the poet, passed by as incidental, did not see, or in their own mind transfigured, the objectionable features that Menzel seized on.   Too little was ascribed to the foreign French element that reached the literature of Germany through Prussia—to Rousseau, Voltaire, Diderot—whose ideas fell in with the unworthier sceptical tendencies of the Kantean system, and polluted the waters of that clear, cold stream; too much was ascribed to the noble idealism that was credited with power to glorify all it touched, and redeem even low things from degradation.   If therefore they apologized for what the sensational moralists blamed, they did it in good faith, not as excusing the indecency, but as surmounting it.   What they admired was the art, and the aspiration it expressed.   The devotees of the French spirit, in its frivolity and meretricious beauty, they turned away from with disdain.   There was enough of the nobler kind to engage them.   When they went to France they went for what France had in common with Germany—an idealism of the wholesome, ethical and spiritual type, which, whether German, French or English, bore always the same characteristics of beauty and nobleness.   Much that was unspiritual, all that was merely speculative, they passed by.   With an appetite for the generous and inspiring only, they sought the really earnest teachers, of whom in France there were a few. The influence of those few was great in proportion to their fewness probably, quite as much as to their merit as philosophers.

IV.

TRANSCENDENTALISM IN FRANCE.

FROM the time of Malebranche, who died in 1715, to
Maine de Biran, Royer-Collard, Ampère and Cousin,
a period of about a century, philosophy in France had
not borne an honorable name.   The French mind was
active ; philosophy was a profession ; the philosophical
world was larger than in Germany, where it was limited
to the Universities.   But France took no lead in speculation, it waited to receive impulse from other lands ;
and even then, instead of taking up the impulse and
carrying it on with original and sympathetic force, it
was content to exhibit and reproduce it.   The office of
expositor, made easy by the perspicacity of its intellect
and the flexibility of its language, was accepted and
discharged with a cleverness that was recognized by
all Europe.   Its histories of philosophy, translations,
expositions, reproductions, were admirable for neatness
and clearness.   The most obscure systems became intelligible in that limpid and lucid speech, which reported
with faultless dexterity the agile movements of the
Gallic mind, and made popular the most abstruse doctrines of metaphysics.   German philosophy in its original dress was outlandish, even to practised students in
German.   The readers of French were many in Eng-

land and the United States, and the readers of French, without severe labor on their part, were put in possession of the essential ideas of the deep thinkers of the race. The best accounts of human speculation are in French. Barthélemy Saint Hilaire interprets Aristotle, and throws important light on Indian Philosophy; Bouillet translates Plotinus; Emil Saisset translates Spinoza; Tissot and Jules Barni perform the same service for Kant; Jules Simon and Etienne Vacherot undertake to make intelligible the School of Alexandria; Paul Janet explains the dialectics of Plato; Adolphe Franck deals with the Jewish Kabbala; Charles de Rémusat with Anselm, Abelard and Bacon; MM. Hauréau and Rousselot with the philosophy of the middle age; M. Chauvet with the theories of the human understanding in antiquity. Cousin published unedited works of Proclus, analyzed the commentaries of Olympiodorus on the Platonic dialogues, made a complete translation of Plato, admirable for clearness and strength, and proposed to present, not of course with his own hand, but by the hands of friendly fellow-workers, and under his own direction, examples of whatever was best in every philosophical system. The philosophical work of France is ably summed up in the report on " Philosophy in France in the nineteenth century," presented by Felix Ravaisson, member of the Institute, and published in 1868, under the auspices of the Ministry of Public Instruction.

The ideas of Locke were brought from London to Paris by Voltaire, who became acquainted with them during a residence in England, and found them effective in his warfare against the ecclesiastical institutions of his country. Through his brilliant interpretations and keen applications, they gained currency, became fashionable among the wits, were domesticated with people of culture and elegance, and worked their way into the religion and politics of the time. It is needless to say that in his hands full justice was done to their external and material aspects.

The system found a more exact and methodical expounder in Condillac, who reduced it to greater simplicity by eliminating from it what in the original marred its unity, namely reflection, the bent of the mind back on itself, whereby it took cognizance of impressions made by the outer world. Taking what remained of the system, the notion that all knowledge came primarily through the senses, and drawing the conclusion that the mind itself was a product of sensation, Condillac fashioned a doctrine which had the merit, such as it was, of utter intelligibleness to the least instructed mind ; a system of materialism naked and unadorned. If he himself forbore to push his principle to its extreme results, declining to assert that we were absolutely nothing else than products of sensation, and surmising that beneath the layers of intelligence and reason there might lurk a principle that sensation could not account for, something stable in the midst of the ceaseless instability, something absolute below everything relative, which might be called action or will, the popular interpretation of his philosophy took no account of such subtleties.

In vain did his disciple Destutt de Tracy declare that " the principle of movement is the will, and that the will is the person, the man himself." The fascination of simplicity proved more than a match for nicety of distinction, and both were ranked among materialists.

Cabanis was at no pains to conceal the most repulsive features of the system. In his work, " The Relations of the Physical and the Moral in Man," he maintained bluntly the theory that there was no spiritual being apart from the body; that mind had no substance, no separate existence of its own, but was in all its parts and qualities a product of the nervous system ; that sensibility of every kind, sentimental, intelligent, moral, spiritual, including the whole domain of conscious and unconscious vitality, was a nervous manifestation ; that man was capable of sensation because he had nerves ; that he was what he was because of the wondrous character of the mechanism of sensation ; that, in a word, the perfection of organization was the perfection of humanity. It was Cabanis who said " the brain secretes thought as the liver secretes bile." Cabanis modified his philosophy before his death, but without effect to break the force of his cardinal positions. The results of such teaching appeared in a morality of selfishness, tending to self-indulgence—a morality destitute of nobleness and sweetness, summing up its lessons in the maxims that good is good to eat ; that the pleasurable thing is right, the painful thing wrong ; that success is the measure of rectitude ; that the aim of life is the attainment of happiness, and that happiness means physical enjoyment;

that virtue and vice are names for prudence and for folly,—Virtue being conformity with the ways of the world, Vice being non-conformity with the ways of the world ; no ideal standard being recognized for the one, no law of rectitude being confessed for the other. Conscience was regarded as an artificial habit created by custom or acquiesced in from tradition ; the "categorical imperative" was pronounced the dogmatism of the fanatic.

From such principles atheism naturally proceeded. Atheism not of opinion merely, but of sentiment and feeling ; for at that time "the potencies" of matter impressed no such awe upon the mind as they have done since ; the "mystery of matter" was unfelt ; physiology was an unexplored region ; the materialist simply denied spirit, putting a blank where believers in religion had been used to find a soul ; and had no alternative but to run sensationalism into sensualism, and to give the senses the flavor of the ground. With us the sensational philosophy has become refined into a philosophy of experience, and the materialist finds himself in a region where to distinguish between matter and spirit is difficult, to say the least. But a hundred years ago matter was clod, and the passion it engendered smelt of the charnel-house. The morbid insanities of the revolution, the orgies in which blood and wine ran together, the savage glee, the delirium that ensued when the uncertainty of life acting on the impulse to enjoy life while it lasted, made men ferocious in clutching at immediate pleasure, attest the consequences that ensued from such frank adoption of the sensational philosophy as was practised among the French. Locke was a man of piety, which even his warmest apologists will hardly claim for Voltaire. The English mind, grave and thoughtful, trained by religious institutions in religious beliefs, was less inclined than the French to drive speculative theories to extreme conclusions. The philosophy of sensationalism culminated, not in the French Revolution, as has been vulgarly asserted, but in the unbelief and sensual extravagance that marked one phase of it.

In this there was nothing original; there was no originality in the reaction that followed, and gave to modern philosophy in France its spiritual character. Laromiguière, educated in the school of Condillac, improved on the suggestion that Condillac had given, and deepened into a chasm the scratch he had made to indicate a distinction between the results of sensation and the faculties of the mind. In his analysis of the mental constitution he came upon two facts that denoted an original activity in advance of sensation—namely, *attention* and *desire :* the former the root of the intellectual, the latter of the moral powers ; both at last resolvable into one principle—attention. This discovery met with wide and cordial welcome, the popularity of Laromiguière's lectures, delivered in 1811, 1812, 1813, revealing the fact that thoughtful people were prepared for a new metaphysical departure.

Maine de Biran, who more than the rest deserves the name of an original investigator, a severe, solitary, independent thinker, pupil of no school and founder of none, brought into strong relief the activity of the intellect. Thought, he maintained, proceeds from will, which is at the base of the personality, is, in fact, the essence of personality. The primary fact is volition. Descartes said, " I think, therefore I am." Maine de Biran said, " I will, therefore I am." " In every one of my determinations," he declared, " I recognize myself as being a cause anterior to its effect and capable of surviving it. I behold myself as outside of the movement I produce, and independent of time ; for this reason, strictly speaking, I do not *become*, I really and absolutely *am.*" " To be, to act, to will, are the same thing under different names." Will as the seat of activity ; will as the core of personality ; will as the soul of causation : here is the corner-stone for a new structure to replace the old one of the " Cyclopædists." Important deductions followed from such a first principle ; the dignity of the moral being, freedom of the moral will, the nobility of existence, the persistency of the individual as a ground for continuous effort and far-reaching hope, the spirituality of man and his destiny. To recover the will from the mass of sensations that had buried it out of sight, was the achievement of this philosopher. It was an achievement by which philosophy was disengaged from physics, and sent forth on a more cheerful way.

The next steps were taken by disciples of the Scotch school—Royer-Collard, Victor Cousin and Theodore Jouffroy. The last translated Reid and Stewart from English into French ; the two former lectured on them. The three, being masters of clear and persuasive speech,

made their ideas popular in France. Cousin's lectures
on the Scotch school, including Reid, were delivered in
1819. The lectures on Kant were given in 1820. Both
courses were full and adequate. Cousin committed himself to neither, but freely criticised both, laying stress on
the sceptical aspect of the transcendental system as
expounded by Kant.

Cousin's own system was the once famous, now discarded eclecticism, under cover of which another phase
of idealism was presented which found favor in America.
The cardinal principle of eclecticism was that truth was
contained in no system or group of systems, but in all
together ; that each had its portion and made its contribution ; and that the true philosophy would be reached
by a process of intellectual distillation by which the essential truth in each would be extracted. A method
like this would have nothing to recommend it but its
generosity, if there were no criterion by which truths
could be tested, no philosophical principle, in short,
to govern the selection of materials. Eclecticism must
have a philosophy before proceeding to make one, must
have arrived at its conclusion before entering on its
process. And this it did. It will be seen by the following
extracts from his writings what the fundamental ideas of
M. Cousin were, and in what respect they aided the
process of rationalism.

The quotations are from his exposition of eclecticism

" Facts are the point of departure, if not the limit of
philosophy. Now facts, whatever they may be, exist
for us only as they come to our consciousness. It is

there alone that observation seizes them and describes them, before committing them to induction, which forces them to reveal the consequences which they contain in their bosom. The field of philosophical observation is consciousness ; there is no other; but in this nothing is to be neglected ; everything is important, for everything is connected ; and if one part be wanting, complete unity is unattainable. To return within our consciousness, and scrupulously to study all the phenomena, their differences and their relations—this is the primary study of philosophy. Its scientific name is psychology. Psychology is then the condition and, as it were, the vestibule of philosophy. The psychological method consists in completely retiring within the world of consciousness, in order to become familiar in that sphere where all is reality, but where the reality is so various and so delicate ; and the psychological talent consists in placing ourselves at will within this interior world, in presenting the spectacle there displayed to ourselves, and in reproducing freely and distinctly all the facts which are accidentally and confusedly brought to our notice by the circumstances of life." . . . . . .

" The first duty of the psychological method is to retire within the field of consciousness, where there is nothing but phenomena, that are all capable of being perceived and judged by observation. Now as no substantial existence falls under the eye of consciousness, it follows that the first effect of a rigid application of method is to postpone the subject of ontology. It postpones it, I say, but does not destroy it. It is a fact, indeed, attested by observation, that in this same consciousness, in which there is nothing but phenomena, there are found notions, whose regular development passes the limits of consciousness and attains the knowledge of actual existences. Would you stop the development of these notions ? You would then arbitrarily limit the compass of a fact, you would attack this fact itself, and thus shake the authority of all other facts. We must either call in

question the authority of consciousness in itself, or admit
this authority without reserve for all the facts attested by
consciousness. The reason is no less certain and real
than the will or the sensibility ; its certainty once admitted
we must follow it wherever it rigorously conducts, though
it be even into the depths of ontology. For example,
it is a rational fact attested by consciousness, that in the
view of intelligence, every phenomenon which is presented supposes a cause. It is a fact, moreover, that
this principle of causality is marked with the characteristics of universality and necessity. If it be universal
and necessary, to limit it would be to destroy it.
Now in the phenomenon of sensation, the principle
of causality intervenes universally and necessarily,
and refers this phenomenon to a cause ; and our
consciousness testifying that this cause is not the
personal cause which the will represents, it follows that
the principle of causality in its irresistible application
conducts to an impersonal cause, that is to say, to an
external cause, which subsequently, and always irresisti-
bly, the principle of causality enriches with the characteristics and laws, of which the aggregate is the Universe.
Here then is an existence ; but an existence revealed by
a principle which is itself attested by consciousness.
Here is a primary step in ontology, but by the path of
psychology, that is to say, of observation. We are led
by similar processes to the Cause of all causes, to the
substantial Cause, to God ; and not only to a God of
Power, but to a God of Justice, a God of Holiness ; so
that this experimental method, which, applied to a
single order of phenomena, incomplete and exclusive,
destroyed ontology and the higher elements of consciousness, applied with fidelity, firmness and completeness, to all the phenomena, builds up that which it had
overthrown, and by itself furnishes ontology with a sure
and legitimate instrument. Thus, having commenced
with modesty, we can end with results whose certainty
is equalled by their importance." . . . .

" What physical inquirer, since Euler, seeks anything in nature but forces and laws ? Who now speaks of atoms ? And even molecules, the old atoms revived— who defends them as anything but an hypothesis ? If the fact be incontestable, if modern physics be now employed only with forces and laws, I draw the rigorous conclusion from it, that the science of Physics, whether it know it or not, is no longer material, and that it became spiritual when it rejected every other method' than observation and induction, which can never lead to aught but forces and laws. Now what is there material in forces and laws ? The physical sciences, then, themselves have entered into the broad path of an enlightened spiritualism ; and they have only to march with a firm step, and to gain a more and more profound knowledge of forces and laws, in order to arrive at more important generalizations. Let us go still further. As it is a law already recognized of the same reason which governs humanity and nature, to refer every finite cause and every multiple law—that is to say, every phenomenal cause and every phenomenal law—to something absolute, which leaves nothing to be sought beyond it in relation to existence, that is to say, to a substance ; so this law refers the external world composed of forces and laws to a substance, which must needs be a cause in order to be the subject of the causes of this world, which must needs be an intelligence in order to be the subject of its laws ; a substance, in fine, which must needs be the identity of activity and intelligence. We have thus arrived accordingly, for the second time, by observation and induction in the external sphere, at precisely the same point to which observation and induction have successively conducted us in the sphere of personality and in that of reason ; consciousness in its triplicity is therefore one ; the physical and moral world is one, science is one, that is to say, in other words, God is One." . . . .

" Having gained these heights, philosophy becomes more luminous as well as more grand; universal har·

mony enters into human thought, enlarges it, and gives
it peace. The divorce of ontology and psychology, of
speculation and observation, of science and common-
sense, is brought to an end by a method which arrives
at speculation by observation, at ontology by psychology,
in order then to confirm observation by speculation,
psychology by ontology, and which starting from the
immediate facts of consciousness, of which the common-
sense of the human race is composed, derives from them
the science which contains nothing more than common-
sense, but which elevates that to its purest and most rigid
form, and enables it to comprehend itself. But I here
approach a fundamental point.

" If every fact of consciousness contains all the human
faculties, sensibility, free activity, and reason, the me,
the not-me, and their absolute identity ; and if every
fact of consciousness be equal to itself, it follows that
every man who has the consciousness of himself possesses
and cannot but possess all the ideas that are necessarily
contained in consciousness. Thus every man, if he
knows himself, knows all the rest, nature and God at the
same time with himself. Every man believes in his own
existence, every man therefore believes in the existence of the world and of God ; every man thinks, every
man therefore thinks God, if we may so express it ;
every human proposition, reflecting the consciousness,
reflects the idea of unity and of being that is essential to
consciousness ; every human proposition therefore contains God ; every man who speaks, speaks of God, and
every word is an act of faith and a hymn. Atheism is a
barren formula, a negation without reality, an abstrac-
tion of the mind which cannot assert itself without self-
destruction ; for every assertion, even though negative,
is a judgment which contains the idea of being, and,
consequently, God in His fulness. Atheism is the illusion of a few sophists, who place their liberty in opposition to their reason, and are unable even to give an account to themselves of what they think ; but the human

race, which is never false to its consciousness and never places itself in contradiction to its laws, possesses the knowledge of God, believes in him, and never ceases to proclaim Him. In fact, the human race believes in reason and cannot but believe in it, in that reason which is manifested in consciousness, in a momentary relation with the me—the pure though faint reflection of that primitive light which flows from the bosom of the eternal substance, which is at once substance, cause, intelligence. Without the manifestation of reason in our consciousness, there could be no knowledge—neither psychological, nor, still less, ontological. Reason is, in some sort, the bridge between psychology and ontology, between consciousness and being; it rests at the same time on both; it descends from God and approaches man; it makes its appearance in the consciousness, as a guest who brings intelligence of an unknown world of which it at once presents the idea and awakens the want. If reason were personal, it would have no value, no authority, beyond the limits of the individual subject. If it remained in the condition of primitive substance, without manifestation, it would be the same for the me which would not know itself, as if it were not. It is necessary therefore that the intelligent substance should manifest itself; and this manifestation is the appearance of reason in the consciousness. Reason then is literally a revelation, a necessary and universal revelation, which is wanting to no man and which enlightens every man on his coming into the world : *illuminat omnem hominem venientem in hunc mundum.* Reason is the necessary mediator between God and man, the λόγος of Pythagoras and Plato, the Word made flesh which serves as the interpreter of God and the teacher of man, divine and human at the same time. It is not, indeed, the absolute God in his majestic individuality, but his manifestation in spirit and in truth; it is not the Being of beings, but it is the revealed God of the human race. As God is never wanting to the human race and never abandons it, so the human race believes in God with an irresistible and unalterable faith, and this unity of faith is its own highest unity. . . . .

" If these convictions of faith be combined in every act of consciousness, and if consciousness be one in the whole human race, whence arises the prodigious diversity which seems to exist between man and man, and in what does this diversity consist ? In truth, when we perceive at first view so many apparent differences between one individual and another, one country and another, one epoch of humanity and another, we feel a profound emotion of melancholy, and are tempted to regard an intellectual development so capricious, and even the whole of humanity, as a phenomenon without consistency, without grandeur, and without interest. But it is demonstrated by a more attentive observation of facts, that no man is a stranger to either of the three great ideas which constitute consciousness, namely, personality or the liberty of man, impersonality or the necessity of nature, and the providence of God. Every man comprehends these three ideas immediately, because he found them at first and constantly finds them again within himself. The exceptions to this fact, by their small number, by the absurdities which they involve, by the difficulties which they create, serve only to exhibit, in a still clearer light, the universality of faith in the human race, the treasure of good sense deposited in truth, and the peace and happiness that there are for a human soul in not discarding the convictions of its kind. Leave out the exceptions which appear from time to time in certain critical periods of history, and you will perceive that the masses which alone have true existence, always and everywhere live in the same faith, of which the forms only vary."

These somewhat too copious extracts have been purposely taken from the first volume of the " Specimens of Foreign Standard Literature," edited by George Ripley

in 1838, rather than from the collected writings of
Cousin, because they show what a leading New England
transcendentalist thought most important in the teaching
of the French school.   His own estimate of the philosophy and his expectations from it may be learned from
the closing passages of the introduction to that volume :

" The objects at which Mr. Coleridge aims, it seems to
me, are in a great measure accomplished by the philosophy of Cousin.   This philosophy demolishes, by one of
the most beautiful specimens of scientific analysis that
is anywhere to be met with, the system of sensation,
against which Mr. Coleridge utters such eloquent and
pathetic denunciations.   It establishes on a rock the
truth of the everlasting sentiments of the human heart.
It exhibits to the speculative inquirer, in the rigorous
forms of science, the reality of our instinctive faith in
God, in virtue, in the human soul, in the beauty of
holiness, and in the immortality of man.

" Such a philosophy, I cannot but believe, will ultimately find a cherished abode in the youthful affections
of this nation, in whose history, from the beginning, the
love of freedom, the love of philosophical inquiry, and
the love of religion, have been combined in a thrice holy
bond.   We need a philosophy like this to purify and
enlighten our politics, to consecrate our industry, to
cheer and elevate society.   We need it for our own use
in the hours of mental misgiving and gloom ; when the
mystery of the universe presses heavily upon our souls ;
when the fountains of the great deep are broken up, and
the
          ' Intellectual power
   Goes sounding on, a dim and perilous way,'

over the troubled waters of the stormy sea.   We need it
for the use of our practical men, who, surrounded on
every side with the objects of sense, engrossed with the

competitions of business, the rivalries of public life, or the cares of professional duty, and accustomed to look at the immediate and obvious utility of everything which appeals to their notice, often acquire a distaste for all moral and religious inquiries, and as an almost inevitable consequence, lose their interest, and often their belief, in the moral and religious faculties of their nature. We need it for the use of our young men, who are engaged in the active pursuits of life, or devoted to the cultivation of literature. How many on the very threshold of manly responsibility, by the influence of a few unhappy mistakes, which an acquaintance with their higher nature, as unfolded by a sound religious philosophy, would have prevented, have consigned themselves to disgrace, remorse, and all the evils of a violated conscience! How many have become the dupes of the sophists' eloquence, or the victims of the fanatics' terrors, for whom the spirit of a true philosophy—a philosophy ' baptized in the pure fountain of eternal love,' would have preserved the charm and beauty of life."

Cousin's "History of Philosophy," translated by H. G. Linberg, was published in 1832. The "Elements of Psychology," by C. S. Henry, appeared in 1834. Thus Cousin was early introduced and recommended, and his expositions of the German schools were received. The volume from which passages have been cited had an important influence on New England thought.

V.

TRANSCENDENTALISM IN ENGLAND

THE prophet of the new philosophy in England was Samuel Taylor Coleridge ; in the early part of the present century, perhaps the most conspicuous figure in our literary world ; the object of more admiration, the centre of more sympathy, the source of more intellectual life than any individual of his time ; the criticism, the censure, the manifold animadversion he was made the mark for, better attest his power than the ovations he received from his worshippers. The believers in his genius lacked words to express their sense of his greatness. He was the " eternal youth," the " divine child." The brilliant men of his period · acknowledged his surpassing brilliancy ; the deep men confessed his depth ; the spiritual men went to him for inspiration. His mind, affluent and profuse, contained within no barriers of conventional form, poured an abounding flood of thoughts over the whole literary domain. He was essayist, journalist, politician, poet, dramatist, metaphysician, philosopher, theologian, divine, critic, expositor, dreamer, soliloquizer ; in all eloquent, in all intense. The effect he produced on the minds of his contemporaries will scarcely be believed now. At present he is little more than a name : his books are pronounced unreadable ; his opinions are not quoted as authority ; his force is spent.   But in 1851, Thomas Carlyle, then past the years of his enthusiasm, and verging on the scornful epoch of his intellectual career, spoke of him, in the "Life of Sterling," as "A sublime man, who, alone in those dark days, had saved his crown of spiritual manhood ; escaping from the black materialisms and revolutionary deluges, with God, freedom, immortality still his ; a king of men.   The practical intellects of the world did not much heed him, or carelessly reckoned him a metaphysical dreamer ; but to the rising spirits of the young generation he had this dusky, sublime character, and sat there as a kind of *Magus*, girt in mystery and enigma, his Dodona oak grove (Mr. Gillman's house at Highgate) whispering strange things, uncertain whether oracles or jargon."   "To the man himself, Nature had given in high measure the seeds of a noble endowment, and to unfold it was forbidden him.   A subtle, lynx-eyed intellect, tremulous, pious sensibility to all good and all beautiful ; truly a ray of empyrean light,—but imbedded in such weak laxity of character, in such indolences and esuriences, as made strange work with it.   Once more, the tragic story of a high endowment with an insufficient will."

The abatement is painfully just ; but while Coleridge lived, this very indolence and moral imbecility added to the interest he excited, and gave a mystic splendor as of a divine inspiration to his mental performances.   The distinction between unhealthiness and inspiration has never been clearly marked, and. the voluble utterances

of the feebly outlined and loosely jointed soul easily
passed for oracles.   Thus his moral deficiencies aided
his influence.   His wonderful powers of conversation or
rather of effusion in the midst of admiring friends helped
the illusion and the fascination.   He really seemed
inspired while he talked; and as his talk ranged through
every domain, the listeners carried away and communicated the impression of a superhuman wisdom.

The impression that Coleridge made on minds of a
very different order from Carlyle's, is given in the following lines by Aubrey de Vere :

> No loftier, purer soul than his hath ever
> With awe revolved the planetary page
>   From infancy to age,
> Of knowledge, sedulous and proud to give her
> The whole of his great heart, for her own sake ;
> For what she is : not what she does, or what can make.

> And mighty voices from afar came to him ;
> Converse of trumpets held by cloudy forms
>   And speech of choral storms.
> Spirits of night and noontide bent to woo him;
> He stood the while lonely and desolate
> As Adam when he ruled a world, yet found no mate.

> His loftiest thoughts were but as palms uplifted ;
> Aspiring, yet in supplicating guise—
>   His sweetest songs were sighs.
> Adown Lethean streams his spirit drifted,
> Under Elysian shades from poppied bank,
> With amaranths massed in dark luxuriance dank.

Coleridge, farewell ! That great and grave transition
Which may not king or priest or conqueror spare.
    And yet a babe can bear,
Has come to thee. Through life a goodly vision
Was thine ; and time it was thy rest to take.
Soft be the sound ordained thy sleep to break ;
When thou art waking, wake me, for thy Master's sake."

In May, 1796,—he was then twenty-four years old,—
Coleridge wrote to a friend, " I am studying German,
and in about six weeks shall be able to read that language with tolerable fluency. Now I have some
thoughts of making a proposal to Robinson, the great
London bookseller, of translating all the works of
Schiller, which would make a portly quarto, on condition that he should pay my journey and my wife's to
and from Jena, a cheap German University where
Schiller resides, and allow me two guineas each quarto
sheet, which would maintain me. If I could realize this
scheme, I should there study chemistry and anatomy, and
bring over with me all the works of Semler and Michaelis,
the German theologians, and of Kant, the great German
metaphysician." In September, 1798, in company
with Wordsworth and his sister, and at the expense of
his munificent friends Josiah and Thomas Wedgewood,
he went to Germany and spent fourteen months in hard
study. There he attended the lectures of Eichhorn and
Blumenbach, made the acquaintance of Tieck, dipped
quite deeply into philosophy and general literature, and
took by contagion the speculative ideas that filled his
imagination with visions of intellectual discovery. Schel-

ling's "Transcendental Idealism," with which Coleridge
was afterwards most in sympathy, was not published till
1800. The "Philosophy of Nature" was published in
1797, the year before Coleridge's visit. In 1817, he tells
the readers of the "Biographia Literaria" that he had
been able to procure only two of Schelling's books—the
first volume of his "Philosophical Writings," and the
"System of Transcendental Idealism;" these and "a
small pamphlet against Fichte, the spirit of which was,
to my feelings, painfully incongruous with the principles,
and which displayed the love of wisdom rather than the
wisdom of love."

The philosophical ideas of Schelling commended themselves at once to Coleridge, who was a born idealist, of au
dacious genius, speculative, imaginative, original, capable
of any such abstract achievement as the German undertook.

"In Schelling's *Natur Philosophie* and the *System
des Transcendentalen Idealismus*, I first found a genial
coincidence with much that I had toiled out for myself,
and a powerful assistance in what I had yet to do.
All the main and fundamental ideas were born and
matured in my mind before I had ever seen a single page
of the German philosopher; and I might indeed affirm
with truth, before the more important works of Schelling
had been written, or at least made public. Nor is this
at all to be wondered at. We had studied in the same
school; been disciplined by the same preparatory
philosophy, namely, the writings of Kant; we had both
equal obligations to the polar logic and dynamic
philosophy of Giordano Bruno; and Schelling has lately,
and, as of recent acquisition, avowed that same affectionate reverence for the labors cf Behmen and other

mystics which I had formed at a much earlier period. God forbid that I should be suspected of a wish to enter into a rivalry with Schelling for the honors so unequivocally his right, not only as a great original genius, but as the *founder* of the Philosophy of Nature, and as the most successful *improver* of the Dynamic system, which, begun by Bruno, was reintroduced (in a more philosophical form, and freed from all its impurities and visionary accompaniments) by Kant, in whom it was the native and necessary growth of his own system. Kant's followers, however, on whom (for the greater part) their master's *cloak* had fallen, without, or with a very scanty portion of his *spirit*, had adopted his dynamic ideas, only as a more refined species of mechanics. With exception of one or two fundamental ideas which cannot be withheld from Fichte, to Schelling we owe the completion and the most important victories of this revolution in philosophy. To me it will be happiness and honor enough, should I succeed in rendering the system itself intelligible to my countrymen, and in the application of it to the most awful of subjects for the most important of purposes. Whether a work is the offspring of a man's own spirit and the product of original thinking, will be discovered by those who are its sole legitimate judges, by better tests than the mere reference to dates."

The question of Coleridge's alleged plagiarism from Schelling does not concern us here. Whether the philosophy he taught was the product of his own thinking, or whether he was merely the medium for communicating the system of Schelling to his countrymen, is of no moment to us. For us it is sufficient to know that the English-speaking people on both shores of the Atlantic received them chiefly through the Englishman. Those who are interested in the other matter will find Coleridge's reputation vindicated in a long and elabo-

rate introduction to the "Biographia Literaria," edition
of 1847, by the poet's son.

Coleridge was a pure Transcendentalist, of the Schelling school. The transcendental phrases came over and
over in book and conversation, "reason" and "under·
standing," "intuition," "necessary truths," "consciousness," and the rest that were used to described the
supersensual world and the faculties by which it was
made visible. He shall speak for himself. The following passage from the "Biographia Literaria," Chapter
XII., will be sufficiently intelligible to those who have
read the previous chapters, or enough of them to comprehend their cardinal ideas:

"The criterion is this: if a man receives as fundamental facts, and therefore of course indemonstratable
and incapable of further analysis, the general notions of
matter, spirit, soul, body, action, passiveness, time, space,
cause and effect, consciousness, perception, memory and
all these, and is satisfied if only he can analyze all other
notions into some one or more of these supposed elements, with plausible subordination and apt arrangement; to such a mind I would as courteously as possible
convey the hint, that for him this chapter was not
written. . . . For philosophy, in its highest sense,
as the science of ultimate truths, and therefore *scientia
scientiarum*, this mere analysis of terms is preparative
only, though as a preparative discipline indispensable.

"Still less dare a favorable perusal be anticipated from
the proselytes of that compendious philosophy which,
talking of mind, but thinking of brick and mortar, or other
images equally abstracted from body, contrives a theory
of spirit by nicknaming matter, and in a few hours can
qualify its dullest disciples to explain the *omne scibile* by
reducing all things to impressions, ideas, and sensations.

" But it is time to tell the truth ; though it requires some courage to avow it in an age and country in which disquisitions on all subjects not privileged to adopt technical terms or scientific symbols, must be addressed to the public. I say, then, that it is neither possible nor necessary for all men, nor for many, to be philosophers. There is a philosophic consciousness which lies beneath or (as it were) behind the spontaneous consciousness natural to all reflecting beings. As the elder Romans distinguished their northern provinces into Cis-Alpine and Trans-Alpine, so may we divide all the objects of human knowledge into those on this side and those on the other side of the spontaneous consciousness. The latter is exclusively the domain of pure philosophy, which is therefore properly entitled *transcendental,* in order to discriminate it at once, both from mere reflection and *re*-presentation on the one hand, and on the other from those flights of lawless speculation which, abandoned by *all* distinct consciousness, because transgressing the bounds and purposes of our intellectual faculties, are justly condemned as *transcendent.*

" The first range of hills that encircles the scanty vale of human life is the horizon for the majority of its inhabitants. On its ridges the sun is born and departs. From them the stars rise, and touching them they vanish. By the many, even this range, the natural limit and bulwark of the vale, is but imperfectly known. Its higher ascents are too often hidden in mists and clouds from uncultivated swamps which few have courage or curiosity to penetrate. To the multitude below these vapors appear, now as the dark haunts of terrific agents, on which none may intrude with impunity ; and now all aglow, with colors not their own, they are gazed at as the splendid palaces of happiness and power. But in all ages there have been a few who, measuring and sounding the rivers of the vale at the feet of their farthest inaccessible falls, have learned that the sources must be far higher and far inward ; a few who, even in the level streams, have detected elements which neither the vale itself nor the surrounding mountains contained or could supply. How and whence to these thoughts, these strong probabilities, the ascertaining vision, the intuitive knowledge may finally supervene, can be learned only by the fact. I might oppose to the question the words with which Plotinus supposes Nature to answer a similar difficulty: 'Should any one interrogate her how she works, if graciously she vouchsafe to listen and speak, she will reply, it behooves thee not to disquiet me with interrogatories, but to understand in silence, even as I am silent, and work without words.'

"They and they only can acquire the philosophic imagination, the sacred power of self-intuition, who within themselves can interpret and understand the symbol, that the wings of the air-sylph are forming within the skin of the caterpillar; those only, who feel in their own spirits the same instinct which impels the chrysalis of the horned fly to leave room in its *involucrum* for *antennæ* yet to come. They know and feel that the potential works in them, even as the actual works in them! In short, all the organs of sense are framed for a corresponding world of sense; and we have it. All the organs of spirit are framed for a correspondent world of spirit; though the latter organs are not developed in all alike. But they exist in all, and their first appearance discloses itself in the moral being. How else could it be that even worldlings, not wholly debased, will contemplate the man of simple and disinterested goodness with contradictory feelings of pity and respect. 'Poor man, he is not made for this world.' Oh, herein they utter a prophecy of universal fulfilment, for man must either rise or sink.

"It is the essential mark of the true philosopher to rest satisfied with no imperfect light, as long as the impossibility of attaining a fuller knowledge has not been demonstrated. That the common consciousness itself will furnish proofs by its own direction that it is connected with master currents below the surface, I shall merely assume as a postulate *pro tempore*. . . . On the

IMMEDIATE which dwells in every man, and on the original intuition or absolute affirmation of it (which is likewise in every man, but does not in every man rise into consciousness), all the *certainty* of our knowledge depends ; and this becomes intelligible to no man by the ministry of mere words from without.　The medium by which spirits understand each other is not the surrounding air, but the *freedom* which they possess in common, as the common ethereal element of their being, the tremulous reciprocations of which propagate themselves even to the inmost of the soul.　Where the spirit of a man is not *filled* with the consciousness of freedom (were it only from its restlessness, as of one struggling in bondage) all spiritual intercourse is interrupted, not only with others, but even with himself. No wonder, then, that he remains incomprehensible to himself as well as to others.　No wonder that in the fearful desert of his consciousness he wearies himself out with empty words to which no friendly echo answers, either from his own heart or the heart of a fellow-being ; or bewilders himself in the pursuit of *notional* phantoms, the mere refractions from unseen and distant truths through the distorting medium of his own unenlivened and stagnant understanding !　To remain unintelligible to such a mind, exclaims Schelling on a like occasion, is honor and a good name before God and man.

" Philosophy is employed on objects of the *inner sense*, and cannot, like geometry, appropriate to every construction a corresponding *outward* intuition. . . . Now the inner sense has its direction determined for the greater part only by an act of freedom.　One man's consciousness extends only to the pleasant or unpleasant sensations caused in him by external impressions ; another enlarges his inner sense to a consciousness of forms and quantity ; a third, in addition to the image, is conscious of the conception or notion of the thing　a fourth attains to a notion of his notions—he reflects on his own reflections ; and thus we may say without impropriety, that the one possesses more or less inner sense than the other. . . .

" The postulate of philosophy, and at the same time the test of philosophical capacity, is no other than the heaven-descended KNOW THYSELF. And this at once practically and speculatively. For as philosophy is neither a science of the reason or understanding only, nor merely a science of morals, but the science of BEING altogether, its primary ground can be neither merely speculative nor merely practical, but both in one. All knowledge rests upon the coincidence of an object with a subject. For we can *know* only that which is true ; and the truth is universally placed in the coincidence of the thought with the thing, of the representation with the object represented."

Coleridge then puts and argues the two alternatives. 1. Either the Objective is taken as primary, and then we have to account for the supervention of the Subjective which coalesces with it, which natural philosophy supposes. 2. Or the Subjective is taken as primary, and then we have to account for the supervention of the objective, which spiritual philosophy supposes. The Transcendentalist accepts the latter alternative.

" The second position, which not only claims but necessitates the admission of its immediate certainty, equally for the scientific reason of the philosopher as for the common-sense of mankind at large, namely, I AM, cannot properly be entitled a prejudice. It is groundless indeed ; but then in the very idea it precludes all ground, and, separated from the immediate consciousness, loses its whole sense and import. It is groundless ; but only because it is itself the ground of all other certainty. Now the apparent contradiction, that the first position—namely, that the existence of things without us, which from its nature cannot be immediately certain—should be received as blindly and as independently of all grounds as the existence of our own being, the transcendental philosopher can solve only by the supposition that the former is unconsciously involved in the latter ; that it is not only coherent, but identical, and one and the same thing with our own immediate self-consciousness. To demonstrate this identity is the office and object of his philosophy.

" If it be said that this is idealism, let it be remembered that it is only so far idealism, as it is at the same time and on that very account the truest and most binding realism."

To follow the exposition further is unnecessary for the present purpose, which is to state the fundamental principles of the philosophy, not to give the processes ot reasoning by which they are illustrated. Had Coleridge been merely a philosopher, his influence on his generation, by this means, would have been insignificant ; for his expositions were fragmentary ; his thoughts were too swift and tumultuous in their flow to be systematically arranged ; his style, forcible and luminous in passages, is interrupted by too frequent episodes, excursions and explanatory parentheses, to be enjoyed by the inexpert. Besides being a philosopher, he was a theologian. His deepest interest was in the problems of theology. His mind was perpetually turning over the questions of trinity, incarnation, Holy Ghost, sin, redemption, salvation. He meditated endless books on these themes, and, in special, one " On the Logos," which was to remove all difficulties and reconcile all contradictions. " On the whole, those dead churches, this dead English church especially, must be brought to life again. Why not ? It was not dead ; the soul of it, in this parched-up body, was tragically asleep only. Atheistic philosophy was, true, on its side ; and Hume and Voltaire could, on their own ground, speak irrefragably for themselves against any church : but lift the church and them into a higher sphere of argument, *they* died into inanition, the church revivified itself into pristine florid vigor, became once more a living ship of the desert, and invincibly bore you over stock and stone."

The philosophy was accepted as a basis for the theology, and apparently only so far as it supplied the basis. Mrs. Coleridge declares, in a note to Chapter IX. of the "Biographia Literaria," that her father, soon after the composition of that work, became dissatisfied with the system of Schelling, considered as a fundamental and comprehensive scheme intended to exhibit the relations of God to the world and man. He objected to it, she insists, as essentially pantheistic, radically inconsistent with a belief in God as himself moral and intelligent, as beyond and above the world, as the supreme mind to which the human mind owes homage and fealty—inconsistent with any just view and deep sense of the moral and spiritual being of man. He was mainly concerned with the construction of a "philosophical system, in which Christianity,—based on the triune being of God, and embracing a primal fall and universal redemption, (to use Carlyle's words) Christianity, ideal, spiritual, eternal, but likewise and necessarily historical, realized and manifested in time,—should be shown forth as accordant, or rather as one with ideas of reason, and the demands of the spiritual and of the speculative mind, of the heart, conscience, reason, which should all be satisfied and reconciled in one bond of peace."

This explains the interest which young and enthusiastic minds in the English Church took in Coleridge, the verses just quoted from Aubrey de Vere, one of the new school of believers, the admiring discipleship of Frederick Denison Maurice, the hearty allegiance of the leaders of the spiritual reformation in England. Coleridge was the real founder of the Broad Church, which attempted to justify creed and sacrament, by substituting the ideas of the spiritual philosophy for the formal authority of traditions which the reason of the age was discarding.

The men who sympathized with the same movement in America felt the same gratitude to their leader. Already in 1829 " The Aids to Reflection " were republished by Dr. James Marsh. Caleb Sprague Henry, professor of philosophy and history in the University of New York in 1839, and before that a resident of Cambridge, an enthusiastic thinker and eloquent talker, loved to dilate on the genius of the English philosopher, and was better than a book in conveying information about him, better than many books in awakening interest in his thought. The name of Coleridge was spoken with profound reverence, his books were studied industriously, and the terminology of transcendentalism was as familiar as commonplace in the circles of divines and men of letters. At present Hegel is the prophet of these believers, Schelling is obsolete, and Coleridge, the English Schelling, has had his day. The change is marked by an all but entire absence of the passionate enthusiasm, the imaginative glow and fervor, that characterized the transcendental phase of the movement Coleridge was a vital thinker; his mind was a flame; his thoughts burned within him, and issued from him in language that trembled and throbbed with the force of the ideas committed to it. He was a divine, a preacher of most wonderful eloquence. At the age of three or four and forty Serjeant Talfourd heard him talk.

"At first his tones were conversational: he seemed to dally with the shallows of the subject and with fantastic images which bordered it; but gradually the thought grew deeper, and the voice deepened with the thought; the stream gathering strength seemed to bear along with it all things which opposed its progress, and blended them with its current; and stretching away among regions tinted with ethereal colors, was lost at airy distance in the horizon of fancy." At five-and-twenty William Hazlitt heard him preach.

"It was in January, 1798, that I rose one morning be-fore daylight, to walk ten miles in the mud, to hear this celebrated person preach. Never, the longest day I have to live, shall I have such another walk as this cold, raw, comfortless one, in the winter of the year 1798. *Il y a des impressions que ni le temps ni les circonstances peuvent effacer. Dusse je vivre des siècles entiers, le doux temps de ma jeunesse ne peut renaître pour moi, ni s'effacer jamais dans ma memoire.* When I got there the organ was playing the hundredth psalm, and when it was done Mr. Coleridge rose and gave out his text, 'He departed again into a mountain himself alone.' As he gave out this text his voice 'rose like a stream of rich distilled perfumes;' and when he came to the last two words, which he pronounced loud, deep, and dis-tinct, it seemed to me, who was then young, as if the sounds had echoed from the bottom of the human heart, and as if that prayer might have floated in solemn silence through the universe. The idea of St. John came into my mind, of one crying in the wilderness, who had his loins girt about, and whose food was locusts and wild honey. The preacher then launched into his subject, like an eagle dallying with the wind. The sermon was upon peace and war, upon church and state, not their alliance, but their separation ; on the spirit of the world and the spirit of Christianity, not as the same, but as opposed to one another. He talked of those who had inscribed the cross of Christ on banners dripping with human gore. He made a poetical and pastoral excursion, and to show the effects of war, drew a striking contrast between the simple shepherd boy, driving his team afield, or sitting under the hawthorn, piping to his flock as though he should never be old ; and the same poor country lad, crimped, kidnapped, brought into town, made drunk at an ale-house, turned into a wretched drummer-boy, with his hair sticking on end with powder and pomatum, a long cue at his back, and tricked out in the finery of the profession of blood.

' Such were the notes our once loved poet sung ; '

and for myself I could not have been more delighted if I had heard the music of the spheres. Poetry and Philosophy had met together, Truth and Genius had embraced, under the eye and with the sanction of Religion. This was even beyond my hopes. I returned home well satisfied."

The influence of Coleridge was greatly assisted by contemporary magazines, which helped by their furious efforts to crush him, and won sympathy for him by their attempts to laugh and hoot him down. Jeffrey handled the "Biographia Literaria" in the Edinburgh Review, August, 1817 ; "as favorable to the book *as could be expected*," the editor quietly says. The numberless varieties of judgment were represented in the Dublin University

Magazine, British and Foreign Quarterly, Fraser, Black-wood, Christian Quarterly, Spectator, Monthly Review, Eclectic, Westminster, most of which contained several articles on different aspects of the subject. In America, Geo. B. Cheever wrote in the North American Review, F. H. Hedge in the Christian Examiner, D. N. Lord in Lord's Theological Journal, H. T. Tuckerman in the Southern Literary Messenger, Noah Porter in the Bibliotheca Sacra. The New York Review, the American Quarterly, American Whig Review, all made contributions to the Coleridgian literature,* and exhibited the extensive reaches of his power. The readers of Lamb, Hazlitt, Wordsworth, Southey and the brilliant essayists that made so fascinating the English literature of the first third of our century must perforce be introduced to Coleridge. The " Ancient Mariner " and " Christabel," which lay on every table, excited interest in the man from whom such astonishing pieces proceeded ; so that many who understood little or nothing of his philosophical ideas, appropriated something of the spirit and tone of them. He had disciples who never heard him speak even in print, and followers who never saw his form even as sketched by critics. His thoughts were in the air ; the mental atmosphere of theological schools was modified by them. They insensibly transplanted establishments and creeds from old to new regions.

In 1851, Thomas Carlyle burlesqued Coleridge, took off his solemn oracular manner, made fun of his "plain-

---

* See for references, Poole's Index to Periodical Literature.

tive snuffle and sing-song," his " om-m-ject and sum-m-ject," his " talk not flowing anywhither like a river, but spreading everywhither in inextricable currents and regurgitations like a lake or sea ; terribly deficient in definite goal or aim, nay often in logical intelligibility ; what you were to believe or do, on any earthly or heavenly thing, obstinately refusing to appear from it, so that, most times, you felt logically lost ; swamped near to drowning in this tide of ingenious vocables spreading out boundless as if to submerge the world." But in his earlier days the " windy harangues " and " dizzying metaphysics " had their charm for him too ; the philosophy of the Highgate sage was in essence and fruit his own. He explained at some length and with considerable frequency, as well as much eloquence, the distinction between " understanding," the faculty that observed, generalized, inferred, argued, concluded, and " reason," the faculty that saw the ideal forms of truth face to face, and beheld the inmost reality of things. He dilated with a disciple's enthusiasm on the principles of the transcendental philosophy, painted in gorgeous colors the promises it held forth, prophesied earnestly respecting the better time for literature, art, social ethics and religious faith it would bring in, preached tempestuously against shams in church and state, from the mount of vision that it disclosed. We have already seen how he could speak of Kant, Fichte, Novalis, of Goethe and Jean Paul. Thirty-five years ago Carlyle was the high priest of the new philosophy. Emerson edited his miscellanies, and the dregs of his ink-bottle were welcomed as the precious sediment of the fountain of inspiration. In 1827 he defended the " Kritik of Pure Reason " against stupid objectors from the sensational side, as, in the opinion of the most competent judges, " distinctly the greatest intellectual achievement of the century in which it came to light," and affirmed as by authority, that the seeker for pure truth must begin with intuition and proceed outward by the light of the revelation thence derived. In 1831 he carried this principle to the extreme of maintaining that a complete surrender to the informing genius, a surrender so entire as to amount to the abandonment of definite purpose and will, was evidence of perfect wisdom ; for such is the interpretation we give to the paradoxical doctrine of " unconsciousness " which implied that in order to save the soul it must be forgotten ; that consciousness was a disease ; that in much wisdom was much grief.

Had Carlyle been more of a philosopher and less of a preacher, more a thinker and less a character, more a patient toiler after truth, and less a man of letters, his first intellectual impulse might have lasted. As it was, the reaction came precisely in middle life, and the apostle of transcendental ideas became the champion of Force. His Transcendentalism seems to have been a thing of sentiment rather than of conviction. A man of tremendous strength of feeling, his youth, as is the case with men of feeling, was romantic, enthusiastic, hopeful, exuberant ; his manhood, as is also the case with men of feeling, was wilful and overbearing, with sadness deepening into moroseness and unhopefulness verging towards despair.

The era of despair had not set in at the period when the mind of New England was fermenting with the ideas of the new philosophy. Then all was brave, humane, aspiring. The denunciations of materialism in philosophy, formalism in religion and utilitarianism in personal and social ethics, rang through the land ; the superb vindications of soul against sense , spirit against letter, faith against rite, heroism and nobleness against the petty expediencies of the market, kindled all earnest hearts. The emphatic declarations that "wonder and reverence are the conditions of insight and the source of strength ; that faith is prior to knowledge and deeper too ; that empirical science can but play on the surface of unfathomable mysteries ; that in the order of reality the ideal and invisible are the world's true adamant, and the laws of material appearance only its alluvial growths ; that in the inmost thought of men there is a thirst to which the springs of nature are a mere mirage, and which presses on to the waters of eternity," fell like refreshing gales from the hills on the children of men imprisoned in custom and suffocated by tradition. The infinitely varied illustrations of the worth of beauty, the grandeur of truth, the excellence of simple, devout sincerity in nature, literature, character ; the burning insistance on the need of fresh inspiration from the region of serene ideas, seemed to proceed from a soul newly awakened, if not especially endowed with the seer's vision. It was better than philosophy ; it was philosophy made vital with sentiment and purpose.

Carlyle early learned the German language, as Coleridge

did, and drank deep from the fountains of its best litera
ture.　To him it opened a new world of thought, which
the ordinary Englishman had no conception of.　Coleridge found himself at home there by virtue of his natural
genius, and also by the introduction given him by Wm.
Law, John Pordage, Richard Saumarez, and Jacob Behmen, so that the suddenly discovered continent broke on
him with less surprise ; but Carlyle was as one taken
wholly unawares, fascinated, charmed, intoxicated with
the sights and sounds about him.　Being unprepared
by previous reflection and overpowered by the gorgeous-
ness of color, the wealth was too much for him ; it palled at last on his appetite, and he experienced a reaction
similar to that of the sensualist whose delirium first per-
suades him that he has found his soul, and then makes
him fear that he has lost it.

With the reactionary stage of Carlyle's career when, as
a frank critic observes, " he flung away with a shriek the
problems his youth entertained, as the fruit by which
paradise was lost ; repented of all knowledge of good and
evil ; clapped a bandage round the open eyes of morals,
religion, art, and saw no salvation but in spiritual sui-
cide by plunging into the currents of instinctive nature
that sweep us we know not whither "—we are not concerned.　His interest for us ceases with his moral enthusiasm.

A more serene and beneficent influence proceeded from
the poet Wordsworth, whose fame rose along with that
of Coleridge, struggled against the same opposition, and
obtained even a steadier lustre.　There was a kindred be-

tween them which Wordsworth did not acknowledge, but which Coleridge more than suspected and tried to divulge. One chapter in the first volume of the " Biographia Literaria " and four chapters in the second volume are devoted to the consideration of Wordsworth's poetry, and effort is made, not quite successfully, to bring Wordsworth's psychological faith into sympathy with his own.

Wordsworth's genius has furnished critics with materials for speculation that must be sought in their proper places. We have no fresh analysis to offer. That the secret of his power over the ingenuous and believing minds of his age is to be found in the sentiment with which he invested homely scenes and characters is a superficial conjecture. What led him to invest homely scenes and characters with sentiment, and what made this circumstance interesting to precisely that class of minds ? What, but the same latent idealism that came to deliberate and formal expression in Coleridge, and suggested in the one what was proclaimed by the other ? For Wordsworth was a metaphysician, though he did not clearly suspect it ; at least, if he did, he was careful not to betray himself by the usual signs. The philosophers recognized him and paid to him their acknowledgments.

In the " Dial," Wordsworth is mentioned with honor ; not discussed as Goethe was, but pleasantly talked about as a well-known friend. The third volume of that magazine, April, 1843, contains an article on " Europe and European Books " in which occurs the following tribute to Wordsworth :

" The capital merit of Wordsworth is that he has

done more for the sanity of this generation than any other writer. Early in life, at a crisis, it is said, in his private affairs, he made his election between assuming and defending some legal rights with the chances of wealth and a position in the world—and the inward promptings of his heavenly genius ; he took his part ; he accepted the call to be a poet, and sat down, far from cities, with coarse clothing and plain fare to obey the heavenly vision. The choice he had made in his will manifested itself in every line to be real. We have poets who write the poetry of society, of the patricians and conventional Europe, as Scott and Moore ; and others, who, like Byron or Bulwer, write the poetry of vice and disease. But Wordsworth threw himself into his place, made no reserves or stipulations ; man and writer were not to be divided. He sat at the foot of Helvellyn and on the margin of Windermere, and took their lustrous mornings and their sublime midnights,for his theme, and not Marlowe nor Massinger, nor Horace, nor Milton nor Dante. He once for all forsook the styles and standards and modes of thinking of London and Paris and the books read there, and the aims pursued, and wrote Helvellyn and Windermere and the dim spirits which these haunts harbored. There was not the least attempt to reconcile these with the spirit of fashion and selfishness, nor to show, with great deference to the superior judgment of dukes and earls, that although London was the home for men of great parts, yet Westmoreland had these consolations for such as fate had condemned to the country life ; but with a complete satisfaction he pitied and rebuked their false lives, and celebrated his own with the religion of a true priest. Hence the antagonism which was immediately felt between his poetry and the spirit of the age, that here not only criticism but conscience and will were parties ; the spirit of literature, and the modes of living, and the conventional theories of the conduct of life were called in question on wholly new grounds, not from Platonism, nor from

Christianity, but from the lessons which the country muse taught a stout pedestrian climbing a mountain, and following a river from its parent rill down to the sea. The Cannings and Jeffreys of the capital, the Court Journals and Literary Gazettes were not well pleased, and voted the poet a bore. But that which rose in him so high as to the lips, rose in many others as high as to the heart. What he said, they were prepared to hear and to confirm. The influence was in the air, and was wafted up and down into lone and populous places, resisting the popular taste, modifying opinions which it did not change, and soon came to be felt in poetry, in criticism, in plans of life, and at last in legislation. In this country it very early found a stronghold, and its effect may be traced on all the poetry both of England and America."

This is truly and well said, though quite inadequate. The slighting allusion to Platonism might have been omitted, for possibly Wordsworth had caught something of the philosophy that was in the air. Mr. Emerson, in "Thoughts on Modern Literature," in the second number of the "Dial," Oct. 1840, touched a deeper chord.

"The fame of Wordsworth" he says, "is a leading fact in modern literature, when it is considered how hostile his genius at first seemed to the reigning taste, and with what feeble poetic talents his great and steadily growing dominion has been established. More than any poet his success has been not his own, but that of the idea which he shared with his coevals, and which he has rarely succeeded in adequately expressing. The Excursion awakened in every lover of nature the right feeling. We saw the stars shine, we felt the awe of mountains, we heard the rustle of the wind in the grass, and knew again the ineffable secret of solitude. It was a great joy. It was nearer to nature than any thing we had before. But the interest of the poem ended almost with the narrative of the influences of nature on the mind of the Boy, in the the first book. Obviously for that passage the poem was written, and with the exception of this and a few strains of like character in the sequel, the whole poem was dull. Here was no poem, but here was poetry, and a sure index where the subtle muse was about to pitch her tent and find the argument of her song. It was the human soul in these last ages striving for a just publication of itself. Add to this, however, the great praise of Wordsworth, that more than any other contemporary bard he is pervaded with a reverence of somewhat higher than (conscious) thought. There is in him that property common to all great poets—a wisdom of humanity, which is superior to any talents which they exert. It is the wisest part of Shakespeare and Milton, for they are poets by the free course which they allow to the informing soul, which through their eyes beholdeth again and blesseth the things which it hath made. The soul is superior to its knowledge, wiser than any of its works."

In the general Preface to his poems, where Wordsworth discusses the principles of the poetic art, he wrote: "The imagination is conscious of an indestructible dominion; the soul may fall away, from its not being able to sustain its grandeur, but if once felt and acknowledged, by no act of any other faculty of the mind can it be relaxed, impaired or diminished. Fancy is given to quicken and to beguile the temporal part of our nature; Imagination to incite and support the eternal." And in the appendix: "Faith was given to man that his affections, detached from the treasures of time, might be inclined to settle on those of eternity: the elevation of his nature, which this habit produces on earth, being to him a presumptive evidence of a future state of existence, and giving him a title to partake of its holiness. The religious man values what he sees, chiefly as an 'imperfect shadowing forth' of what he is incapable of seeing." Was this an echo from the German Jacobi, whose doctrine of Faith had been some time abroad in the intellectual world?

The ode "Intimations of Immortality from Recollections of Early Childhood," was a clear reminiscence of Platonism. This famous poem was the favorite above all other effusions of Wordsworth with the Transcendentalists, who held it to be the highest expression of his genius, and most characteristic of its bent. Emerson in his last discourse on Immortality, calls it "the best modern essay on the subject." Many passages in the longer poems attest the transcendental character of the author's faith. Coleridge quotes from "Tintern Abbey:"

> For I have learned
> To look on nature, not as in the hour
> Of thoughtless youth, but hearing oftentimes
> The still sad music of humanity,
> Nor harsh nor grating, though of ample power
> To chasten and subdue. And I have felt
> A presence that disturbs me with the joy
> Of elevated thoughts; a sense sublime
> Of something far more deeply interfused,
> Whose dwelling is the light of setting suns,
> And the round ocean and the living air,
> And the blue sky, and in the mind of man;
> A motion and a spirit that impels
> All thinking things, all objects of all thought,
> And rolls through all things."

This passage from the " Excursion " suggests language of Fichte in his *Bestimmung des Menschen,* " In der Liebe nur ist das Leben, ohne Sie ist Tod und Vernichtung."

> This is the genuine course, the aim, the end,
> Of prescient Reason ; all conclusions else
> Are abject, vain, presumptuous and perverse,
> The faith partaking of those holy times.
>
> Life, I repeat, is energy of Love,
> Divine or human; exercised in pain,
> In strife and tribulation ; and ordained,
> If so approved and sanctified, to pass
> Through shades and silent rest, to endless joy.

Another extract recalls the " pantheism " of Schelling.

> Thou—who didst wrap the cloud
> Of infancy around us, that Thyself
> Therein with our simplicity awhile
> Might'st hold, on earth, communion undisturbed,
> Who from the anarchy of dreaming sleep,
> Or from its death-like void, with punctual care,
> And touch as gentle as the morning light,
> Restorest us, daily, to the powers of sense
> And reason's steadfast rule,—Thou, thou alone
> Art everlasting, and the blessed Spirits,
> Which Thou includest, as the Sea her Waves.
> For adoration Thou endurest ; endure
> For consciousness the motions of Thy will ;
> For apprehension those transcendent truths
> Of the pure Intellect, that stand as laws ;
> Submission constituting strength and power,
> Even to Thy Being's infinite majesty !

Having before me a copy of Wordsworth's poems, once the possession of an earnest Transcendentalist, I find these, and many lines of similar import, underlined; showing how dear the English poet was to the American reader.

There were others who held and enunciated the new faith that came from Germany, the transfigured protestantism of the land of Luther. But these three names will suffice to indicate the wealth of England's contribution to the spiritual life of the New World—Coleridge, Carlyle, Wordsworth—the philosopher, the preacher, the poet ; the man of thought, the man of letters, the man of imagination. These embrace all the methods by which the fresh enthusiasm for the soul communicated its power. These three were everywhere read, and everywhere talked of. They occupied prominent places in the public eye. They sank into the shadow only when the faith that glorified them began to decline.

It is remarkable that Emerson in the paper just quoted, written in 1840, passes from Wordsworth to Landor ; while the author of the other paper, written in 1843, passes, and almost with an expression of relief, from Wordsworth to Tennyson, the new poet whose breaking glory threatened the morning star with eclipse. By this time Transcendentalism was on the wane. The " Dial " marked for one year longer the hours of the great day, and then was removed from its place, and the scientific method of measuring progress was introduced. Wordsworth from year to year had a diminishing proportion of admirers : from year to year the admirers of Tennyson increased. As early as 1843 the passion for music, color, and external polish was manifest. Tennyson's elegance and subtlety, his rich fancy, his mastery of language, his metrical skill, his taste for the sumptuous and gorgeous, were winning their way to popularity. The critic in the "Dial" has misgivings: " In these boudoirs of damask and alabaster one is further off from stern nature and human life than in "Lalla Rookh" and "The Loves of the Angels." Amid swinging censers and perfumed lamps, amidst velvet and glory, we long for rain and frost. Otto of roses is good, but wild air is better." But the sweets have been tasted, and have spoiled the relish for the old homeliness. For the man who loved him the charm of Wordsworth was idyllic; for the few who bent the head to him it was mystical and prophetic. The idyllic sentiment palled on the taste. It was a reaction from artificial forms of sensibility, and having enjoyed its day, submitted to the law of change that called it into being. The moral earnestness, the mystic idealism became unpopular along with the school of philosophy from which it sprung, and gave place to the realism of the Victorian bards, who expressed the sensuous spirit of a more external age. Transcendentalism lurks in corners of England now. The high places of thought are occupied by men who approach the great problems from the side of nature, and through matter feel after mind ; by means of the senses attempt the heights of spirit.

VI.

TRANSCENDENTALISM IN NEW ENGLAND.

THE title of this Chapter is in a sense misleading. For with some truth it may be said that there never was such a thing as Transcendentalism out of New England. In Germany and France there was a transcendental philosophy, held by cultivated men, taught in schools, and professed by many thoughtful and earnest people ; but it never affected society in its organized institutions or practical interests. In old England, this philosophy influenced poetry and art, but left the daily existence of men and women untouched. But in New England, the ideas entertained by the foreign thinkers took root in the native soil and blossomed out in every form of social life. The philosophy assumed full proportions, produced fruit according to its kind, created a new social order for itself, or rather showed what sort of social order it would create under favoring conditions. Its new heavens and new earth were made visible, if but for a moment, and in a wintry season. Hence, when we speak of Transcendentalism, we mean New England Transcendentalism.

New England furnished the only plot of ground on the planet, where the transcendental philosophy had a chance to show what it was and what it proposed. The forms of life there were, in a measure, plastic. There were no immovable prejudices, no fixed and unalterable traditions. Laws and usages were fluent, malleable at all events. The sentiment of individual freedom was active; the truth was practically acknowledged, that it takes all sorts of people to make a world, and the many minds of the many men were respected. No orders of men, no aristocracies of intellect, no privileged classes of thought were established. The old world supplied such literature as there was, in science, law, philosophy, ethics, theology; but an astonishing intellectual activity seized upon it, dealt with it in genuine democratic fashion, classified it, accepted it, dismissed it, paying no undue regard to its foreign reputation. Experiments in thought and life, of even audacious description, were made, not in defiance of precedent—for precedent was hardly respected enough to be defied—but in innocent unconsciousness of precedent. A feeling was abroad that all things must be new in the new world. There was call for immediate application of ideas to life. In the old world, thoughts remained cloistered a generation before any questioned their bearing on public or private affairs. In the new world, the thinker was called on to justify himself on the spot by building an engine, and setting something in motion. The test of a truth was its availability. The popular faith in the capacities of men to make states, laws, religions for themselves, supplied a ground work for the new philosophy. The philosophy of sensation, making great account, as it did, of circumstances, arrangements, customs usages, rules of education and discipline, was alien and disagreeable to people who, having just emancipated themselves from political dependence on the mother country, were full of confidence in their ability to set up society for themselves. The philosophy that laid its foundations in human nature, and placed stress on the organic capacities and endowments of the mind, was as congenial as the opposite system was foreign. Every native New Englander was at heart, whether he suspected it or not, radically and instinctively a disciple of Fichte or Schelling, of Cousin or Jouffroy.

The religion of New England was Protestant and of the most intellectual type. Romanism had no hold on the thinking people of Boston. None beside the Irish laboring and menial classes were Catholics, and their religion was regarded as the lowest form of ceremonial superstition. The Congregational system favored individuality of thought and action. The orthodox theology, in spite of its arbitrary character and its fixed type of supernaturalism, exercised its professors severely in speculative questions, and furnished occasions for discernment and criticism which made reason all but supreme over faith. This theology too had its purely spiritual side—nay, it was essentially spiritual. Its root ran back into Platonism, and its flower was a mysticism which, on the intellectual side, bordered closely on Transcendentalism. The charge that the Trinitarian system, in its distinguishing features, was of Platonic, and not of Jewish origin, was a confession that it was born of the noblest idealism of the race. So in truth it was, and so well-instructed Trinitarians will confess that it was. The Platonic philosophy being transcendental

in its essence and tendency, communicated this character to Christian speculation.   The skeletons of ancient polemics were buried deep beneath the soil of
orthodoxy, and were not supposed to be a part of the
structure of modern beliefs, but there nevertheless they
were.   The living faith of New England, in its spiritual
aspects, betrayed its ancestry.   The speculation had become Christian, the powers claimed by pagan philosophers
for the mind were ascribed to the influences of the Holy
Spirit and the truths revealed in consciousness were
truths of the Gospel ; but the fact of immediate communication between the soul of the believer and its Christ
was so earnestly insisted on, the sympathy was represented as being of so kindred and organic a nature, that
in reading the works of the masters of New England
theology, it requires an effort to forget that the speculative basis of their faith was not the natural basis of the
philosopher, but the supernatural one of the believer.
The spiritual writings of Jonathan Edwards, the
"Treatise on the Religious Affections" especially,
breathe the sweetest spirit of idealism.   Indeed, whenever orthodoxy spread its wings and rose into the
region of faith, it lost itself in the sphere where the
human soul and the divine were in full concurrence.
Transcendentalism simply claimed for all men what
Protestant Christianity claimed for its own elect.

That adherents of the sensuous philosophy professed
the orthodox doctrines, is a circumstance that throws the
above statement into bolder relief.   For these people
gave to the system the hard, external, dogmatical charac-

ter which in New England provoked the Unitarian reaction. The beliefs in scripture inspiration, incarnation, atonement, election, predestination, depravity, fall, regeneration, redemption, deprived of their interior meaning, became ragged heaps of dogmatism, unbeautiful, incredible, hateful. Assault came against them from the quarter of common intelligence and the rational understanding. The sensuous philosophy associated with the school of Locke,—which Edwards and the like of him scorned,—fell upon the fallen system and plucked it unmercifully. Never was easier work than that of the early Unitarian critics. The body of orthodoxy having lost its soul, was a very unsightly carcass,—so evidently, to every sense, a carcass, that they who had respected it as a celestial creation, and could not be persuaded that this was all they respected, allowed the scavengers to take it away, only protesting that the thing disposed of was not the revealed gospel, or anything but a poor effigy of it.

The Unitarians as a class belonged to the school of Locke, which discarded the doctrine of innate ideas, and its kindred beliefs. Unitarianism from the beginning showed affinity with this school, and avowed it more distinctly than idealists avowed Trinitarianism. Paul of Samosata, Arius, Pelagius, Socinus, the Swiss, Polish, English advocates of the same general theology and christology were, after their several kinds, disciples of the same philosophical system. Unitarianism, it was remarked, has rarely, if ever, been taught or held by any man of eminence in the church who was a Platonist.

The Unitarians of New England, good scholars, careful reasoners, clear and exact thinkers, accomplished men of letters, humane in sentiment, sincere in moral intention, belonged, of course with individual exceptions, to the class which looked without for knowledge, rather than within for inspiration. The Unitarian in religion was a whig in politics, a conservative in literature, art and social ethics. The Unitarian divine was more familiar with Tillotson than with Cudworth, and more in love with William Paley than with Joseph Butler. He was strong in the " Old English" classics, and though a confessed devotee to no school in philosophy, was addicted to the prevailing fashion of intelligent, cultivated good sense. The Unitarian was disquieted by mysticism, enthusiasm and rapture. Henry More was unintelligible to him, and Robert Fludd disgusting. He had no sympathy with Helvetius, D'Holbach, Diderot or Voltaire, those fierce disturbers of intellectual peace; he had as little with William Law and Coleridge, dreamers and visionaries, who substituted vapor for solid earth. The Unitarian leaders were distinguished by practical wisdom, sober judgment, and balanced thoughtfulness, that weighed opinions in the scale of evidence and argument. Even Dr. Channing clung to the philosophical traditions that were his inheritance from England. The splendid things he said about the dignity of human nature, the divinity of the soul, the moral kinship with Christ, the inspiration of the moral sentiment, the power of moral intuition, habitual and characteristic as they were, scarcely justify the ascription to him of sympathy with philosophical idealism. His tenacious adherence to the record of miracle as attesting the mission of the Christ, and his constant exaltation of the Christ above humanity, suggest that the first principles of the transcendental philosophy had not been distinctly accepted, even if they were distinctly apprehended. The following extract from a letter written in 1819, expresses Dr. Channing's feeling toward Christ, a feeling never essentially altered: " Jesus Christ existed before he came into the world, and in a state of great honor and felicity. He was known, esteemed, beloved, revered in the family of heaven. He was entrusted with the execution of the most sublime purposes of his Father." About the same time he wrote: " Jesus ever lives, and is ever active for mankind. He is Mediator, Intercessor, Lord, and Saviour ; He has a permanent and constant connection with mankind. He is through all time, now as well as formerly, the active and efficient friend of the human race." The writer of such words was certainly not a Transcendentalist in philosophy. His biographer, himself a brilliant Transcendentalist, admits as much. " His soul" he says, " was illuminated with the idea of the absolute immutable glory of the Moral Good ; and reverence for conscience is the key to his whole doctrine of human destiny and duty. Many difficult metaphysical points he passed wholly by, as being out of the sphere alike of intuition and of experience. He believed, to be sure, in the possibility of man's gaining some insight of Universal Order, and respected the lofty

aspiration which prompts men to seek a perfect knowledge of the Divine laws ; but he considered pretensions
to absolute science as quite premature saw more
boastfulness than wisdom in ancient and modern
schemes of philosophy, and was not a little amused at
the complacent confidence with which quite evidently
fallible theorists assumed to stand at the centre, and to
scan and depict the panorama of existence." In a letter
of 1840, referring to the doctrines of Mr. Parker and
that school of thinkers, he writes : " I see and feel the
harm done by this crude speculation, whilst I also see
much nobleness to bind me to its advocates. In its
opinions generally I see nothing to give me hope. I am
somewhat disappointed that this new movement is to do
so little for the spiritual regeneration of society." A
year later, he tells James Martineau that the spiritualists (meaning the Transcendentalists) " in identifying
themselves a good deal with Cousin's crude system, have
lost the life of an original movement. They are anxious
to defend the soul's immediate connection with God,
and are in danger of substituting private inspiration
for Christianity." What he knew of Kant, Schelling
and Fichte, through Mad. de Stael and Coleridge, he
welcomed as falling in with his own conceptions of the
grandeur of the human mind and will ; but his aquaint-
ance with them was never complete, and if it had been,
he would perhaps have been repelled by the intellectual,
as strongly as he was attracted by the moral teaching.

In this matter the sentiment of Channing went beyond
his philosophy. The following extracts taken at random

from a volume of discourses edited in 1873 by his nephew, under the title " The Perfect Life," show that Channing was a Transcendentalist in feeling, whatever he may have been in thought.

" The religious principle, is, without doubt, the noblest working of human nature. This principle God implanted for Himself. Through this the human mind corresponds to the Supreme Divinity."

" The idea of God is involved in the primitive and most universal idea of Reason ; and is one of its central principles."

" We have, each of us, the spiritual eye to see, the mind to know, the heart to love, the will to obey God."

" A spiritual light, brighter than that of noon, pervades our daily life. The cause of our not seeing is in ourselves."

" The great lesson is, that there is in human nature an element truly Divine, and worthy of all reverence ; that the Infinite which is mirrored in the outward universe, is yet more brightly imaged in the inward spiritual world."

" They who assert the greatness of human nature, see as much of guilt as the man of worldly wisdom. But amidst the passions and selfishness of men they see another element—a Divine element—a spiritual principle."

" This moral principle—the supreme law in man—is the Law of the Universe, the very Law to which the highest beings are subject, and in obeying which they find their elevation and their joy."

" The Soul itself,—in its powers and affections, in its unquenchable thirst and aspiration for unattained good, gives signs of a Nature made for an interminable progress, such as cannot be now conceived."

The debt which Transcendentalism owed to Unitarianism was not speculative ; neither was it immediate or direct. The Unitarians, clergy as well as laity, so far as the latter comprehended their position, acknowledged themselves to be friends of free thought in religion. This was their distinction. They disavowed sympathy with dogmatism, partly because such dogmatism as there was existed in the minds of their theological foes, and was felt in such persecution as society permitted ; and partly because they honestly respected the human mind, and valued thought for its own sake. They had no creed, and no system of philosophy on which a creed could be, by common consent, built. Rather were they open inquirers, who asked questions and waited for rational answers, having no definite apprehension of the issue to which their investigations tended, but with room enough within the accepted theology to satisfy them, and work enough on the prevailing doctrines to keep them employed. Under these circumstances, they honestly but incautiously professed a principle broader than they were able to stand by, and avowed the absolute freedom of the human mind as their characteristic faith ; instead of a creed, the right to judge all creeds ; instead of a system, authority to try every system by rules of evidence. The intellectual among them were at liberty to entertain views which an orthodox mind instinctively shrank from ; to read books which an orthodox believer would not have touched with the ends of his fingers. The literature on their tables represented a wide mental activity. Their libraries contained authors never found before on ministerial shelves. Skepticism throve by what it fed on ; and, before they had become fully aware of the possible results of their diligent study, their powers had acquired a confidence that encouraged ventures beyond the walls of Zion. This profession of free inquiry, and the practice of it within the extensive area of Protestant theology, opened the door to the new speculation which carried unlooked-for heresies in its bosom ; and before the gates could be closed the insidious enemy had penetrated to the citadel.

There was idealism in New England prior to the introduction of Transcendentalism. Idealism is of no clime or age. It has its proportion of disciples in every period and in the apparently most uncongenial countries; a full proportion might have been looked for in New England. But when Emerson appeared, the name of Idealism was legion. He alone was competent to form a school, and as soon as he rose, the scholars trooped about him. By sheer force of genius Emerson anticipated the results of the transcendental philosophy, defined its axioms and ran out their inferences to the end. Without help from abroad, or with such help only as none but he could use, he might have domesticated in Massachusetts an idealism as heroic as Fichte's, as beautiful as Schelling's ; but it would have lacked the dialectical basis of the great German systems.

Transcendentalism, properly so called, was imported in foreign packages. Few read German, but most read French. As early as 1804, Degerando lectured on Kant's philosophy, in Paris ; and as early as 1813 Mad. de Stael gave an account of it. The number of copies of the original works of either Kant, Fichte, Jacobi or

Schelling, that found their way to the United States, was inconsiderable. Half a dozen eager students obtained isolated books of Herder, Schleiermacher, De Wette and other theological and biblical writers, read them, translated chapters from them, or sent notices of them to the Christian Examiner. The works of Coleridge made familiar the leading ideas of Schelling. The foreign reviews reported the results and processes of French and German speculation. In 1827, Thomas Carlyle wrote, in the Edinburgh Review, his great articles on Richter and the State of German Literature; in 1828 appeared his essay on Goethe. Mr. Emerson presented these and other papers as "Carlyle's Miscellanies" to the American public. In 1838 George Ripley began the publication of the "Specimens of Foreign Standard Literature," a series which extended to fourteen volumes; the first and second comprising philosophical miscellanies by Cousin, Jouffroy and Constant, translated with introductions by Mr. Ripley himself; the third devoted to Goethe and Schiller, with elaborate and discriminating prefaces by John S. Dwight; the fourth giving Eckermann's Conversations with Goethe, done into English by Margaret Fuller; the three next containing Menzel's German Literature, by Prof. C. C. Felton; the eighth and ninth introducing Wm. H. Channing's version of Jouffroy's Introduction to Ethics; the tenth and eleventh, DeWette's Theodor, by James Freeman Clarke; the twelfth and thirteenth, DeWette's Ethics, by Samuel Osgood; and the last offering samples of German Lyrics, by Charles T. Brooks. These volumes, which were remarkably attractive, both in form and contents, brought many readers into a close acquaintance with the teaching and the spirit of writers of the new school.

The Philosophical Miscellanies of Cousin were much noticed by the press, George Bancroft in especial sparing no pains to commend them and the views they presented. The spiritual philosophy had no more fervent or eloquent champion than he. No reader of his " History of the United States," has forgotten the noble tribute paid to it under the name of Quakerism, or the striking parallel between the two systems represented in the history by John Locke and Wm. Penn, both of whom framed constitutions for the new world. For keenness of apprehension and fullness of statement the passages deserve to be quoted here. They occur in the XVI. chapter of the History.

" The elements of humanity are always the same, the inner light dawns upon every nation, and is the same in every age ; and the French revolution was a result of the same principles as those of George Fox, gaining domin-inion over the mind of Europe. They are expressed in the burning and often profound eloquence of Rousseau ; they reappear in the masculine philosophy of Kant. The professor of Königsberg, like Fox and Barclay and Penn, derived philosophy from the voice in the soul ; like them, he made the oracle within the categorical rule of practical morality, the motive to disinterested virtue ; like them, he esteemed the Inner Light, which discerns universal and necessary truths, an element of humanity ; and therefore his philosophy claims for humanity the right of ever renewed progress and reform. If the Quakers disguised their doctrine under the form of theology, Kant concealed it for a season under the jargon of a nervous but unusual diction. But Schiller has reproduced the great idea in beautiful verse; Chat-eaubriand avowed himself its advocate; Coleridge has repeated the doctrine in misty language; it beams through the poetry of Lamartine and Wordsworth; while in the country of beautiful prose, the eloquent Cousin, listening to the same eternal voice which connects humanity with universal reason, has gained a wide fame for " the divine principle," and in explaining the harmony between that light and the light of Christianity, has often unconsciously borrowed the language, and employed the arguments of Barclay and Penn."

A few pages later is the brilliant passage describing the essential difference between this philosophy and that of Locke :

" Locke, like William Penn, was tolerant; both loved freedom, both cherished truth in sincerity. But Locke kindled the torch of liberty at the fires of tradition ; Penn at the living light in the soul. Locke sought truth through the senses and the outward world ; Penn looked inward to the divine revelations in every mind. Locke compared the soul to a sheet of white paper, just as Hobbes had compared it to a slate on which time and chance might scrawl their experience. To Penn the soul was an organ which of itself instinctively breathes divine harmonies, like those musical instruments which are so curiously and perfectly formed, that when once set in motion, they of themselves give forth all the melodies designed by the artist that made them. To Locke, conscience is nothing else than our own opinion of our own actions ; to Penn, it is the image of God and his oracle in the soul. . . . In studying the understanding Locke begins with the sources of knowledge ; Penn with an inventory of our intellectual treasures. . . . The system of

Locke lends itself to contending factions of the most opposite interests and purposes; the doctrine of Fox and Penn, being but the common creed of humanity, forbids division and insures the highest moral unity. To Locke, happiness is pleasure, and things are good and evil only in reference to pleasure and pain; and to "inquire after the highest good is as absurd as to dispute whether the best relish be in apples, plums or nuts." Penn esteemed happiness to lie in the subjection of the baser instincts to the instinct of Deity in the breast; good and evil to be eternally and always as unlike as truth and falsehood; and the inquiry after the highest good to involve the purpose of existence. Locke says plainly that, but for rewards and punishments beyond the grave, 'it is certainly right to eat and drink, and enjoy what we delight in.' Penn, like Plato and Fenelon, maintained the doctrine so terrible to despots, that God is to be loved for His own sake, and virtue to be practised for its intrinsic loveliness. Locke derives the idea of infinity from the senses, describes it as purely negative, and attributes it to nothing but space, duration and number; Penn derived the idea from the soul, and ascribed it to truth and virtue and God. Locke declares immortality a matter with which reason has nothing to do; and that revealed truth must be sustained by outward signs and visible acts of power; Penn saw truth by its own light and summoned the soul to bear witness to its own glory."

The justice of the comparison, in the first part of the above extract, of Quakerism with Transcendentalism, may be disputed. Some may be of opinion that inasmuch as Quakerism traces the source of the Inner Light to the supernatural illumination of the Holy Spirit, while Transcendentalism regards it as a natural endowment of the human mind, the two are fundamentally opposed while superficially in agreement. However this may be, the practical issues of the two coincide, and the truth of the contrast presented between the philosophies, designated by the name of Locke on the one side, and of Penn on the other, will not be disputed. Mr. Bancroft's statement, though dazzling, is exact. It was made in 1837. The third edition from which the above citation was made, was published in 1838, the year of Mr. Emerson's address to the Divinity students at Cambridge.

Mr. Emerson had shown his hand plainly several years before. In 1832 he raised the whole issue in the "epoch making" sermon, in which he advanced the view of the communion service that led to his resignation of the Christian ministry. His elder brother, William, returning from his studies in Germany, was turned from the profession of the church which he had purposed entering, to the law, by similar scruples. In 1834, James Walker printed in the " Christian Examiner " an address, which was the same year published as a tract, by the American Unitarian Association, entitled " The Philosophy of Man's Spiritual Nature in regard to the foundations of Faith," wherein he took frankly the transcendental ground, contending :

" That the existence of those spiritual faculties and capacities which are assumed as the foundation of religion in the soul of man, is attested, and put beyond controversy by the revelations of consciousness ; that religion in the soul, consisting as it does, of a manifestation and development of these spiritual faculties and capacities, is as much a reality in itself, and enters as essentially into our idea of a perfect man, as the corresponding manifestation and development of the reasoning faculties, a sense of justice, or the affections of sympathy and benevolence; and that " from the acknowledged existence and reality of spiritual impressions or perceptions, we may and do assume the existence and reality of the spiritual world; just as from the acknowledged existence and reality of sensible impressions or perceptions, we may and do assume the existence and realities of the sensible world."

In this discourse, for originally it was a discourse, the worst species of infidelity is charged to the " Sensational " philosophy, and at the close, the speaker in impressive language, said:

" Let us hope that a better philosophy than the degrading sensualism out of which most forms of infidelity have grown, will prevail, and that the minds of the rising generation will be thoroughly imbued with it. Let it be a philosophy which recognizes the higher nature of man, and aims, in a chastened and reverential spirit, to unfold the mysteries of his higher life. Let it be a philosophy which comprehends the soul, a soul suscept-ible of religion, of the sublime principle of faith, of a faith which ' entereth into that within the veil.' Let it be a philosophy which continually reminds us of our intimate relations to the spiritual world; which opens to us new sources of consolation in trouble, and new sources of life in death—nay, which teaches us that what we call *death* is but the dying of all that is mortal, that nothing but life may remain."

In 1840, the same powerful advocate of the transcend-ental doctrine, in a discourse before the alumni of the Cambridge Divinity School, declared that the return to a higher order of ideas, to a living faith in God, in Christ, and in the church, had been promoted by such

men as Schleiermacher and De Wette ; gave his opinion
that the religious community had reason to look with
distrust and dread on a philosophy which limited the
ideas of the human mind to the information imparted
by the senses, and denied the existence of spiritual
elements in the nature of man ; and again welcomed the
philosophy taught in England by Butler, Reid· and
Coleridge ; in Germany, by Kant, Jacobi and Schleiermacher ; in France, by Cousin, Jouffroy and Degerando.
Such words from James Walker, always a favorite
teacher with young men, a mind of judicial authority
in the liberal community, and at that time Professor of
Moral Philosophy at Harvard College, made a deep
impression.   When he said : " Men may put down Transcendentalism .if they can, but they must first deign to
comprehend its principles," the most conservative began
to surmise that there must be something in Transcendentalism.

But before this the movement was well under way.
In 1836, Emerson's " Nature " broke through the
shell of accepted opinions on a very essential subject :
true, but five hundred copies were sold in twelve years ;
critics and philosophers could make nothing of it ; but
those who read it recognized signs of a new era, even if
they could not describe them ; and many who did not read
it felt in the atmosphere the change it introduced.   The
idealism of the little book was uncompromising.

" In the presence of ideas we feel that the outward
circumstance is a dream and a shade.   Whilst we wait

in this Olympus of gods, we think of nature as an appendix to the soul. We ascend into their region, and know that these are the thoughts of the Supreme Being." * * * "Idealism is an hypothesis to account for nature by other principles than those of carpentry and chemistry. It acquaints us with the total disparity between the evidence of our own being, and the evidence of the world's being. The world is a divine dream, from which we may presently awake to the glories and certainties of day."

The same year, George Ripley reviewed in the "Christian Examiner," Martineau's "Rationale of Religious Enquiry." The article was furiously assailed in the Boston Daily Advertiser. Mr. Ripley replied in the paper of the next day, vindicating the ideas of the review and of the book as being strictly in consonance with the principles of liberal Christianity.

In 1838 came the wonderful "address" before the Cambridge Divinity School, which stirred the soul of aspiring young men, and, wakened the wrath of sedate old ones. It was idealism in its full blaze, and it made the germs of Transcendentalism struggle in the sods.

The next year Andrews Norton attacked the new philosophy in a discourse before the same audience, on "The Latest Form of Infidelity." The doctrine of that discourse was "Sensationalism" in its boldest aspect.

"Christ was commissioned by God to speak to us in His name, and to make known to us, on His authority, those truths which it most concerns us to know; and there can be no greater miracle than this. No proof of His divine commission could be afforded but through miraculous displays of God's power. Nothing is left that can be called Christianity, if its miraculous character be denied. Its essence is gone ; its evidence is annihilated." * * * " To the demand for certainty let it come from whom it may, I answer that I know of no absolute certainty beyond the limit of momentary consciousness ; a certainty that vanishes the instant it exists, and is lost in the region of metaphysical doubt." . . . " There can be no intuition, no direct perception of the truth of Christianity, no metaphysical certainty." . . . " Of the facts on which religion is founded, we can pretend to no assurance except that derived from the testimony of God from the Christian revelation."

A pamphlet defending the discourse contained passages like the following : " The doctrine that the mind possesses a faculty of intuitively discovering the truths of religion, is not only utterly untenable, but the proposition is of such a character that it cannot well bear the test of being distinctly stated. The question respecting the existence of such a faculty is not difficult to be decided. We are not conscious of possessing any such faculty ; and there can be no other proof of its existence. Its defenders shrink from presenting it in broad daylight. They are disposed to keep it out of view behind a cloud of words." . . . " Consciousness or intuition can inform us of nothing but what exists in our own minds, including the relations of our own ideas. It is therefore not an intelligible error, but a mere absurdity to maintain that we are conscious, or have an intuitive knowledge of the being of God, of our own immortality, of the revelation of God through Christ, or of any other fact of religion." . . . " The religion of which they (the Transcendentalists) speak, therefore, exists merely, if it exist at all, in undefined and unintelligible feelings, having reference, perhaps, to certain imaginations, the result of impressions communicated in childhood or produced by the visible signs of religious belief existing around us, or awakened by the beautiful and magnificent spectacles which nature presents."

Mr. Norton spoke with biting severity of the masters of German philosophy, criticism, and literature, and exhausted his sarcasm on the address of Mr. Emerson delivered the previous year. To Mr. Norton, Mr. Ripley made prompt and earnest, though temperate, reply in three long and powerful letters, devoted mainly to a refutation of his adversary's accusations against Spinoza, Schleiermacher, De Wette, and the philosophic theologians of Germany. Not till the end does he take issue with the fundamental positions of Mr. Norton's philosophy; then he brands as " revolting " the doctrine that " there can be no intuition, no direct perception of the truth of Christianity ;" that " the feeling or direct perception of religious truth " is an " imaginary faculty ;" and affirms his conviction that " the principle that the soul has no faculty to perceive spiritual truth, is contradicted by the universal consciousness of man."

" Does the body see," he asks, " and is the spirit blind ? No, man has the faculty for feeling and perceiving religious truth. So far from being imaginary, it is the highest reality of which the pure soul is conscious. Can I be more certain that I am capable of looking out and admiring the forms of external beauty, ' the frail and weary weed in which God dresses the soul that he has called into time,' than that I can also look within, and commune with the fairer forms of truth and holiness which plead for my love, as visitants from Heaven ? "

The controversy was taken up by other pens. In 1840, Theodore Parker, speaking as a plain man under the name of Levi Blodgett, " moved and handled the

Previous Question" after a fashion that betrayed the practised thinker and scribe. Mr. Parker occupied substantially the same ground that was taken by James Walker in 1834.

"The germs of religion, both the germs of religious principle and religious sentiment, must be born in man, or innate, as our preacher says. I reckon that man is by nature a religious being, *i. e.* that he was made to be religious, as much as an ox was made to eat grass. The existence of God is a fact given in our nature : it is not something discovered by a process of reasoning, by a long series of deductions from facts ; nor yet is it the last generalization from phenomena observed in the universe of mind or matter. But it is a truth fundamental in our nature ; given outright by God ; a truth which comes to light as soon as self-consciousness begins. Still further, I take a sense of dependence on God to be a natural and essential sentiment of the soul, as much as feeling, seeing and hearing are natural sensations of the body. Here, then, are the religious instincts which lead man to God and religion, just as naturally as the intellectual instincts lead him to truth, and animal instincts to his food. As there is light for the eye, sound for the ear, food for the palate, friends for the affections, beauty for the imagination, truth for the reason, duty for conscience—so there is God for the religious sentiment or sense of dependence on Him. Now all these presuppose one another, as a want essential to the structure of man's mind or body presupposes something to satisfy it. And as the sensation of hunger presupposes food to satisfy it, so the sense of dependence on God presupposes his existence and character."

From these premises Mr. Parker proceeds to discuss the questions about miracles, inspiration, revelation, the character and functions of Jesus, the Christ, and kindred matters belonging to the general controversy. The year following, he preached the sermon on the "Transient and Permanent in Christianity," which brought out the issues between the "Sensationalists" and the "Transcendentalists," and was the occasion of detaching the latter from the original body.

The first series of Emerson's "Essays" containing "Self Reliance," "Compensation," "Spiritual Laws," "The Over Soul," "Circles," "Intellect," was published during that year, and was followed almost immediately by "The Transcendentalist," a lecture read in Masonic Temple, Boston. In this lecture occurs the following allusion to Kant:

"The Idealism of the present day acquired the name of Transcendental from the use of that term by Immanuel Kant of Königsberg, who replied to the skeptical philosophy of Locke, which insisted that there was nothing in the intellect which was not previously in the experience of the senses, by showing that there was a very important class of ideas or imperative forms, which did not come by experience, but through which experience was acquired; that these were intuitions of the mind itself; and he denominated them *Transcendental* forms. The extraordinary profoundness and precision of that man's thinking have given vogue to his nomenclature in Europe and America, to that extent that whatever belongs to the class of intuitive thought is popularly called, at the present day, Transcendental." * * *
"The Transcendentalist adopts the whole connection of spiritual doctrine. He believes in miracles, in the perpetual openness of the human mind to new influx of light and power; he believes in inspiration and ecstasy.

He wishes that the spiritual principle should be suffered to demonstrate itself to the end, in all possible applications to the state of man, without the admission of anything unspiritual, that is, anything positive, dogmatic, personal."

From what has been said it may be inferred that Transcendentalism in New England was a movement within the limits of "liberal" Christianity or Unitarianism as it was called, and had none but a religious aspect. Such an inference would be narrow. In 1838, Orestes Augustus Brownson started "The Boston Quarterly Review," instituted for the discussion of questions in politics, art, literature, science, philosophy and religion. The editor who was the principal, and almost the sole writer, frankly declares that "he had no creed, no distinct doctrines to support whatever;" that he "aimed to startle, and made it a point to be as paradoxical and extravagant as he could, without doing violence to his own reason or conscience." This avowal was made in 1857, after Mr. Brownson had become a Roman Catholic. The pages of the Review prove the writer to have been a pronounced Transcendentalist. A foreign journal called him "the Coryphœus of the sect," a designation which, at the time, was meekly accepted.

Mr. Brownson was a remarkable man, remarkable for intellectual force, and equally for intellectual wilfulness. His mind was restless, audacious, swift; his self assertion was immense; his thoughts came in floods; his literary style was admirable for freshness, terseness and vigor. Of rational stability of principle he had nothing, but was completely at the mercy of every novelty in speculation. That others thought as he did, was enough to make him think otherwise; that he thought as he had six months before was a signal that it was time for him to strike his tent and move on. An experimenter in systems, a taster of speculations, he passed rapidly from one phase to another, so that his friends ascribed his steadfastness to Romanism, to the fatigue of intellectual travelling. Mr. Brownson was born in Stockbridge, Vt., Sept. 16, 1803. His education was scanty; his nurture was neglected; his discipline, if such it can be called, was to the last degree unwise. The child had visions, fancied he had received communications from the Christ, and held spiritual intercourse with the Virgin Mary, Angels and Saints. Of a sensitive nature on the moral and spiritual side, interested from boyhood in religious speculations, he had, before he reached man's estate, asked and answered, in his own passionate way, all the deepest questions of destiny. At the age of 21, he passed from Supernaturalism to Rationalism; at 22 became a Universalist minister; at 28 adopted what he called "The Religion of Humanity;" the year following, joined the Unitarian ministry. At this time he studied French and German, and became fervidly addicted to philosophy. Benjamin Constant's theory of religion fascinated him by its brilliant generalizations, and its novel readings of Mythology, and was immediately adopted because it interested him and fell in with his mood of mind. In 1833, he accepted Cousin's philosophy as he had accepted

Constant's, "attending to those things that I could appropriate to my purposes." In 1836 he organized the "Society for Christian Union and Progress" in Boston, and continued to be its minister till 1843. All this time he was dallying with Socialism, principally in the form of St. Simonianism; thought of himself as possibly the precursor of the Messiah; threw out strange heresies on the subject of property and the modern industrial system; and was suspected, he declared afterwards unjustly suspected, of holding loose opinions on love and marriage. "New Views of Christianity, Society and the Church," appeared in 1836, a little book, written in answer to objections brought against Christianity as being a system of extravagant spiritualism. This idea Mr. Brownson combated, by pointing out the true character of the religion of Jesus as contrasted with the schemes that had borne his name, exposing the corruptions it had undergone, during the succeeding ages, from Protestantism as well as from Romanism, and indicating the method and the signs of a return to the primeval faith which reconciled God and man, spirit and matter, soul and body, heaven and earth, in the establishment of just relations between man and man, the institution of a simply human state of society.

"Charles Elwood, or The Infidel Converted," was published in 1840. Two or three passages from this theological discussion, thinly masked in the guise of a novel, will suffice to class the author with Transcendentalists of the advanced school.

"They who deny to man all inherent capacity to know God, all immediate perception of spiritual truth, place man out of the condition of ever knowing any thing of God." . . . . "There must be a God within to recognize and vouch for the God who speaks to us from without." . . . . "I hold that the ideas or conceptions which man attempts to embody or realize in his forms of religious faith and worship, are intuitions of reason." "I understand by inspiration the spontaneous revelations of the reason; and I call these revelations divine, because I hold the reason to be divine. Its voice is the voice of God, and what it reveals without any aid from human agency, is really and truly a divine revelation." . . . . "This reason is in all men. Hence the universal beliefs of mankind, the universality of the belief in God and religion. Hence, too, the power of all men to judge of supernatural revelations." . . . "All are able to detect the supernatural, because all have the supernatural in themselves."

The "Boston Quarterly," was maintained five years,— from 1838 to 1842 inclusive,—and consequently covered this period. It would therefore be safe to assume, what the volumes themselves attest, that whatever subject was dealt with,—and all conceivable subjects were dealt with,—were handled by the transcendental method. In the "Christian World," a short-lived weekly, published by a brother of Dr. W. E. Channing, Mr. Brownson began the publication of a series of articles on the "Mission of Jesus." Seven were admitted; the eighth was declined as being "Romanist" in its outlook. In 1844, the writer avowed himself a Roman Catholic, and was confirmed in Boston, October 20th. The "Convert," which contains the spiritual biography of this extraordinary man, and from which the above facts in his mental history are partly taken, was published in 1857. The Romanist was at that time essentially a Transcendentalist. "Truth," he writes, "is the mind's object, and it seeks and accepts it intuitively, as the new-born child seeks the mother's breast from which it draws its nourishment. The office of proof or even demonstration is negative rather than affirmative." Mr. Brownson was the most eminent convert to Romanism of this period, when conversions were frequent in Boston; and his influence was considerable in turning uneasy minds to the old faith. He was a powerful writer and lecturer, an occasional visitor at Brook Farm, but his mental baselessness perhaps repelled nearly as many as his ingenuity beguiled.

The literary achievements of Transcendentalism are best exhibited in the "Dial," a quarterly "Magazine for Literature, Philosophy and Religion," begun July, 1840, and ending April, 1844. The editors were Margaret Fuller and R. W. Emerson; the contributors were the bright men and women who gave voice in literary form to the various utterances of the transcendental genius. Mr. Emerson's bravest lectures and noblest poems were first printed there. Margaret Fuller, besides numerous pieces of miscellaneous criticism, contributed the article on Goethe, alone enough to establish her fame as a discerner of spirits, and the paper on "The Great Lawsuit; Man versus Men—Woman versus Women," which was afterwards expanded into the book "Woman in the XIXth century." Bronson

Alcott sent in chapters the " Orphic Sayings," which were an amazement to the uninitiated and an amusement to the profane. Charles Emerson, younger brother of the essayist, whose premature death was bewailed by the admirers of intellect and the lovers of pure character, proved by his " Notes from the Journal of a Scholar," that genius was not confined to a single member of his family. George Ripley, James Freeman Clarke, Theodore Parker, Wm. H. Channing, Henry Thoreau, Eliot Cabot, John S. Dwight the musical critic, C. P. Cranch the artist-poet, Wm. E. Channing, were liberal of contributions, all in characteristic ways ; and unnamed men and women did their part to fill the numbers of this most remarkable magazine. The freshest thoughts on all subjects were brought to the editors' table ; social tendencies were noticed ; books were received ; the newest picture, the last concert, was passed upon ; judicious estimates were made of reforms and reformers abroad as well as at home ; the philosophical discussions were able and discriminating ; the theological papers were learned, broad and fresh. The four volumes are exceedingly rich in poetry, and poetry such as seldom finds a place in popular magazines. The first year's issue contained sixty-six pieces ; the second, thirty-five ; the third, fifty ; the fourth, thirty-three ; among these were Emerson's earliest inspirations. The " Problem," " Wood-notes," " The Sphinx," " Saadi," " Ode to Beauty," " To Rhea," first appeared in the " Dial." Harps that had long been silent, unable to make themselves heard amid the din of the later generation, made their music here. For Transcendentalism was essentially poetical and put its thoughts naturally into song. The poems in the " Dial," even leaving out the famous ones that have been printed since with their authors' names, would make an interesting and attractive volume. How surprised would some of those writers be if they should now in their prosaic days read what then they wrote under the spell of that fine frenzy !

The following mystic poem, which might have come from an ancient Egyptian, dropped from one who has since become distinguished for something very different from mysticism. Has he seen it these many years ? Can he believe that he was ever in the mood to write it ? It is called

VIA SACRA.

Slowly along the crowded street I go,
Marking with reverent look each passer's face,
Seeking and not in vain, in each to trace
That primal soul whereof he is the show.
For here still move, by many eyes unseen,
The blessed gods that erst Olympus kept.
Through every guise these lofty forms serene
Declare the all-holding life hath never slept,
But known each thrill that in man's heart hath been,
And every tear that his sad eyes have wept.
Alas for us ! the heavenly visitants,—
We greet them still as most unwelcome guests
Answering their smile with hateful looks askance,
Their sacred speech with foolish, bitter jests ;
But oh ! what is it to imperial Jove
That this poor world refuses all his love ?

A remarkable feature of the "Dial" were the chapters of "Ethnical Scriptures," seven in all, containing texts from the Veeshnu Sarma, the laws of Menu, Confucius, the Desatir, the Chinese "Four Books," Hermes Trismegistus, the Chaldæan Oracles. Thirty-five years ago, these Scriptures, now so accessible, and in portions so familiar, were known to the few, and were esteemed by none but scholars, whose enthusiasm for ancient literature got the better of their religious faith. To read such things then, showed an enlightened and courageous mind; to print them in a magazine under the sacred title of "Scriptures" argued a most extraordinary breadth of view. In offering these chapters to its readers, without apology and on their intrinsic merits, Transcendentalism exhibited its power to overpass the limits of all special religions, and do perfect justice to all expressions of the religious sentiment.

The creed of Transcendentalism has been sufficiently indicated. It had a creed, and a definite one. In his lecture on "The Transcendentalist," read in 1841, Mr. Emerson seems disposed to consider Transcendentalism merely as a phase of idealism.

" Shall we say then that Transcendentalism is the Saturnalia or excess of Faith; the presentment of a faith proper to man in his integrity, excessive only when his imperfect obedience hinders the satisfaction of his wit. Nature is Transcendental, exists primarily, necessarily, ever works and advances; yet takes no thought for the morrow. Man owns the dignity of the life which throbs around him in chemistry, and tree, and animal, and in the involuntary functions of his own body; yet

he is balked when he tries to fling himself into this
enchanted circle, where all is done without degradation.
Yet genius and virtue predict in man the same absence
of private ends, and of condescension to circumstances,
united with every trait and talent of beauty and
power." * * * " This way of thinking, falling on
Roman times, made stoic philosophers ; falling on despotic times made patriot Catos and Brutuses ; falling
on superstitious times, made prophets and apostles ;
on popish times, made protestants and ascetic monks ;
preachers of Faith against preachers of Works ; on
prelatical times, made Puritans and Quakers ; and falling
on Unitarian and commercial times, makes the peculiar
shades of Idealism which we know."

It is audacious to criticize Mr. Emerson on a point
like this ; but candor compels the remark that the above
description does less than justice to the definiteness of
the transcendental movement. It was something more
than a reaction against formalism and tradition, though
it took that form. It was more than a reaction against
Puritan Orthodoxy, though in part it was that. It was
in a very small degree due to study of the ancient
pantheists, of Plato and the Alexandrians, of Plutarch,
Seneca and Epictetus, though one or two of the leaders
had drunk deeply from these sources. Transcendentalism
was a distinct philosophical system. Practically it was
an assertion of the inalienable worth of man ; theoreti-
cally it was an assertion of the immanence of divinity
in instinct, the transference of supernatural attributes to
the natural constitution of mankind.

Such a faith would necessarily be protean in its aspects.
Philosopher, Critic, Moralist, Poet, would give it voice

according to cast of genius. It would present in turn all the phases of idealism, and to the outside spectator seem a mass of wild opinions; but running through all was the belief in the Living God in the Soul, faith in immediate inspiration, in boundless possibility, and in unimaginable good.

The editors and reviewers of its day could make nothing of it. The most entertaining part of the present writer's task has been the reading of articles on Transcendentalism in the contemporaneous magazines. The reviewers were unable to resist the temptation to make themselves ridiculous. The quarterlies and monthlies are before me, looking as if they resented the exposure of their dusty and musty condition, and would conceal if they could the baldness of their wit. It would be cruel to exhume those antique judgments, so honest, yet so imbecile and so mistaken. The doubts and misgivings, the bitternesses and the horrors, the sinkings of heart and the revolvings of soul may be estimated by any who will consult the numbers of the Christian Examiner, the Biblical Repository, the Princeton Review, the New Englander, the Whig Review, Knickerbocker, (Knickerbocker is especially facetious), but we advise none to do it who would retain their respect for honorable names. The writers, let us hope, did the best they knew, and it would be unkind to expose the theological prejudice, the polemical acrimony, the narrowness and flippancy they would have been ashamed of had they been aware of it.

A good example of the courteous kind of injustice

may be found in the Christian Examiner for January, 1837, in a review of "Nature" from the pen of a Cambridge Professor, who writes in a kindly spirit and with an honest intention to be fair to a movement with which he had no intellectual sympathy :

"The aim of the Transcendentalists is high. They profess to look not only beyond facts, but, without the aid of facts, to principles. What is this but Plato's doctrine of innate, eternal and immutable ideas on the consideration of which all science is founded ? Truly, the human mind advances but too often in a circle. The New School has abandoned Bacon, only to go back and wander in the groves of the Academy, and to bewilder themselves with the dreams which first arose in the fervid imagination of the Greeks. Without questioning the desirableness of this end, of considering general truths without any previous examination of particulars, we may well doubt the power of modern philosophers to attain it. Again, they are busy in the enquiry (to adopt their own phraseology) after the Real and Abso-lute, as distinguished from the Apparent. Not to repeat the same doubt as to their success, we may at least request them to beware lest they strip the truth of its relation to Humanity, and thus deprive it of its usefulness."

We quote this passage not merely to show how inevita-bly the best intentioned critics of Transcendentalism fell into sarcasm, nor to illustrate the species of error into which the " Sensational" philosophy betrayed even can-did minds ; but to call attention to another point, namely, the general misconception of the practical aims and purposes of the new school. It was a common preju-

dice that Transcendentalists were visionaries and enthu
siasts, who in pursuit of principles neglected duties,
and while seeking for The Real and The Absolute forgot
the actual and the relative. Macaulay puts the case
strongly in his article on Lord Bacon :

" To sum up the whole ; we should say that the aim of
the Platonic philosophy was to exalt man into a God.
The aim of the Baconian philosophy was to provide
man with what he requires while he continues to be man.
The aim of the Platonic philosophy was to raise us far
above vulgar wants. The aim of the Baconian philosophy
was to supply our wants. The former aim was noble ;
but the latter was attainable. Plato drew a good bow ;
but, like Acestes in Virgil, he aimed at the stars ; and
though there was no want of strength and skill, the shot
was thrown away. Bacon fixed his eye on a mark which
was placed on the earth, and within bow shot, and hit
it in the white. The philosophy of Plato began in
words and ended in words—noble words indeed ; words
such as were to be expected from the finest of human
intellects exercising boundless control over the finest of
human languages. The philosophy of Bacon began in
observations and ended in arts. The smallest actual
good is better than the most magnificent promises of
impossibilities. The truth is, that in those very matters
for the sake of which they neglected all the vulgar
interests of mankind, the ancient philosophers did nothing
or worse than nothing—they promised what was impracticable ; they despised what was practicable ; they filled
the world with long words and long beards ; and they left
it as wicked and as ignorant as they found it."

Substitute Idealism for Platonism, and Transcendentalists for ancient philosophers, and this expresses the
judgment of " sensible men " of the last generation, on

Transcendentalism. It was not perceived that the two schools of philosophy aimed at producing the same results, but by different methods ; that the " Sensationalist " worked up from beneath by material processes, while the "Idealist " worked downward from above by intellectual ones ; that the former tried to push men up by mechanical appliances, and the latter endeavored to draw them up by spiritual attraction ; that while the disciples of Bacon operated on man as if he was a complex animal, a creature of nature and of circumstances, who was borne along with the material progress of the planet, but had no independent power of flight, the disciples of Kant and Fichte assumed that man was a creative, recreative force, a being who had only to be conscious of the capacities within him to shape circumstances according to the pattern shown him on the Mount. The charge of shooting at stars is puerile. The only use they would make of stars was to " hitch wagons " to them. The Transcendentalists of New England were the most strenuous workers of their day, and at the problems which the day flung down before them. The most strenuous, and the most successful workers too. They achieved more practical benefit for society, in proportion to their numbers and the duration of their existence, than any body of Baconians of whom we ever heard. Men and women are healthier in their bodies, happier in their domestic and social relations, more contented in their estate, more ambitious to enlarge their opportunities, more eager to acquire knowledge, more kind and humane in their sympathies, more reasonable in their expectations, than they would have been if Margaret Fuller and Ralph Waldo Emerson and Theodore Parker and George Ripley and Bronson Alcott, and the rest of their fellow believers and fellow workers had not lived. It is the fashion of our generation to hold that progress is, and must of necessity be, exceedingly gradual; and that no safe advance is ever made except at snail's pace. But ever and anon the mind of man refutes the notion by starting under the influence of a thought, and leaping over long reaches of space at a bound. Transcendentalism gave one of these demonstrations, sufficient to refute the vulgar prejudice. Its brief history may have illustrated the truth of Wordsworth's lines,

> " That 'tis a thing impossible to frame
> Conceptions equal to the Soul's desires;
> And the most difficult of tasks to keep
> Heights which the Soul is competent to gain."

The heights were gained nevertheless, and kept long enough for a view of the land of promise; and ever since, though the ascent is a dim recollection, and the great forms have come to look like images in dreams, and the mighty voices are but ghostly echoes, men and women have been happy in laboring for the heaven their fathers believed they saw.

VII.

PRACTICAL TENDENCIES

MR. EMERSON—we find ourselves continually appealing to him as the finest interpreter of the transcendental movement—made a confession which its enemies were quick to seize on and turn to their purpose.

" It is a sign of our times, conspicuous to the coarsest observer, that many intelligent and religious persons withdraw themselves from the common labors and competitions of the market and the caucus, and betake themselves to a certain solitary and critical way of living, from which no solid fruit has yet appeared to justify their separation. They hold themselves aloof; they feel the disproportion between themselves and the work offered them, and they prefer to ramble in the country and perish of ennui, to the degradation of such charities and such ambitions as the city can propose to them. They are striking work and crying out for somewhat worthy to do. They are lonely; the spirit of their writing and conversation is lonely; they repel influences; they shun general society; they incline to shut themselves in their chamber in the house; to live in the country rather than in the town; and to find their tasks and amusements in solitude. They are not good citizens; not good members of society; unwillingly they bear their part of the public and private burdens; they do not willingly share in the public charities, in the public religious rites, in the enterprises of education, of missions, foreign or domestic, in the abolition of the slave trade, or in the temperance society. They do not even like to vote. The philanthropists inquire whether Transcendentalism does not mean sloth; they had as lief hear that their friend is dead as that he is a Transcendentalist; for then is he paralyzed, and can do nothing for humanity."

This extreme statement must not be taken as eithe1 complete or comprehensive. They who read it in the lecture on "The Transcendentalist" must be careful to notice Mr. Emerson's qualifications, that "this retirement does not proceed from any whim on the part of the separators;" that "this part is chosen both from temperament and from principle; with some unwillingness too, and as a choice of the less of two evils;" that "they are joyous, susceptible, affectionate;" that "they wish a just and even fellowship or none;" that "what they do is done because they are overpowered by the humanities that speak on all sides;" that "what you call your fundamental institutions, your great and holy causes, seem to them great abuses, and, when nearly seen, paltry matters." But even this apology does not quite exonerate his friends.

Transcendentalism certainly did produce its share ot idle, dreamy, useless people—as "Sensationalism" produced its share of coarse, greedy, low-lived and bestial ones. But its legitimate fruit was earnestness, aspiration and enthusiastic energy.

We must begin with the philosophy of Man. The Transcendentalist claims for all men as a natural endowment what "Evangelical" Christianity ascribes to the few as a special gift of the Spirit. This faith comes to

expression continually. The numbers of the "Dial"
are alight with it.

"Man is a rudiment and embryon of God : Eternity
shall develop in him the Divine Image."

"The Soul works from centre to periphery, veiling her
labors from the ken of the senses."

"The sensible world is spirit in magnitude outspread
before the senses for their analysis, but whose synthesis
is the soul herself, whose prothesis is God."

"The time may come, in the endless career of the
soul, when the facts of incarnation, birth, death, descent
into matter, and ascension from it, shall comprise no
part of her history ; when she herself shall survey this
human life with emotions akin to those of the naturalist
on examining the relics of extinct races of beings."

"Of the perception now fast becoming a conscious
fact,—that there is one mind, and that also the powers
and privileges which lie in any, lie in all; that I, as a
man, may claim and appropriate whatever of true or fair
or good or strong has anywhere been exhibited ; that
Moses and Confucius, Montaigne and Leibnitz are not so
much individuals as they are parts of man and parts of
me, and my intelligence proves them my own,—literature is far the best expression."

Thus Mr. Alcott and Mr. Emerson. Thomas T. Stone,
—a modest, retiring, deep and interior man, a child of the
spiritual philosophy, which he faithfully lived in and up
to, and preached with singular fulness and richness of
power—makes his statement thus, in an article entitled
"Man in the Ages," contributed to the third number of
the "Dial":

"Man is man, despite of all the lies which would convince him he is not, despite of all the thoughts which

would strive to unman him. There is a spirit in man, an inspiration from the Almighty. What is, is. The eternal is eternal ; the temporary must pass it by, leaving it to stand evermore. There is now, there has been always, power among men to subdue the ages, to dethrone them, to make them mere outgoings and servitors of man. It is needed only that we assert our prerogative,—that man do with hearty faith affirm : ' I am ; in me being is. Ages, ye come and go; appear and disappear ; products, not life ; vapors from the surface of the soul, not living fountain. Ye are of me, for me, not I of you or for you. Not with you my affinity, but with the Eternal. I am ; I live ; spirit I have not ; spirit am I.' "

Samuel D. Robbins, another earnest prophet of the spiritual man, utters the creed again in the way peculiar to himself.

"There is an infinity in the human soul which few have yet believed, and after which few have aspired. There is a lofty power of moral principle in the depths of our nature which is nearly allied to Omnipotence ; compared with which the whole force of outward nature is more feeble than an infant's grasp. There is a spiritual insight to which the pure soul reaches, more clear and prophetic, more wide and vast than all telescopic vision can typify. There is a faith in God, and a clear perception of His will and designs, and providence, and glory, which gives to its possessor a confidence and patience and sweet composure, under every varied and troubling aspect of events, such as no man can realize who has not felt its influences in his own heart. There is a communion with God, in which the soul feels the presence of the unseen One, in the profound depths of its being, with a vivid distinctness and a holy reverence such as no word can describe. There is a state of union with God, I do not say often reached, yet it has been

attained in this world, in which all the past and present
and future seem reconciled, and eternity is won and
enjoyed : and God and man, earth and heaven, with all
their mysteries are apprehended in truth as they lie in
the mind of the Infinite."

The poet chimes in with the prophet.   We marked
for quotation several passages from the " Dial," but a few
detached stanzas must suffice.   C. P. Cranch opens his
lines to the ocean thus :

> Tell me, brothers, what are we ?
> Spirits bathing in the sea
>   of Deity.
> Half afloat, and half on land,
> Wishing much to leave the strand,
> Standing, gazing with devotion,
> Yet afraid to trust the ocean,
>   Such are we.

And thus he closes lines to the Aurora Borealis :

> But a better type thou art
> Of the strivings of the heart,
> Reaching upwards from the earth
> To the *Soul* that gave it birth.
> When the noiseless beck of night
> Summons out the inner light
> That hath hid its purer ray
> Through the lapses of the day,—
> Then like thee, thou Northern Morn,
> Instincts which we deemed unborn

Gushing from their hidden source
Mount upon their heavenward course,
And the spirit seeks to be
Filled with God's eternity.

That a philosophy like this will impel to aspiration need not be said; aspiration is the soul of it. The Transcendentalist was constantly on the wing.

"On all hands men's existence is converted into a preparation for existence. We do not properly live, in these days; but everywhere with patent inventions and complex arrangements are getting ready to live. The end is lost in the means, life is smothered in appliances. We cannot get to ourselves, there are so many external comforts to wade through. Consciousness stops half way. Reflection is dissipated in the circumstances of our environment. Goodness is exhausted in aids to goodness, and all the vigor and health of the soul is expended in quack contrivances to build it up." * * * What the age requires is not books, but example, high, heroic example; not words but deeds; not societies but men—men who shall have their root in themselves, and attract and convert the world by the beauty of their fruits. All truth must be living, before it can be adequately known or taught. Men are anterior to systems. Great doctrines are not the origin, but the product of great lives. The Cynic practice must precede the Stoic philosophy, and out of Diogenes's tub came forth in the end the wisdom of Epictetus, the eloquence of Seneca, and the piety of Antonine." * * *
"The religious man lives for one great object; to perfect himself, to unite himself by purity with God, to fit himself for heaven by cherishing within him a heavenly disposition. He has discovered that he has a soul; that his soul is himself; that he changes not with the changing things of life, but receives its discipline

from them; that man does not live by bread alone, but that the most real of all things, inasmuch as they are the most enduring, are the things which are not seen; that faith and love and virtue are the sources of his life, and that one realises nothing, except he lay fast hold on them. He extracts a moral lesson, a lesson of endurance or of perseverance for himself, or a new evidence of God and of his own immortal destiny, from every day's hard task."

That last strain came from the man who for many years has been known as the foremost musical critic of New England, if not of America, John S. Dwight. Another writes:

" The soul lies buried in a ruined city, struggling to be free and calling for aid. The worldly trafficker in life's caravan hears its cries, and says, it is a prisoned maniac. But one true man stops and with painful toil lifts aside the crumbling fragments; till at last he finds beneath the choking mass a mangled form of exceeding beauty. Dazzling is the light to eyes long blind; weak are the limbs long prisoned; faint is the breath long pent. But oh! that mantling flush, that liquid eye, that elastic spring of renovated strength. The deliverer is folded to the breast of an angel."

The duty of self-culture is made primary and is eloquently preached. The piece from which this extract is taken, entitled " The Art of Life " is anonymous, but supposed to be from Emerson's pen:

" The work of life, so far as the individual is concerned, and that to which the scholar is particularly called, is

Self-Culture, the perfect unfolding of our individual nature. To this end above all others, the art of which I speak directs our attention and points our endeavor. There is no man, it is presumed, to whom this object is wholly indifferent, who would not willingly possess this too, along with other prizes, provided the attainment of it were compatible with personal ease and worldly good. But the business of self-culture admits of no compromise. Either it must be made a distinct aim or wholly abandoned."

But it is time wasted to speak on this point. It has been objected to Transcendentalism that it made self-culture too important, carrying it to the point of selfishness, sacrificing in its behalf, sympathy, brotherly love, sentiments of patriotism, personal fidelity and honor, and rejoicing in the production of a " mountainous Me " fed at the expense of life's sweetest humanities ; and Goethe is straightway cited as the Transcendental apostle of the gospel of heartless indifference. But allowing the charge against Goethe to rest unrefuted, it must be made against him as a man, not as a Transcendentalist ; and even were it true of him as a Transcendentalist, it was not true of Kant or Fichte, of Schleiermacher or Herder ; of Jean Paul or Novalis ; of Coleridge, Carlyle or Wordsworth ; and who ever intimated that it was true of Emerson, who has been one of the most industrious teachers of his generation, and one of the most earnest worshippers of the genius of his native land ;—of Margaret Fuller, whose life was a quickening flood of intellectual influence ;—of Bronson Alcott, who, every winter for years, has carried his seed corn to the far West, seeking only a receptive furrow for his treasured being ;—of Theodore Parker, who sacrificed precious days of study, his soul's passion for knowledge, his honorable ambition to achieve a scholar's fame, in order that his country, in her time of trial, might not want what he was able to give ;—of Wm. Henry Channing, to whom the thought of human · ity is an inspiration, and "sacrifice an all sufficing joy ;"— of George Ripley, who offered himself, all that he had and was, that the experiment of an honest friendly society might be fairly tried ? By "self-culture" these and the rest of their brotherhood meant the culture of that nobler self which includes heart, and conscience, sympathy and spirituality, not as incidental ingredients, but as essential qualities. Self-hood they never identified with selfishness ; nor did they ever confound or associate its attainment with the acquisition of place, power, wealth, or eminent repute ; the person was more to them than the individual ; they sought no reward except for service ; and the consciousness of serving faithfully was their best reward.

To Transcendentalism belongs the credit of inaugurating a theory and practice of dietetics which is preached assiduously now by the vegetarian physiologists. The people who regarded man as a soul, first taught the wisdom that is now inculcated by people who regard man as a body. The doctrine that human beings live on air and light ; that food should be simple and nutritious ; that coarse meats should be discarded and fiery liquors abolished ; that wines should be substituted

for " spirits," light wines for heavy, and pure water for
wines;—has in all ages been taught by mystics and
idealists. The ancient master of it was Pythagoras.
Their idea was, that as the body was, for the time being,
the dwelling-place of the soul, its lodging and home, its
prison or its palace, its organ, its instrument, its box of
tools, the medium of its activity, it must be kept in
perfect condition for these high offices. They honored
the flesh in the nobility of their care of it. No sour
ascetics they, but generous feeders on essences and
elixirs ; no mortifiers of matter, but purifiers and
refiners of it; regarding it as too exquisitely mingled
and tempered a substance to be tortured and imbruted.
The materialist prescribes temperance, continence, so-
briety, in order that life may be long, and comfortable,
and free from disease. The idealist prescribes them, in
order that life may be intellectual, serene, pacific,
beneficent.

The chief mystic of the transcendental band has
been the chief prophet of this innocent word. " The
New Ideas," wrote Mr. Alcott, " bear direct on all the
economies of life. They will revise old methods, and
institute new cultures. I look with special hope to their
effect on the regimen of the land. Our present modes
of agriculture exhaust the soil, and must, while life is
made thus sensual and secular; the narrow covetousness
which prevails in trade, in labor, in exchanges, ends in
depraving the land ; it breeds disease, decline, in the
flesh,—debauches and consumes the heart." " The
Soul's Banquet is an art divine. To mould this statue

of flesh from chaste materials, kneading it into comeliness and strength, this is Promethean; and this we practise, well or ill, in all our thoughts, acts, desires. I would abstain from the fruits of oppression and blood, and am seeking means of entire independence. This, were I not holden by penury unjustly, would be possible. One miracle we have wrought nevertheless, and shall soon work all of them;—our wihe is water,—flesh, bread;—drugs, fruits;—and we defy, meekly, the satyrs all, and Esculapius."

" It was the doctrine of the Samian Sage, that whatsoever food obstructs divination, is prejudicial to purity and chastity of mind and body, to temperance, health, sweetness of disposition, suavity of manners, grace of form and dignity of carriage, should be shunned. Especially should those who would apprehend the deepest wisdom, and preserve through life the relish for elegant studies and pursuits, abstain from flesh, cherishing the justice which animals claim at men's hands, nor slaughtering them for food or profit." " A purer civilization than ours can yet claim to be, is to inspire the genius of mankind with the skill to deal dutifully with soils and souls, exalt agriculture and manculture into a religion of art; the freer interchange of commodities which the current world-wide intercourse promotes, spreads a more various, wholesome, classic table, whereby the race shall be refined of traits reminding too plainly of barbarism and the beast." Said Timotheus of Plato, " they who dine with the philosopher have nothing to complain of the next morning." That the doctrine has its warm, glowing side, appears in a characteristic poem in the little volume called " Tablets."

The anchorite's plea was not always as good as his practice. Arguing the point once with a sagacious man of the world, he urged as a reason for abstinence from animal food that one thereby distanced the animal. For the eating of beef encouraged the bovine quality, and the pork diet repeats the trick of Circe, and changes men into swine. But, rejoined the friend, if abstinence from animal food leaves the animal out, does not partaking of vegetable food put the vegetable in? I presume the potato diet will change man into a potato. And what if the potatoes be small! The philosopher's reply is not recorded. But in his case the beast did disappear, and the leek has never become prominent. In his case health, strength, agility, sprightliness, cheerfulness, have been wholly compatible with disuse of animal food. Few men have preserved the best uses of body and mind so long unimpaired. Few have lost so few days ; have misused so few ; are able to give a good account of so many. The vegetarian of seventy-six shames many a cannibal of forty.

The Transcendentalist was by nature a reformer. He could not be satisfied with men as they were. His doctrine of the capacities of men, even in its most moderate statement, kindled to enthusiasm his hope of change. However his disgust may have kept him aloof for a time, his sympathy soon brought him back, and his faith sent him to the front of the battle. In beginning his lecture on " Man The Reformer," Mr. Emerson does not dissemble his hope that each person whom he addresses has "felt his own call to cast aside all evil customs, timidities and limitations, and to be in his place a free and helpful man, a reformer, a benefactor, not content to slip through the world like a footman or a spy, escaping by his nimbleness and apologies as many knocks as he can, but a brave and upright man, who must find or cut a straight path to everything excellent in the earth, and not only go honorably himself, but make it easier for all who follow him, to go in honor and with benefit." "The power," he declares," which is at once spring and regulator in all efforts of reform, is the conviction that there is an infinite worthiness in man, which will appear at the call of worth, and that all particular reforms are the removing of some impediment. Is it not the highest duty that man should be honored in us? "In the history of the world" the same great teacher remarks, "the doctrine of Reform had never such scope as at the present hour. Lutherans, Herrnhütters, Jesuits, Monks, Quakers, Knox, Wesley, Swedenborg, Bentham, in their accusations of society, all respected something,—church or state, literature or history, domestic usages, the market town, the dinner table, coined money. But now all these and all things else hear the the trumpet and must rush to judgment,— Christianity, the laws, commerce, schools, the farm, the laboratory: and not a kingdom, town, statute, rite, calling, man, or woman but is threatened by the new spirit." "Let me feel that I am to be a lover. I am to see to it that the world is the better for me, and to find my reward in the act. Love would put a new face on this weary old world in which we dwell as pagans and enemies too long, and it would warm the heart to see how fast the vain diplomacy of statesmen, the impotence of armies, and navies, and lines of defence, would be superseded by this unarmed child."

The method of reform followed from the principle. It was the method of individual awakening and regeneration, and was to be conducted " through the simplest ministries of family, neighborhood, fraternity, quite wide of associations and institutions." The true reformer," it was proclaimed, " initiates his labor in the precincts of private life, and makes it, not a set of measures, not an utterance, not a pledge merely, but a life ; and not an impulse of a day, but commensurate with human existence : a tendency towards perfection of being." The Transcendentalist might easily become an enthusiast from excess of faith ; but a fanatic, with a tinge of melancholy in his disposition, a drop of malignity in his blood, he could not be. He was less a reformer of human circumstance than a regenerator of the human spirit, and he was never a destroyer except as destruction accompanied the process of regeneration.

This fine positive purpose appeared in all he undertook. With movements that did not start from this primary assumption of individual dignity, and come back to that as their goal, he had nothing to do. Was he an anti-slavery man--and he was certain to be one at heart— the Transcendentalists were glowing friends of that reform, —he was so because his philosophy compelled him to see in the slave the same humanity that appeared in the master; in the African the same possibilities that were confessed in the Frank, the Anglo-Saxon, and the Celt. Did he take up the cause of education, it was as a believer in the latent capacity of every child, boy or girl; as an earnest wisher that such capacity might be stimulated by the best methods, and directed to the best ends. What he effected, or tried to effect in this way will be understood by the reader of the record of Mr. Alcott's school; that bold and original attempt at educating, leading or drawing out young minds, which showed such remarkable promise, and would have achieved such remarkable results had more faithful trial of its method been possible. Was he a reformer of society, it was as a vitalizer, not as a machinist.

In no respect does the Transcendentalist's idea of social reform stand out more conspicuously than in this. With an incessant and passionate aspiration after a pure social state,—deeply convinced of the mistakes, profoundly sensible of the miseries of the actual condition, he would not be committed to experiments that did not assume his first principle—the supreme dignity of the individual man. The systems of French socialism he distrusted from the first; for they proceeded on the ground that man is not a self determined being, but a creature of circumstance. Mr. Albert Brisbane's attempt to domesticate Fourierism among us was cordially considered, but not cordially welcomed. He seemed to have no spiritual depth of foundation; his proposition to imprison man in a Phalanx, was rejected; his omission of moral freedom in the scheme was resented; no sincerity, no keenness of criticism, no exposure of existing evils or indignation of protest against then, disarmed the jealousy of endeavors to reconstruct society, as if human beings were piles of brick or lumps of mortar.

In 1841 a community was planned in Massachussetts, by Liberal Christians of the Universalist sect. Though never put in operation it did not escape the criticism of the " Dial." The good points were recognized and commended; the moral features were praised as showing a deep insight into the Christian idea, and the articles of confederation were pronounced admirable in judgment and form, with a single exception, which however was fatal. Admittance of members was conditioned on pledges of non-resistance, abolition, temperance, abstinence from voting, and such like. Though these conditions were easy enough in themselves, and were expressed in the most conciliatory spirit, they were justly regarded as giving to the community the character of a church or party, much less than world embracing. "A true community," it was declared, " can be founded on nothing short of faith in the universal man, as he comes out of the hands of the Creator, with no law over his liberty but the eternal ideas that lie at the foundation of his being." " The final cause of human society is the unfolding of the individual man, into every form of perfection, without let or hindrance according to the inward nature of each."

When the Brook Farm experiment was under way at West Roxbury, its initiators were warned against three dangers : the first, *Organization*, which begins by being an instrument and ends by being a master; the second, *Endowment*, which promises to be a swift helper, and is, ere long, a stifling encumbrance; the third, the spirit of *Coterie*, which would in no long time, shrink their rock of ages to a platform, diminish their brotherhood to a clique, and reduce their aims to experiences.

Brook Farm, whereof it is not probable that a history will ever be written, for the reason that there were in it slender materials for history,—though there were abundant materials for thought,—was projected on the purest transcendental basis. It was neither European nor English, neither French nor German in its origin. No doubt, among the supporters and friends of it were some who had made themselves acquainted with the writings of St. Simon and Chevalier, of Proudhon and Fourier; but it does not appear that any of these authors shaped or prescribed the plan, or influenced the spirit of the enterprise. The Constitution which is printed herewith explains sufficiently the project, and expresses the spirit in which it was undertaken. The jealous regard for the rights of the individual is not the least characteristic feature of this remarkable document. The By-Laws, which want of space excludes from these pages, simply confirm the provisions that were made to guard the person against unnecessary infringement of independence.

CONSTITUTION.

In order more effectually to promote the great purposes of human culture ; to establish the external relations of life on a basis of wisdom and purity ; to apply the principles of justice and love to our social orgnization in accordance with the laws of Divine Providence ; to substitute a system of brotherly cöoperation for one of selfish competition ; to secure to our children and those who may be entrusted to our care, the benefits of the highest physical, intellectual and moral education, which in the progress of knowledge the resources at our command will permit ; to institute an attractive, efficient, and productive system of industry ; to prevent the exercise of worldly anxiety, by the competent supply of our necessary wants ; to diminish the desire of excessive accumulation, by making the acquisition of individual property subservient to upright and disinterested uses ; to guarantee to each other forever the means of physical support, and of spiritual progress ; and thus to impart a greater freedom, simplicity, truthfulness, refinement, and moral dignity, to our mode of life ;—we the undersigned do unite in a voluntary Association, and adopt and ordain the following articles of agreement, to wit :

ARTICLE I.

NAME AND MEMBERSHIP.

SEC. 1. The name of this Association shall be " THE BROOK-FARM ASSOCIATION FOR INDUSTRY AND EDUCATION. " All persons who shall hold one or more shares in its stock, or whose labor and skill shall be considered an equivalent for capital, may be admitted by the vote of two-thirds of the Association, as members thereof.

SEC. 2.   No member of the Association shall ever be subjected to any religious test ; nor shall any authority be assumed over individual freedom of opinion by the Association, nor by one member over another ; nor shall any one be held accountable to the Association, except for such overt acts, or omissions of duty, as violate the principles of justice, purity, and love, on which it is founded ; and in such cases the relation of any member may be suspended or discontinued, at the pleasure of the Association.

ARTICLE II.

CAPITAL STOCK.

SEC. 1.   The members of this Association shall own and manage such real and personal estate in joint stock proprietorship, divided into shares of one hundred dollars each, as may from time to time be agreed on.

SEC. 2.   No shareholder shall be liable to any assessment whatever on the shares held by him ; nor shall he be held responsible individually in his private property on account of the Association ; nor shall the Trustees, or any officer or agent of the Association, have any authority to do any thing which shall impose personal responsibility on any shareholder, by making any contracts or incurring any debts for which the shareholders shall be individually or personally responsible.

SEC. 3.   The Association guarantees to each shareholder the interest of five per cent. annually on the amount of stock held by him in the Association, and this interest may be paid in certificates of stock and credited on the books of the Association ; provided that each shareholder may draw on the funds of the Association for the amount of interest due at the third annual settlement from the time of investment.

SEC. 4.   The shareholders on their part, for themselves, their heirs and assigns, do renounce all claim on any profits accruing to the Association for the use of their capital invested in the stock of the Association, except five per cent. interest on the amount of stock held by them, payable in the manner described in the preceding section.

ARTICLE III.

GUARANTIES.

SEC. 1. The Association shall provide such employment for all its members as shall be adapted to their capacities, habits, and tastes ; and each member shall select and perform such operations of labor, whether corporal or mental, as shall be deemed best suited to his own endowments and the benefit of the Association.

SEC. 2. The Association guarantees to all its members, their children and family dependents, house-rent, fuel, food, and clothing, and the other necessaries of life, without charge, not exceeding a certain fixed amount to be decided annually by the Association ; no charge shall ever be made for support during inability to labor from sickness or old age, or for medical or nursing attendance, except in case of shareholders, who shall be charged therefor, and also for the food and clothing of children, to an amount not exceeding the interest due to them on settlement ; but no charge shall be made to any members for education or the use of library and public rooms.

SEC. 3. Members may withdraw from labor, under the direction of the Association, and in that case, they shall not be entitled to the benefit of the above guaranties.

SEC. 4. Children over ten years of age shall be provided with employment in suitable branches of industry ; they shall be credited for such portions of each annual dividend, as shall be decided by the Association, and on the completion of their education in the Association at the age of twenty, shall be entitled to a certificate of stock to the amount of credits in their favor, and may be admitted as members of the Association.

ARTICLE IV.

DISTRIBUTION OF PROFITS.

SEC. 1 The net profits of the Association, after the payment of all expenses, shall be divided into a number of shares corresponding to the number of days' labor; and every member shall be entitled to one share of every day's labor performed by him.

SEC. 2. A full settlement shall be made with every member once a year, and certificates of stock given for all balances due; but in case of need, to be decided by himself, every member may be permitted to draw on the funds in the Treasury to an amount not exceeding the credits in his favor for labor performed.

ARTICLE V.

GOVERNMENT.

SEC. 1. The government of the Association shall be vested in a board of Directors, divided into four departments, as follows; 1st, General Direction; 2d, Direction of Education; 3d, Direction of Industry; 4th, Direction of Finance; consisting of three persons each, provided that the same person may be elected member of each Direction.

SEC. 2. The General Direction and Direction of Education shall be chosen annually, by the vote of a majority of the members of the Association. The Direction of Finance shall be chosen annually, by the vote of a majority of the share-holders and members of the Association. The direction of Industry shall consist of the chiefs of the three primary series.

SEC. 3. The chairman of the General Direction shall be the President of the Association, and together with the Direction of Finance, shall constitute a board of Trustees, by whom the property of the Association shall be held and managed.

SEC. 4 The General Direction shall oversee and manage the affairs of the Association, so that every department shall be carried on in an orderly and efficient manner.

SEC. 5. The departments of Education and Finance shall be under the control each of its own Direction, which shall select, and in concurrence with the General Direction, shall appoint such teachers, officers, and agents, as shall be necessary to the complete and systematic organization of the department. No Directors or other officers shall be deemed to possess any rank superior to the other members of the Association, nor shall they receive any extra remuneration for their official services.

SEC. 6. The department of industry shall be arranged in groups and series, as far as practicable, and shall consist of three primary series; to wit, Agricultural, Mechanical, and Domestic Industry. The chief of each series shall be elected every two months by the members thereof, subject to the approval of the general Direction. The chief of each group shall be chosen weekly by its members.

ARTICLE VI.

MISCELLANEOUS.

SEC. 1. The Association may from time to time adopt such by-laws, not inconsistent with the spirit and purpose of these articles, as shall be found expedient or necessary.

SEC. 2. In order to secure to the Association the benefits of the highest discoveries in social science, and to preserve its fidelity to the principles of progress and reform, on which it is founded, any amendment may be proposed to this Constitution at a meeting called for the purpose ; and if approved by two-thirds of the members at a subsequent meeting, at least one month after the date of the first, shall be adopted.

From this it appears that the association was simply an attempt to return to first principles, to plant the seeds of a new social order, founded on respect for the dignity, and sympathy with the aspirations of man. It was open to all sects; it admitted, welcomed, nay, demanded all kinds and degrees of intellectual culture. The most profound regard for individual opinion, feeling and inclination, was professed and exhibited. Confidence that surrender to the spontaneous principle, with no more restriction than might be necessary to secure its development, was wisest, lay at the bottom of the scheme.

It was felt at this time, 1842, that, in order to live a religious and moral life in sincerity, it was necessary to leave the world of institutions, and to reconstruct the social order from new beginnings. A farm was bought in close vicinity to Boston ; agriculture was made the basis of the life, as bringing man into direct and simple relations with nature, and restoring labor to honest conditions. To a certain extent, it will be seen, the principle of community in property was recognized, community of interest and coöperation requiring it ; but to satisfy the claims and insure the rights of the individual, members were not required to impoverish themselves, or to resign the fruit of their earnings.

Provisions were either raised on the farm or purchased at wholesale. Meals were eaten in " commons." It

was the rule that all should labor—choosing their occupations, and the number of hours, and receiving wages
according to the hours. No labor was hired that could
be supplied within the community ; and all labor was
rewarded alike, on the principle that physical labor is
more irksome than mental, more absorbing and exacting,
less improving and delightful. Moreover, to recognize
practically the nobility of labor in and of itself, none
were appointed to special kinds of work. All took their
turn at the several branches of employment. None were
drudges or menials. The intellectual gave a portion of
their time to tasks such as servants and handmaidens
usually discharge. The unintellectual were allowed a
portion of their time for mental cultivation. The benefits
of social intercourse were thrown open to all. The aim
was to secure as many hours as practicable from the
necessary toil of providing for the wants of the body,
that there might be more leisure to provide for the deeper
wants of the soul. The acquisition of wealth was no
object. No more thought was given to this than the
exigencies of existence demanded. To live, expand,
enjoy as rational beings, was the never-forgotten aim.

The community trafficked by way of exchange and
barter with the outside world ; sold its surplus produce ;
sold its culture to as many as came or sent children to
be taught. It was hoped that from the accumulated
results of all this labor, the appliances for intellectual and
spiritual health might be obtained ; that books might be
bought, works of art, scientific collections and apparatus,
means of decoration and refinement, all of which should

be open on the same terms to every member of the association.   The principle of coöperation was substituted
for the principle of competition ; self development for
selfishness.   The faith was avowed in every arrangement
that the soul of humanity was in each man and woman.

The reputation for genius, accomplishment and wit,
which the founders of the Brook Farm enterprise enjoyed
in society, attracted towards it the attention of the public,
and awakened expectation of something much more than
ordinary in the way of literary advantages.   The settlement became a resort for cultivated men and women who
had experience as teachers and wished to employ their
talent to the best effect ;   and for others who were tired of
the conventionalities, and sighed for honest relations with
their fellow-beings.   Some took advantage of the easy
hospitality of the association, and came there to live
mainly at its expense—their unskilled and incidental
labor being no compensation for their entertainment.
The most successful department was the school.   Pupils
came thither in considerable numbers and from considerable distances.   Distinguished visitors gave charm and
reputation to the place.

The members were never numerous ; the number
varied considerably from year to year.   Seventy was a
fair average ; of these, fewer than half were young persons
sent thither to be educated.   Several adults came for
intellectual assistance.   Of married people there were, in
1844, but four pairs.   A great deal was taught and
learned at Brook Farm.   Classics, mathematics, general
literature, æsthetics, occupied the busy hours.   The most

productive work was done in these ideal fields, and the best result of it was a harvest in the ideal world, a new sense of life's elasticity and joy, the delight of freedom, the innocent satisfaction of spontaneous relations.

The details above given convey no adequate idea of the Brook Farm fraternity. In one sense it was much less than they imply; in another sense it was much more. It was less, because its plan was not materially successful; the intention was defeated by circumstances; the hope turned out to be a dream. Yet, from another aspect, the experiment fully justified itself. Its moral tone was high; its moral influence sweet and sunny. Had Brook Farm been a community in the accepted sense, had it insisted on absolute community of goods, the resignation of opinions, of personal aims interests or sympathies; had the principle of renunciation, sacrifice of the individual to the common weal, been accepted and maintained, its existence might have been continued and its pecuniary basis made sure. But asceticism was no feature of the original scheme. On the contrary, the projectors of it were believers in the capacities of the soul, in the safety, wisdom and imperative necessity of developing those capacities, and in the benign effect of liberty. Had the spirit of rivalry and antagonism been called in, the sectarian or party spirit, however generously interpreted, the result would probably have been different. But the law of sympathy being accepted as the law of life, exclusion was out of the question; inquisition into beliefs was inadmissible; motives even could not be closely scanned; so while some were enthusiastic friends

of the principle of association, and some were ardent
devotees to liberty, others thought chiefly of their
private education and development; and others still
were attracted by a desire of improving their social condition, or attaining comfort on easy terms.   The idea,
however noble, true, and lovely, was unable to grapple
with elements so discordant.   Yet the fact that these
discordant elements did not, even in the brief period
of the fraternity's existence, utterly rend and abolish
the idea; that to the last, no principle was compromised,
no rule broken, no aspiration bedraggled, is a confession
of the purity and vitality of the creative thought.   That
a mere aggregation of persons, without written compact,
formal understanding, or unity of purpose, men, women
and children, should have lived together, four or five
years, without scandal or reproach from dissension or
evil whisper, should have separated without rancor or
bitterness, and should have left none but the pleasantest
savor behind them—is a tribute to the Transcendental
Faith.

In 1844, the Directors of the Association, George Ripley, Minot Pratt, and Charles Anderson Dana, published a statement, declaring: that every step had strengthened the faith with which they set out; that their
belief in a divine order of human society had in their
minds become an absolute certainty ; that, in their judgment, considering the state of humanity and of social
science, the world was much nearer the attainment of
such a condition than was generally supposed. They here
said emphatically that Fourier's doctrine of universal

unity commanded their unqualified assent, and that their whole observation had satisfied them of the practical arrangements which he deduced therefrom, of the correspondence of the law of groups and series with the law of human nature. At this time the farm contained two hundred and eight acres, and could be enlarged to any extent necessary. The Association held property worth nearly or quite thirty thousand dollars, of which about twenty-two thousand was invested, either in the stock of the company or in permanent loans to it at six per cent, which could remain as long as the Association might wish. The organization was pronounced to be in a satisfactory working condition ; the Department of Education, on which much thought had been bestowed, was flourishing. With a view to an ultimate expansion into a perfect Phalanx, it was proposed to organize the three primary departments of labor, namely, Agriculture, Domestic Industry, and the Mechanical Arts. Public meetings had awakened an interest in the community. Appeals for money had been generously answered. The numbers had been increased by the accession of many skilful and enthusiastic laborers in various departments. About ten thousand dollars had been added by subscription to the capital. A work-shop sixty feet by twenty-eight had been erected ; a Phalanstery, or unitary dwelling on a large scale, was in process of erection, to meet the early needs of the preparatory period, until success should authorize the building of a Phalanstery "with the magnificence and permanence proper to such a structure." The prospect was, or looked, encouraging.

The experiment had been tested by the hard discipline of more than two years; the severest difficulties had apparently been conquered; the arrangements had attained systematic form, as far as the limited numbers permitted; the idea was respectfully entertained; socialism was spreading; it embraced persons of every station in life; and in its extent, and influence on questions of importance, it seemed, to enthusiastic believers, to be fast assuming in the United States a national character. This was in October 1844. At this time the Brook Farm Associationists connected themselves with the New York Socialists who accepted the teachings of Fourier; and the efforts described were put forth in aid of the new and more systematic plans that had been adopted. But this coalition, which promised so much, proved disastrous in its result. The Association was unable to sustain industrial competition with established trades. The expenses were more than the receipts. In the spring of 1847 the Phalanstery was burned down; the summer was occupied in closing up the affairs; and in the autumn the Association was broken up. The members betook themselves to the world again, and engaged in the ordinary pursuits of life. The farm was bought by the town of West Roxbury, and afterwards passed into private hands. During the civil war the government used it for military purposes. The main building has since been occupied as a hospital. The leaders of the Association removed to New York, and for about a year, till February 1849, continued their labors of propagandism by means of the "Harbinger," till that expired : then their dream faded away.

The full history of that movement can be written only by one who belonged to it, and shared its secret: and it would doubtless have been written before this, had the materials for a history been more solid. Aspirations have no history. It is pleasant to hear the survivors of the pastoral experiment talk over their experiences, merrily recall the passages in work or play, revive the impressions of country rambles, conversations, discussions, social festivities, recount the comical mishaps, summon the shadows of friends dead, but unforgotten, and describe the hours spent in study or recreation, unspoiled by carefulness. But it is in private alone that these confidences are imparted. To the public very little has been, or will be, or can be told.

Mr. Hawthorne was one of the first to take up the scheme. He was there a little while at the beginning in 1841, and his note-books contain passages that are of interest. But Hawthorne's temperament was not congenial with such an atmosphere, nor was his faith clear or steadfast enough to rest contented on its idea. His, however, were observing eyes; and his notes, being soliloquies, confessions made to himself, convey his honest impressions :

BROOK FARM, April 13th, 1841. "I have not taken yet my first lesson in agriculture, except that I went to see our cows foddered, yesterday afternoon. We have eight of our own; and the number is now increased by a Transcendental heifer belonging to Miss Margaret Fuller. She is very fractious, I believe, and apt to kick over the milk pail . . . I intend to convert myself

into a milk-maid this evening, but I pray Heaven that
Mr. Ripley may be moved to assign me the kindliest
cow in the herd, otherwise I shall perform my duties
with fear and trembling.   I like my brethren in affliction
very well, and could you see us sitting round our table
at meal times, before the great kitchen fire, you would
call it a cheerful sight."

"April 14. I did not milk the cows last night, because
Mr. R. was afraid to trust them to my hands, or me to
their horns, I know not which. But this morning I have
done wonders.   Before breakfast I went out to the barn
and began to chop hay for the cattle, and with such
"righteous vehemence," as Mr. R. says, did I labor,
that in the space of ten minutes I broke the machine.
Then I brought wood and replenished the fires ; and
finally went down to breakfast, and ate up a huge mound
of buckwheat cakes. After breakfast Mr. R. put a four-
pronged instrument into my hands, which he gave me to
understand was called a pitchfork ; and he and Mr.
Farley being armed with similar weapons, we all three
commenced a gallant attack on a heap of manure. This
office being concluded, and I having purified myself, I
sit down to finish this letter. Miss Fuller's cow hooks
other cows, and has made herself ruler of the herd, and
behaves in a very tyrannical manner."

"April 16th. I have milked a cow !!! The herd has
rebelled against the usurpation of Miss Fuller's heifer ;
and whenever they are turned out of the barn, she is
compelled to take refuge under our protection.   So
much did she impede my labors by keeping close to me,
that I found it necessary to give her two or three gentle
pats with a shovel. She is not an amiable cow ; but she
has a very intelligent face, and seems to be of a reflective cast of character.

I have not yet been twenty yards from our house and
barn ; but I begin to perceive that this is a beautiful
place. The scenery is of a mild and placid character,
with nothing bold in its aspect ; but I think its beauties

will grow upon us, and make us love it the more the longer we live here. There is a brook so near the house that we shall be able to hear its ripple in the summer evenings,—but for agricultural purposes it has been made to flow in a straight and rectangular fashion which does it infinite damage as a picturesque object. Mr. R. has bought four black pigs."

"April 22nd. What an abominable hand do I scribble; but I have been chopping wood and turning a grindstone all the forenoon; and such occupations are apt to disturb the equilibrium of the muscles and sinews. It is an endless surprise to me how much work there is to be done in the world; but thank God I am able to do my share of it, and my ability increases daily. What a great, broad-shouldered, elephantine personage I shall become by and by!

I read no newspapers, and hardly remember who is President, and feel as if I had no more concern with what other people trouble themselves about, than if I dwelt in another planet."

"May 1st. All the morning I have been at work, under the clear blue sky, on a hill side. Sometimes it almost seemed as if I were at work in the sky itself, though the material in which I wrought was the ore from our gold-mine. There is nothing so disagreeable or unseemly in this sort of toil as you could think. It defiles the hands indeed, but not the soul.

The farm is growing very beautiful now,—not that we yet see anything of the peas and potatoes which we have planted, but the grass blushes green on the slopes and hollows.

I do not believe that I should be so patient here if I were not engaged in a righteous and heaven-blessed way of life. We had some tableaux last evening. They went off very well."

"May 11th. This morning I arose at milking time, in good trim for work; and we have been employed partly in an Augean labor of clearing out a wood-shed, and partly in carting loads of oak.   This afternoon I hope to have something to do in the field, for these jobs about the house are not at all suited to my taste."

"June 1st.   I think this present life of mine gives me an antipathy to pen and ink, even more than my Custom-house experience did.   In the midst of toil, or after a hard day's work, my soul obstinately refuses to be poured out on paper.   It is my opinion that a man's soul may be buried and perish under a dung heap, just as well as under a pile of money."

"August 15th.   Even my Custom-house experience was not such a thraldom and weariness as this.   O, labor is the curse of the world, and nobody can meddle with it, without becoming proportionably brutified!   Is it a praiseworthy matter that I have spent five golden months in providing food for cows and horses ?   It is not so."

"Salem, Sept. 3d.   Really I should judge it to be twenty years since I left Brook Farm ; and I take this to be one proof that my life there was an unnatural and un-suitable, and therefore an unreal one.   It already looks like a dream behind me.   The real Me was never an as-sociate of the community ; there had been a spectral Ap-pearance there, sounding the horn at daybreak, and milking the cows, and hoeing the potatoes, and raking hay, toiling in the sun, and doing me the honor to assume my name.   But this spectre was not myself."

Mr. Hawthorne was elected to high offices, to those of Trustee of the Brook Farm estate, and Chairman of the Committee of Finance ; but he told Mr. Ripley that he could not spend another winter there.   If we could inspect all the note-books of the community, supposing all to be as frank as Hawthorne, our picture of Brook Farm life would be fascinating.   But his was, perhaps, the only note-book kept in the busy brotherhood, and his rather sombre view must be accepted as the impression of one peculiar mind. In the "Blithedale Romance," Hawthorne disclaimed any purpose to describe persons or events at Brook Farm, and expressed a hope that some one might yet do justice to a movement so full of earnest aspiration. But he, himself, declined the task. "The old and affectionately remembered home at Brook Farm—certainly the most romantic episode of his own life—essentially a day dream, and yet a fact—thus offering an available foothold between fiction and reality," merely supplied the scenery for the romance. More than twenty years have passed since Hawthorne's appeal to his associates, but it has not been answered.

The characteristic nature of transcendental reform was exhibited in the temper of its agitation for the enfranchisement of women, and the enlargement of her sphere of duty and privilege. More definitely than any other, this reform can trace its beginnings and the source of its inspiration to the disciples of the transcendental philosophy. The transcendentalists gave it their countenance to some extent, to a man and a woman, conceding the truth of its idea even when criticising the details of its application. With almost if not quite equal unanimity, the other school regarded it with disfavor. The cause of woman, as entertained by the reformers, was not likely to commend itself to people who consulted custom, law, or institution; who accepted the authority of tradition, took history to be revelation, deferred to the decree of circumstance, or, under any other open or disguised form, bowed to the doctrine that might makes right. The philosophical conservatives and the social conservatives struck hands on this ; for both, the one party in deference to established usage, the other party in deference to the opinion that mind followed organization, defended things as they were, and hoped for a better state of things, if they hoped for it at all, as a result of changes in the social environment. The disciples of the same philosophy now hold the same view of this particular reform. From them comes the charge of unsexing women and demoralizing the sex. In the belief of the transcendentalist, souls were of no sex. Men and women were alike human beings, with human capacities, longings, and destinies ; and the condition of society that doomed them to hopelessness in regard to the complete and perfect justification of their being, was, in his judgment—not in his feeling, or sentiment, but in his judgment—unsound.

The ablest and most judicial statement on the question was made by Margaret Fuller in the "Dial" of July 1843. The paper entitled the "Great Law Suit" was afterwards expanded into the little volume called "Woman in the XIXth Century," which contains all that is best worth saying on the subject, has been the storehouse of argument and illustration from that time to this, and should be read by all who would understand the cardinal points in the case. The careful student of that book will be amazed at the misapprehensions in respect to its doctrine that are current even in intelligent circles. Certainly Miss Fuller does claim everything that may fairly be comprehended under woman's education ; everything that follows, or may be honestly and rationally held as following in the course of her intellectual development. But she claims it by rigorous fidelity to a philosophical idea; not passionately or hastily. Not as a demand of sentiment, not as a right under liberty, not as a conclusion from American institutions, but as the spiritual prerogative of the spiritual being. Her argument moves on this high table-land of thought; and moves with a steadiness, a serenity, an ease that little resemble the heated debates on later platforms. Miss Fuller was thoroughly feminine in her intuitions. It was impossible for her to treat any subject, to say nothing of a subject so complex and delicate as this, with any but the finest tempered tools. Her sympathies were with women; she attracted women by the power of her intelligence and fellow feeling. Women of feeling and aspiration— pure feeling and beautiful aspiration,—came to her. The secrets of the best hearts were revealed to her, as they could not have been, had she failed to reach or attract them on their own level. Her idea of womanly character as displayed in sentiment and action was as gracious as it was lofty.

" We would have every arbitrary barrier thrown down. We would have every path laid open to women as freely as to man. Were this done, and a slight temporary fermentation allowed to subside, we believe that the Divine would ascend into nature to a height unknown in the history of past ages ; and nature, thus instructed, would regulate the spheres, not only so as to avoid collision, but to bring forth ravishing harmony."

Yet then, and only then, will human beings, in her judgment, be ripe for this, when inward and outward freedom for woman as much as for man, shall be acknowledged as a right, not yielded as a concession.

" What woman needs is not as a woman to act or rule, but as a nature to grow, as an intellect to discern, as a soul to live freely, and unimpeded to unfold such powers as were given her when we left our common home. If fewer talents were given her, yet, if allowed the full and free employment of these, so that she may render back to the giver his own with usury, she will not complain, nay, I dare to say, she will bless and rejoice in her earthly birth-place her earthly lot."

" Man is not willingly ungenerous. He wants faith and love because he is not yet himself an elevated being. He cries with sneering skepticism : Give us a sign ! But if the sign appears, his eyes glisten, and he offers not merely approval but homage."

The Transcendental idea makes her just to all, to the Hebrews who "greeted with solemn rapture all great and holy women as heroines, prophetesses, nay judges in Israel, and if they made Eve listen to the serpent, gave Mary to the Holy Ghost ; " to the Greeks whose feminine deities were types of dignity and loveliness ; to the Romans, whose glorious women are " of threadbare celebrity ; " to Asiatics, Russians, English. It gave her generous interpretations for laws, institutions, customs, bidding her look on the bright side of history.

" Whatever may have been the domestic manners of the ancient nations, the idea of woman was nobly manifested in their mythologies and poems, where she appeared as Sita in the Ramayana, a form of tender purity ; in the Egyptian Isis, of divine wisdom never yet surpassed. In Egypt too, the sphinx, walking the earth with lion tread, looked out upon its marvels in the calm, inscrutable beauty of a virgin face, and the Greek could only add wings to the great emblem." "In Sparta the women were as much Spartans as the men. Was not the calm equality they enjoyed well worth the honors of chivalry? They intelligently shared the ideal life of their nation." "Is it in vain that the truth has been recognized that woman is not only a part of man, bone of his bone, and flesh of his flesh, born that man might not be lonely, but in themselves possessors of and possessed by immortal souls? This truth undoubtedly received a greater outward stability from the belief of the church that the earthly parent of the Saviour of souls was a woman."

"Woman cannot complain that she has not had her share of power. This in all ranks of society, except the lowest, has been hers to the extent that vanity could crave, far beyond what wisdom would accept. It is not the transient breath of poetic incense that women want; each can receive that from a lover. It is not life-long sway; it needs to become a coquette, a shrew, or a good cook, to be sure of that. It is not money, nor notoriety, nor the badges of authority that men have appropriated to themselves. It is for that which includes all these and precludes them; which would not be forbidden power, lest there be temptation to steal and misuse it; which would not have the mind perverted by flattery from a worthiness of esteem. It is for that which is the birthright of every being capable to receive it,—the freedom, the religious, the intelligent freedom of the universe, to use its means, to learn its secret as far as nature has enabled them, with God alone for their guide and their judge."

"The only reason why women ever assume what is more appropriate to men, is because men prevent them from finding out what is fit for themselves. Were they free, were they wise fully to develop the strength and beauty of woman, they would never wish to be men or manlike. The well instructed moon flies not from her orbit to seize on the glories of her partner."

" Give the soul free course, let the organization be freely developed, and the being will be fit for any and every relation to which it may be called."

" Civilized Europe is still in a transition state about marriage, not only in practice but in thought. A great majority of societies and individuals are still doubtful whether earthly marriage is to be a union of souls, or merely a contract of convenience and utility. Were woman established in the rights of an immortal being, this could not be." But " those who would reform the world, must show that they do not speak in the heat of wild impulse ; their lives must be unstained by passion- ate error ; they must be severe lawgivers to themselves. As to their transgressions of opinions, it may be observed, that the resolve of Eloise to be only the mistress of Abelard, was that of one who saw the contract of mar- riage a seal of degradation. Wherever abuses of this sort are seen, the timid will suffer, the bold will protest ; but society has the right to outlaw them, till she has revised her law, and she must be taught to do so, by one who speaks with authority, not in anger or haste."

" Whether much or little has been or will be done ; whether women will add to the talent of narration, the power of systematizing ; whether they will carve marble as well as iron, is not important. But that it should be acknowledged that they have intellect which needs developing, that they should not be considered complete, if beings of affection and habit alone, is important. Earth knows no fairer, holier relation than that of mother. But a being of infinite scope must not be treated with an exclusive view to any one relation."

" In America women are much better situated than men. Good books are allowed, with more time to read them. They have time to think, and no traditions chain them. Their employments are more favorable to the inward life than those of men. Men are courteous to them ; praise them often ; check them seldom. In this country, is venerated, wherever seen, the character which Goethe spoke of as an Ideal : 'The excellent woman is she, who, if her husband dies, can be a father to the children.'"

Nothing can be more reasonable than this ; and this is the tone of transcendental feeling and thought on the subject. The only criticism that can fairly be made on the Transcendentalist's idea of woman, is that it has more regard for essential capacities and possibilities, than for incidental circumstances, more respect for the ideal than for the actual woman. However grave a sin this may be against common sense, it is none against purity, noble-ness, or the laws of private or public virtue. The dream, if it be no more than a dream, is beautiful and inspiring.

The Transcendentalist believed in man's ability to apprehend absolute ideas of Truth, Justice, Rectitude, Goodness ; he spoke of The Right, The True, The Beautiful, as eternal realities which he perceived. The "Sensational" philosophy was shut up in the relative and conditioned ; knew nothing higher than expediency ; held prudence, caution, practical wisdom in highest rank among the virtues ; consulted the revelations of history ; recognized no law above established usage ; went for guidance to the book, the record, the statute ; it could not speak therefore with power, but could only consider, surmise, cast probabilities, devise plans and work care-fully towards their execution. The Sensationalist dis-trusted the seer, rejected the prophet, and disliked the reformer. His aim was low ; his work within easy distance ; his object, some plainly visible and appreciable satisfaction. His faith in men and women was small ; his trust in circumstances and conditions was unbounded ; but as this faith had no wings, it could neither raise its possessor from the ground, nor speed him faster than a walking pace. He was easily satisfied with the world as it was; or if dissatisfied, had little hope of its being made better by anything he could do. His helplessness and hopelessness will make him in opinion an optimist, who finds it easier to assume that the order of the world is perfect and will so appear by and by, than that it is made imperfect for him to mend. Optimism is perhaps oftener the creed of the indolent than of the earnest.

The Transcendentalist was satisfied with nothing so long as it did not correspond to the ideal in the enlightened soul; and in the soul recognized the power to make all things new. Nothing will content him short of the absolute right, the eternally true, the unconditioned excellence. He prays for the kingdom of Heaven, lives in expectation of it; would not be surprised at its coming any day. For though the distance is immense between the world as it is and his vision of the world as it should be—a distance that the Evolutionist despairs of seeing traversed in thousands of years, if he believes it will be traversed at all,—still, as the power of regeneration is supposed to be in the soul itself, which is possessed of infinite capacities and is open continually to inspirations from the world of soul, the transformation may begin when least expected, and may be completed before preparation for it can be made. Hence his boundless enthusiasm and hope; hence the ardor of his feeling, the glow of his language. Hence his disposition to exaggerate the force of tendencies that point in his direction; to take the brightest view of events, and put the happiest construction on the signs of the times. In the anti-slavery period the Transcendentalist glorified the negro beyond all warrant of fact, seeing in him an imprisoned. soul struggling to be free. The same soul he sees in woman oppressed by limitations; the same in the drunkard, the gambler, the libertine. His eye is ever fixed on the future.

VIII.

RELIGION

IT was by no accident that the transcendental philosophy addressed itself at once to the questions of religion. It did so at the beginning, in Germany, and later, in England, and did so from the nature of the case. Its very name implied that it maintained the existence of ideas in the mind which transcended sensible experience. Such ideas fall within the domain of religion; ideas of the infinite, the eternal, the absolute; and the significance and import of these ideas exercised the minds of transcendental thinkers, according to their genius. Kant felt it necessary to reopen the problem of God and immortality; Fichte followed, Schelling and Hegel moved on the same plane.

Transcendentalism was, in fact, a reaction against the moral and political skepticism which resulted directly from the prevailing philosophy of sensation. Since Bacon's day, religious beliefs had been losing hold on the enlightened mind of England and Europe. The drift of speculation was strongly against, not the Christian system alone, but natural religion, and the ideal foundation of morality. The writings of Collins, Dodwell, Mandeville, expressed more skepticism than they created, and betrayed a deeply-seated and widely-spread misgiving in regard to the fundamental truths of theology. Hume's argument against the credibility of miracles was never answered, and the anxiety to answer it was a confession of alarm from the heart of the church. The famous XVIth chapter of Gibbon's " Decline and Fall of the Roman Empire " was assailed furiously, but in vain, each assault exposing the weakness of the assailants ; and it was only by adopting his history, and editing it with judicious notes, that the church silenced the enemy it could not crush. The deists of the seventeenth century in no wise balanced their denials by their affirmations, but left Christianity fearfully shattered by their blows. The champions of the church fought skepticism with skepticism, conceding in substance the points they superficially attacked. Towards the close of the seventeenth century Cudworth confronted atheism with idealism, retreating upon Plato when the foe had carried the other works ; early in the century following, Butler, in the celebrated "Analogy," fought infidelity with weapons that infidelity might have turned, and since has turned with deadly effect, against himself. The ablest representative of Unitarianism was Joseph Priestley, a materialist of the school of Hartley. The cardinal beliefs of religion were debated in a way that was quite unsatisfactory in the light of reason, showing the extent to which faith had been undermined. Indeed, had it not been for the power of institutions, customs, respectability, and tradition, the popular beliefs would have all but disappeared, so deep into the heart of the people unbelief had penetrated. The church stood fast, because it was allied with power and fashion, not because it was supported by reason or faith. The whole tone of feeling on sacred and ethical topics was low; divine ideas were defended by considerations of expediency; God was a probability; the immortality of the soul a possibility, a supplement to skepticism, an appendix to a philosophy which, finding no God here, presumed there must be one hereafter. There is no more soulless reading than the works of the Christian apologists of the seventeenth century. The infidels had more ideas, and apparently more sincerity, but in neither was there any spiritual impulse or fervor.

In Germany the philosophy of Bacon and Locke did not strike deep root. The day of Germany was to come later. Her thoughts were pent up in her own breast. She was isolated, and almost speechless. Her genius awoke with the new philosophy. Under the influence of idealism it bloomed in the richest of modern literatures. Her very skepticism, the much talked-of rationalism, had an ideal origin. Strauss was a disciple of Hegel. Baur, and the "historical school" of Tübingen worked out their problem of New Testament criticism from the Hegelian idea, the constructive force whereof was so powerful, that the negations lost their negative character, and showed primarily as affirmations of reason. By being adopted into the line of intellectual development of mankind, Christianity, though dethroned and disenchanted, was dignified as a supreme moment in the autobiography of God.

Frederick the Great, in the middle of the eighteenth century, attracted literary celebrities to his court, and gave an impulse, so far, to the German mind ; but the French genius found more encouragement there than the German, and in his time French genius was speeding fast in the way of skepticism. Condillac, Cabanis, d'Holbach, Helvetius, were of that generation. The " Encyclopæ-dists," the most brilliant men and women of the generation, were planning their work of demolition. Voltaire was the great name in contemporary literature. The books of Volney were popular towards the end of the century. Skepticism and materialism had the floor. It was fashionable to ridicule the belief in personal immortality, and in enlightened circles to deny the existence of God. The doctrines of Christianity were abandoned to priests and women ; philosophers deemed them too absurd to be argued against. Had the assault been less witty and more scientific, less acrimonious and more reasonable, less scornful and more consistent, its apparent success might have been permanent. As it was, a change of mood occurred ; a conservative spirit succeeded the destructive ; order prevailed over anarchy ; and the Catholic church, which had only been temporarily thrust aside—not fatally wounded, not by any means disposed of—regained its suspended power.

But rational or intellectual Christianity—in other words the system of Protestantism, in whatever form held—received a severe blow in France from these audacious hands. Religion took refuge in institutions and ceremonial forms ; and there remained little else except a kernel of sentiment in a thin shell of tradition. What beliefs were entertained were accepted on authority ; reason sought other fields of exercise, scientific, philosophical, literary ; and a chill of indifference crept over the once religious world. From France, opinions adverse to Christianity were brought to America by travelled or curious people ; they pervaded the creative minds of our earliest epoch, and penetrated far into the popular intelligence. The habit of thinking independently of authority and tradition became confirmed, and as a matter of course led to doubts and denials ; for thinking was done in a temper of defiance, which constrained the thought to obey the wish. Such philosophical ideas as there were, came from France and England. Paley's was the last word in morals ; the " Bridgewater Treatises " were the received oracles in religion ; the rules of practical judgment had usurped the dominion of faith.

What pass things had come to in New England, in the centre of its culture, has been described in a previous chapter. It was time for a reaction to set in ; and it came in the form of Transcendentalism. The " sensational " philosophy, it was contended, could not supply a basis for faith. Its first principle was *"Nihil in intellectu quod non prius in sensu."* " There is nothing in the intellect that was not first in the senses." From this principle nothing but skepticism could proceed. How, for instance, asks the Transcendentalist, can the sensational philosophy of Locke and his disciples give us anything approaching to a certainty of the existence of God ? The senses furnish no evidence of it. God is not an

object of sensation. He is not seen, felt, heard, tasted
or smelt. The objects of sense are material, local, incidental; God is immaterial, universal, eternal. The
objects of sense are finite; but a finite God is no God; for
God is infinite. Is it said that by men of old, bible men,
God was seen, heard, clasped in human arms? The reply
is, that whatever Being was so apparent and tangible,
could not have been God. To the assertion that the
Being announced himself as God,—the infinite, the eternal
God,—the challenge straightway is given: To whom did
he say it? How can it be proved that he said it? Is
the record of his saying it authentic? Might not the
Being have made a false statement? Can we be certain
there was no mental hallucination? Suppose these and
other doubts of a similar character dispelled, still, hearing is not knowing. All we have is a tradition of God,
a legend, a rumor, a dim reminiscence, that passes like
a shadow across men's minds. The appeal to miracle is
set aside by historical skepticism. The wonder lacks
evidence; and to prove the wonder a miracle, is
beyond achievement. A possibility, or at most, a probability of God's existence is all that sensationalism, with
every advantage given it, can supply.

And if this philosophy fails to give an assurance of
God's existence, the failure to throw light on his attributes is more signal. The senses report things as they
exist in relations, not as they exist in themselves.
Neither absolute power, absolute wisdom nor absolute
goodness is hinted at by the senses. The visible system
of things abounds in contradictions that we cannot

reconcile, puzzles we cannot explain, mysteries we cannot penetrate, imperfections we cannot account for, wrongs we cannot palliate, evils we cannot cover up or justify. That a vein of wisdom, an element of goodness, an infusion of loving-kindness is in the world is evident; but to show that, is to go very little way towards establishing the attributes of a Perfect Being. A God of limited power, wisdom or goodness, is no God, and no other does Sensationalism offer. Transcendentalism points to the fact that under the auspices of this philosophy atheism has spread; and along with atheism the intellectual demoralization that accompanies the disappearance of a cardinal idea.

From this grave peril the Transcendentalist found an escape in flight to the spiritual nature of man, in virtue of which he had an intuitive knowledge of God as a being, infinite and absolute in power, wisdom and goodness; a direct perception like that which the senses have of material objects; a perception that gains in distinctness, clearness and positiveness as the faculties through which it is obtained increase in power and delicacy. To the human mind, by its original constitution, belongs the firm assurance of God's existence, as a half latent fact of consciousness, and with it a dim sense of his moral attributes. To minds capacious and sensitive the truth was disclosed in lofty ranges that lifted the horizon line, in every direction, above the cloud land of doubt; to minds cultivated, earnest, devout, aspiring, the revelation came in bursts of glory. The experiences of inspired men and women were repeated. The prophet, the seer, the saint, was no longer a favored person whose sayings and doings were recorded in the Bible, but a living person, making manifest the wealth of soul in all human beings. Communication with the ideal world was again opened through conscience ; and communion with God, close and tender as is anywhere described by devotees and mystics, was promised to the religious affections.

The Transcendentalist spoke of God with authority. His God was not possible, but real; not probable, but certain. In his high confidence he had small respect for the labored reasonings of " Natural Religion ; " the argument from design, so carefully elaborated by Paley, Brougham and the writers of the " Bridgewater Treatises," was interesting and useful as far as it went, but was remanded to an inferior place. The demonstration from miracle was dismissed with feelings bordering on contempt, as illogical and childish.

Taking his faith with him into the world of nature and of human life, the Transcendentalist, sure of the divine wisdom and love, found everywhere joy for mourning and beauty for ashes. Passing through the valley of Baca, he saw springs bubbling up from the sand, and making pools for thirsty souls. Wherever he came, garments of heaviness were dropped and robes of praise put on. Evil was but the prophecy of good, wrong the servant of right, pain the precursor of peace, sorrow the minister to joy. He would acknowledge no exception to the rule of an absolute justice and an inexorable love. It was certain that all was well, appear-

ances to the contrary notwithstanding. He was, as we
have said, an optimist—not of the indifferent sort that
make the maxim "Whatever is, is right" an excuse for
idleness—but of the heroic kind who, by refreshing their
minds with thoughts of the absolute goodness, keep alive
their faith, hope, endeavor, and quicken themselves to
efforts at understanding, interpreting and bringing to
the surface the divine attributes. For himself he had
no misgivings, and no alarm at the misgivings of others;
believing them due, either to some misunderstanding that
might be corrected, or to some moral defect that could
be cured. Even Atheism, of the crudest, coarsest,
most stubborn description, had no terrors for him. It
was in his judgment a matter of definition mainly.
Utter atheism was all but inconceivable to him; the
essential faith in divine things under some form of
mental perception being too deeply planted in human
nature to be eradicated or buried.

Taking his belief with him into the world of history,
the Transcendentalist discovered the faith in God beneath
all errors, delusions, idolatries and superstition. He
read it into unintelligible scriptures; he drew it forth
from obsolete symbols; he dragged it to the light from
the darkness of hateful shrines and the bloody mire of
pagan altars. Mr. Parker meditated a work on the
religious history of mankind, in which the development
of the theistic idea was to be traced from its shadowy
beginnings to its full maturity; and this he meant should
be the crowning work of his life. Sure of his first principle, he had no hesitation in going into caves and among

the ruins of temples. Had that work been completed, the Transcendentalist's faith in God would have received its most eloquent statement.

The other cardinal doctrine of religion—the immortality of the soul,—Transcendentalism was proud of having rescued from death in the same way. The philosophy of sensation could give no assurance of personal immortality. Here, too, its fundamental axiom, "*Nihil in intellectu quod non prius in sensu,*" was discouraging to belief. For immortality is not demonstrable to the senses. Experience affords no basis for conviction, and knowledge cannot on any pretext be claimed. The sensational school was divided into two parties. The first party confessed that the immortality of the soul was a thing not only unprovable, but a thing easily disproved, a thing improbable, and, to a clear mind, impossible to believe. The soul being a product of organization, at all events fatally implicated in organization, conditioned by it in all respects, must perish with organization, as the flower perishes with the stem. Of a spirit distinct from body there is, according to this school, no evidence, either before death or after. Man's prospect, therefore, is bounded by this life. Dreamers may have visions of another; mourners may sigh for another; ardent natures may hope for another; but to believe in another is, to the rational mind, according to this philosophy, impossible. The sentence "dust thou art, and to dust thou shalt return," may seem a hard one; but as it cannot be reversed or modified, it must be accepted with submission; and in default of another life, the honest man will make the most of the life he has; not necessarily saying with the sensualist: " Let us eat and drink, for to-morrow we die ;" but with the hero reminding himself that he must " Work while it is day, for the night cometh in which no man can work." The modern disciples of this doctrine of annihilation speak in a tone of lofty courage of their destiny, and disguise under shining and many colored garments of anticipation, the fact of their personal cessation. The thinkers find refuge in the intellectual problems of the present ; the workers pile up monuments that shall endure when they are gone ; poets like George Eliot, make grand music on the harp-strings of the common humanity ; but the fact remains that the philosophy of experience abandons, or did before the advent of spiritualism—the expectation of an existence after death.

The other branch of the Sensational school fell back on authority, and received on the tradition of history what could not be verified by science. Immortality was accepted as a doctrine of instituted religion, taken on the credit of revelation, and sealed by the resurrection of Jesus. As an article of faith it was accepted without comment. If we have not seen the glorified dead, others have, and their witness is recorded in the Scriptures. Beyond that believers did not care to go ; beyond that advised no one else to go. To question the genuineness of the Scriptures, to cast doubt on the resurrection of Jesus, to intimate that the tradition of the church is a thin stream that murmurs pleasantly in the shade of the sacred groves, but would dry up if the sun-light were let in, was resented as an offence against reverence and morality. By such as these the belief that slipped away from the reason was detained by the will.

But beliefs thus appropriated are insecurely held. The inactivity of the mind cannot be guaranteed ; a slight disturbance of its tamely acquiescent condition may set its whole scheme of opinions afloat. A sentence on a printed page, a word let fall in conversation, a discovered fact, an awakened suspicion, a suggestion of doubt by a friend, may stir the thought whose movement will bring the whole structure down. There being no certainty, only arbitrary consent ; no personal conviction, only formal acquiescence ; there was nothing to prevent the belief from disappearing altogether, and leaving the mind vacant.

Even when retained, beliefs thus held have no vitality. They are not living faiths in any intelligent sense. Useful they may be for pulpit declamation and closet discussion ; serviceable on funeral occasions and in chambers of sorrow ; available for purposes of moral impression; but inspiring they are not; actively sustaining and consoling they are not. Their effect on the conduct of life is almost imperceptible. They are appendages to the mind, not parts of it ; proprieties, not properties. They are to be reckoned as part of a man's stock in trade, not as part of his being.

Transcendentalism, by taking the belief in immortality out of these incidental and doubtful associations, and making it a constituent element in the constitution of the mind itself, thought to rescue it from its precarious position, and place it beyond the reach of danger. No belief was, on the whole, so characteristic of Transcendentalism as this; none was so steadfastly assumed, so constantly borne in view. Immortality was here a postulate, a first principle. Theodore Parker called it a fact of consciousness—the intensity of his conviction rendering him careless of precision in speech. The writings of Emerson are redolent of the faith. Even when he argues in his way against the accepted creed, and casts doubt on every form in which the doctrine is entertained, the loftiness of his language about the soul carries the presage of immortality with it. The "Dial" has no argument about immortality; no paper in the whole series is devoted to the subject; the faith was too deep and essential to be talked about—it was assumed. The Transcendentalist was an enthusiast on this article. He spoke, not as one who surmises, conjectures, is on the whole inclined to think; but as one who knows beyond cavil or question. We never met a man whose assurance of immortality was as strong as Theodore Parker's. The objections of materialists did not in the least disturb him. In the company of the most absolute of them he avowed his conviction. What others clung to as supports—the church tradition, the story of the raising of Lazarus, the account of the resurrection of Jesus—were to him stumbling blocks in the way of spiritual faith, for they drew attention away from the witness of the soul.

The preaching of Transcendentalists caused, in all

parts of the country, a revival of interest and of faith
in personal immortality; spiritualized the idea of it;
enlarged the scope of the belief, and ennobled its character; established an organic connection between the
present life and the future, making them both one in substance; disabused people of the coarse notion that the
next life was an incident of their experience, and compelled them to think of it as a normal extension of their
being; substituted aspiration after spiritual deliverance
and perfection, for hope of happiness and fear of misery;
recalled attention to the nature and capacity of the soul
itself; in a word, announced the natural immortality of
the soul by virtue of its essential quality. The fanciful
reasoning of Plato's *"Phædon"* was supplemented by
new readings in psychology, and strengthened by powerful moral supports; the highest desires, the purest feelings,
the deepest sympathies, were enlisted in its cause; death
was made incidental to life; lower life was made subordinate to higher; and men who were beginning to
doubt whether the demand for personal immortality was
entirely honorable in one who utterly trusted in God,
thoroughly appreciated the actual world, and fairly respected his own dignity, were reassured by a faith which
promised felicity on terms that compromised neither
reason nor virtue. The very persons who had let go
the hope of immortality because they could not accept
it at the cost of sacrificing their confidence in God's instant justice, were glad to recover it as a promise of
fulfilment to their dearest desire for spiritual expansion.

The Sensational philosophy had done a worse harm

to the belief in immortality, than by rendering the pros
pect of it uncertain ; it had rendered the character of it
pusillanimous and plebeian ; it had demanded it on the
ground that God must explain himself, must correct his
blunders and apologize for his partiality in distributing
sugar plums ; it had argued for it from personal, social,
sectarian, and other sympathies and antipathies ; it had
expected it on the strength of a rumor that a specially
holy man, a saint of Judea, had appeared after death to
his peculiar friends ; it had pleaded for it, as children
beg for dessert after bread and meat. The transcendental philosophy dismissed these unworthy claims,
made no demand, put up no petition, but simply made
articulate the prophecy of the spiritual nature in man,
and trusted the eternal goodness for its fulfilment.
Other arguments might come to the support of this
anticipation ; history might bring its contribution of
recorded facts ; suffering and sorrow might add their
pathetic voices, bewailing the oppressive power of circumstance, and crying for peace out of affliction ; the biographies of Jesus might furnish illustration of the victory
of the greatest souls over death ; but considerations of
this kind received their importance from the light they
threw on the immortal attributes of spirit. Apart from
these their significance was gone.

The pure Transcendentalists saw everywhere evidence
of the greatness of the soul. Christianity they regarded
as its chief manifestation. Imperfect Transcendentalists
there were, who used the fundamental postulates of the
transcendental philosophy to confirm their faith in super-

natural realities. Their Transcendentalism amounted merely to this, that man had a natural capacity for *receiving* supernatural truths, when presented by revelation. The *possession* of such truths, even in germ; the power to unfold them naturally, by process of mental or spiritual growth; the faculty to seize, define, shape, legitimate and enthrone them, they denied. The soul, according to them, was recipient, not originating or creative. They continued to be Christians of the " Evangelical " stamp; champions of special intervention of light and grace; hearty believers in the divinity of the Christ and the saving influence of the Holy Ghost; holding to the peculiar inspiration of the Bible, and the personal need of regeneration. The wisest teachers of orthodoxy belonged to this school.

The pure Transcendentalist went much further. According to him, the seeds of truth, if not the outline forms of truth, were contained in the soul itself, all ready to expand in bloom and beauty, as it felt the light and heat of the upper world. Sir Kenelm Digby relates that in Padua he visited the laboratory of a famous physician, and was there shown a small pile of fine ashes under a glass. On the application of a gentle heat, it arose, assumed the shape of its original flower, all its parts being perfectly distinct in form and well defined in character. During the application of the heat, the spectral plant preserved its delicate outline ; but on withdrawal of the heat, it became dust again. So, according to the Transcendentalist, the spiritual being of man—which apparently is a heap of lifeless ashes on the surface of material existence—when graciously shone upon by knowledge and love, puts on divine attributes, glows with beauty, palpitates with joy, gives out flashes of power, distils odors of sanctity, and exhibits the marks of a celestial grace. The soul, when thus awakened, utters oracles of wisdom, sings, prophesies, thunders decalogues, pronounces beatitudes, discourses grandly of God and divine things, performs wonders of healing on sick bodies and wandering minds, rises to heights of heroism and saintliness.

From this point of vision, it was easy to survey the history of mankind, and, in the various religions of the world, see the efforts of the soul to express itself in scriptures, emblems, doctrines, altar forms, architecture, painting, moods and demonstrations of piety. The Transcendentalist rendered full justice to all these, studied them, admired them, confessed their inspiration. Of these faiths Christianity was cheerfully acknowledged to be the queen. The supremacy of Jesus was granted with enthusiasm. His teachings were accepted as the purest expressions of religious truth; His miracles were regarded as the natural achievements of a soul of such originality and force. In his address to the senior class in Divinity College, 1838, Mr. Emerson spoke of Christ's miracles as being "one with the blowing clover and the falling rain," and urged the young candidates for the ministry to let his life and dialogues "lie as they befel, active and warm, part of human life, and of the landscape, and of the cheerful day." When, in 1840, Theodore Parker wrote his "Levi Blodgett" letter, he believed in miracles, the miracles of the New Testament and many others besides, more than the Christians about him were willing to accept.

" It may be said these religious teachers (Zoroaster, Buddha, Fo) pretended to work miracles. I would not deny that they *did* work miracles. If a man is obedient to the law of his mind, conscience and heart, since his intellect, character and affections are in harmony with the laws of God, I take it he can do works that are impossible to others, who have not been so faithful, and consequently are not " one with God" as he is; and this is all that is meant by a miracle." " The possession of this miraculous power, when it can be proved, as I look at the thing, is only a *sign*, which may be uncertain, of the superior genius of a religious teacher, or a *sign* that he will utter the truth, and never a *proof* thereof."

The Transcendentalist was a cordial believer in marvels, as being so hearty a believer in the potency of the spiritual laws. Parker's opposition to the miracles of the New Testament was provoked by the exclusive claim that was put forward by their defenders, and by the position they were thrust into as pillars of doctrine. His wish to make it appear that truth could stand without them, impelled him to strain at their overthrow. Later, his studies in New Testament criticism confirmed his suspicion that the testimony in their favor was altogether inadequate to sustain their credibility. The theory of Baur and his disciples of the Tübingen school seemed to him unanswerable, and he abandoned, as a scholar, much that as a Transcendentalist he might have been disposed to retain. W. H. Furness, author of several biographical studies on the life and character of Jesus—a Transcendentalist of the most impassioned school, but no adept in historical criticism—maintained to the last the credibility of the Christian miracles, and purely on the ground of their perfect naturalness as performed by a person so spiritually exalted as Jesus was. The more ardent his admiration of that character, the more unshrinking his belief in these manifestations of its superiority. Dr. Furness is prepared to think that if no miracles had been recorded, nevertheless miracles must have been wrought, and would, but for some blindness or skepticism, have been mentioned.

The charge that Transcendentalism denied the reality of supernatural powers and influences shows how imperfectly it was apprehended. It seemed to deny them because it transferred them to another sphere. It regarded man himself as a supernatural being; not the last product of nature, but the lord of nature; not the *creature* of organization, but its creator. In its extreme form, Transcendentalism was a deification of nature, in the highest aspects of Beauty. It raised human qualities to the supreme power; it ascribed to extraordinary virtue in its exalted states the efficient grace that is commonly attributed to the Holy Spirit. The pure Transcendentalist spoke of the experiences and powers of the illuminated soul with as much extravagance of rapture as one of the newly redeemed ever expressed. The profane made sport of his fanaticisms and fervors in the same way that they made sport of the wild over-gush of a revival meeting. The demonstrations of feeling were in fact, precisely similar; only in the one case the excitement was traced to the Christ in the skies, in the other to the Christ who was the soul of the man; in the one case a superhuman being was imagined as operating on the soul; in the other case the soul was supposed to be giving expression to itself.

The Transcendentalist was not careful enough in making this distinction, and was, therefore, to blame for a portion of the misapprehension that ensued. He often found in sacred literature, thoughts which he himself put there. Parker, discoursing of inspiration, cites Paul and John as holding the same doctrine with himself; though it is plain to the single mind that their doctrine was in no respect the same, but so different as to be in contradiction. Paul and John, it is hardly too much to say, set up their doctrine in precise opposition to the doctrine of the Transcendentalists. Paul declared that the natural man could *not* discern divine things; that they were foolishness to him; that they must be spiritually discerned; that the Christian was able to discern them spiritually *because he had* the " mind of Christ." The eighth chapter of the Epistle to the Romans contains sentences that, taken singly, apart from their connection, comfort the cockles of the transcendental heart; but the writer is glorifying Christ the inspirer; not the soul the inspired. He opens the chapter with the affirmation that " there is no condemnation to them which are in CHRIST JESUS, who walk not after the flesh, but after the spirit," and follows it with the saying that " if any man have not the *Spirit of Christ,* he is none of his." This is the spirit that "quickens mortal bodies," that makes believers to be "Sons of God," giving them the spirit of adoption whereby they cry "Abba, Father," bearing witness with their spirit that they are "the children of God." This is the spirit that "helpeth our infirmities," and "maketh intercession with groanings which cannot be uttered." Transcendentalism deliberately broke with Christianity. Paul said "other foundation can no man lay than that is laid, which is Jesus Christ." Transcendentalism responded: "Jesus Christ built on my foundation, the soul;" and, for thus answering, was classed with those who used as building materials "wood, hay, stubble," which the fire would consume. In the view of Transcendentalism, Christianity was an illustrious form of natural religion—Jesus was a noble type of human nature; revelation was disclosure of the soul's mystery; inspiration was the filling of the soul's lungs; salvation was spiritual vitality.

Transcendentalism carried its appeal to metaphysics. At present physics have the floor. Our recent studies have been in the natural history of the soul. Its spiritual history is discredited. But the human mind ebbs and flows. The Bains and Spencers and Taines may presently give place to other prophets; psychology may come to the front again, and with it will reappear the sages and seers. In that event, the religion of Transcendentalism will revive, and will have a long and fair day.

For it can hardly be supposed that the present movement in the line of observation is the final one: that henceforth we are to continue straight on till, by the path of physiology, we arrive at absolute truth; that idealism is dead and gone for ever, and materialism of a refined type holds the future in its hand. The triumphs of the scientific method in the natural world are wonderful. The law of evolution has its lap full of promise. But one who has studied at all the history of human thought; who has seen philosophies crowned and discrowned, sceptred and outcast; who has followed the changing fortunes of opposing schools, and witnessed the alternate victories and defeats that threatened, each in its turn, to decide the fate of philosophy, will be slow to believe that the final conflict has been fought, or is to be, for hundreds of years to come. The principles of the " Sensational " philosophy have, within the last half century, been revived and restated with great power by Mill, Bain, Spencer, Taine, and other leaders of speculative opinion both in England and Europe. Recent discoveries and generalizations in physical science have lent countenance to them. The investigations in physiology and biology, the researches in the regions of natural history, the revelations of chemistry, have all combined to confirm their truth. Psychology, in the hands of its latest masters, has worked successfully in their interest. The thinness, shallowness and dry technicality of the original school have given place to a rich and varied exposition of the facts of organic life in its origin, development and results. The original form of the Sensational philosophy as it prevailed in Europe is described by Mill as " the shallowest set of doctrines which perhaps, were ever passed off upon a cultivated age as a complete psychological system; a system which affected to resolve all the phenomena of the human mind into sensation, by a process which essentially consisted in merely *calling* all states of mind, however heterogeneous, by that name; a philosophy now acknowledged to consist solely of a set of verbal generalizations, explaining nothing, distinguishing nothing, leading to nothing." The " Sensational " philosophy is now presented as the philosophy of "experience." Its occupation is to resolve into results of experience and processes of organic life the *à priori* conceptions that have been accepted as simple and primitive data of consciousness, by the Ideal philosophy. Mill was one of the first to undertake this from the psychological side, analyzing the processes of reason, and making account of the contents of the mind. Lewes, Spencer, Tyndall have approached the same problem from the side of organization. In the first edition of the Logic, Mill clearly indicated the ground he took in the controversy between the two schools; in the last edition, he defined his position more clearly, against Whewell, and in agreement with Bain.

In the article on Coleridge, published in the *London and Westminister Review*, March, 1840, and republished in the second volume of " Dissertations and Discussions," Mill declares explicitly, that in his judgment, the truth on the much-debated question between the two philosophies lies with the school of Locke and Bentham :

" The nature of laws and things in themselves, or the hidden causes of the phenomena which are the objects of experience, appear to us radically inaccessible to the human faculties. We see no ground for believing that any thing can be the object of our knowledge except our experience, and what can be inferred from our experience by the analogies of experience itself; nor that there is any idea, feeling or power in the human mind, which, in order to account for it, requires that its origin should be referred to any other source. We are, therefore, at issue with Coleridge on the central idea of his philosophy; and we find no need of, and no use for, the peculiar technical terminology which he and his masters, the Germans, have introduced into philosophy, for the double purpose of giving logical precision to doctrines which we do not admit, and of marking a relation between those abstract doctrines and many concrete experimental truths, which this language, in our judgment, serves not to elucidate, but to disguise and obscure."

In the examination of Sir William Hamilton's Philosophy, he still more emphatically expressed his dissent from Schelling, Cousin, and every school of idealism, rejecting the doctrine of intuitive knowledge; taking the eternal ground from beneath the ideas of the Infinite and Absolute; sharply questioning the well-conceded interpretations of consciousness; resolving the "first principles" into mental habits; and even going so far as to doubt whether twice two necessarily made four.*

The system of Spencer and other expositors of the doctrine of evolution is, in its general features and its ultimate tendency, too familiar to be stated. Its hostili-

---

* Vol. 1, page 89, 90.

ty to the intuitive philosophy must be obvious even to unpractised minds. The atomic theory of the constitution of matter, which, in one or another form, is accepted by the majority of scientific men, gives ominous prediction of disaster to every scheme that is built on the necessary truths of pure reason.

But the philosophers of the experimental school are by no means in accord among themselves, on a matter so cardinal as the relation of mind to organization. In the latest edition of the Logic, Mill repeats the language used in the first :*

" That every mental state has a nervous state for its immediate antecedent, though extremely probable, cannot hitherto be said to be proved, in the conclusive manner in which this can be proved of sensations ; and even were it certain, yet every one must admit that we are wholly ignorant of the characteristics of these nervous states ; we know not, and have no means of knowing, in what respect one of them differs from another. . . . The successions, therefore, which obtain among mental phenomena, do not admit of being deduced from the physiological laws of our nervous organization." "It must by no means be forgotten that the laws of mind may be derivative laws resulting from laws of animal life, and that their truth, therefore, may ultimately depend on physical conditions ; and the influence of physiological states or physiological changes in altering or counteracting the mental successions, is one of the most important departments of psychological study. But on the other hand, to reject the resource of psychological analysis, and construct the theory of mind solely on such data as physiology affords at present, seems to me as

---

* Logic, p. 591.   Amer. Edition.

great an error in principle, and an even more serious one in practice. Imperfect as is the science of mind, I do not scruple to affirm that it is in a considerably more advanced state than the portion of physiology which corresponds with it ; and to discard the former for the latter appears to me to be an infringement of the true canons of inductive philosophy."

In a previous chapter * Mill had said :

" I am far from pretending that it may not be capable of proof, or that it is not an important addition to our knowledge, if proved, that certain motions in the particles of bodies are the *conditions* of the production of heat or light ; that certain assignable physical modifications of the nerves may be the conditions, not only of our sensations and emotions, but even of our thoughts ; that certain mechanical and chemical conditions may, in the order of nature, be sufficient to determine to action the physiological laws of life. All I insist upon, in common with every thinker who entertains any clear idea of the logic of science, is, that it shall not be supposed that by proving these things, one step would be made toward a real explanation of heat, light, or sensation ; or that the generic peculiarity of those phenomena can be in the least degree evaded by any such discoveries, however well established. Let it be shown, for instance, that the most complex series of physical causes and effects succeed one another in the eye and in the brain, to produce a sense of color ; rays falling on the eye, refracted, converging, crossing one another, making an inverted image on the retina ; and after this a motion—let it be a vibration, or a rush of nervous fluid, or whatever else you are pleased to suppose, along the optic nerve—a propagation of this motion to the brain itself, and as many more different motions as you

---

* Logic, p. 548. Amer. Edition.

choose; still, at the end of these motions there is something which is not motion, there is a feeling or sensation of color. The mode in which any one of the motions produces the next, may possibly be susceptible of explanation by some general law of motion; but the mode in which the last motion produces the sensation of color cannot be explained by any motion; it is the law of color, which is, and must always remain a peculiar thing. Where our consciousness recognizes between two phenomena an inherent distinction; where we are sensible of a difference, which is not merely of degree; and feel that no adding one of the phenomena to itself will produce the other; any theory which attempts to bring either under the laws of the other must be false."

To precisely the same effect, DuBois Reymond, in an address to the Congress of German Naturalists given in Leipsic:

"It is absolutely and forever inconceivable that a number of carbon, hydrogen, nitrogen and oxygen atoms, should be otherwise than indifferent to their own position and motion, past, present, or future. It is utterly inconceivable how consciousness should result from their joint action."

The position of John Tyndall is well understood. It was avowed in 1860 in the *Saturday Review;* again in his address to the Mathematical and Physical Section of the British Association in 1868, wherein he declared that

"The passage from the physics of the brain to the corresponding facts of consciousness is unthinkable. Granted

that a thought and a definite molecular action in the
brain occur simultaneously, we do not possess the organ,
nor, apparently, any rudiment of the organ, which would
enable us to pass by a process of reasoning from the one
phenomenon to the other. They appear together, but
we do not know why."

In 1875, reviewing Martineau in the *Popular Science
Monthly* for December, Tyndall calls attention to these
declarations, and quotes other language of his own to
the same purpose:

"You cannot satisfy the understanding in its demand
for logical continuity between molecular processes and
the phenomena of consciousness. This is a rock on
which materialism must inevitably split whenever it pre-
tends to be a complete philosophy of the human mind."

Mr. John Fiske, a disciple of Herbert Spencer, and an
exceedingly able expositor of the philosophy of which
Spencer is the acknowledged chief, makes assertions
equally positive : *

"However strict the parallelism may be within the
limits of our experience, between the phenomena of
the mind, and the segment of the circle of motions, the
task of transcending or abolishing the radical antithesis
between the phenomena of mind and the phenomena of
matter, must always remain an impracticable task ; for,
in order to transcend or abolish this radical antithesis,
we must be prepared to show how a given quantity of
molecular motion in nerve tissue can be transformed into

---

* Outlines of Cosmic Philosophy, Vol. II., p. 442.

a definable amount of ideation or feeling.   But this, it is quite safe to say, can never be done."

There are of course, distinguished names on the other side.   The work on " Intelligence," by Mr. Taine, which Mr. Mill warmly commends as the " the first serious effort (in France) to supply the want of a better than the official psychology," cannot be wisely overlooked by any one interested in this problem.   Taine objects to Tyndall's statement of the problem, declares that by approaching it from another point, it is soluble, and frankly undertakes to solve it.*

" When we consider closely any one of our conceptions—that of a plant, an animal, a mineral—we find that the primitive threads of which it is woven, are sensations, and sensations only. We have proof of this already if we recollect that our ideas are only reviving sensations, that our ideas are nothing more than images which have become signs, and that thus this elementary tissue subsists in a more or less disguised form at all stages of our thought."   " It is true that we cannot conceive the two events otherwise than as irreducible to one another; but that may depend on the way we conceive them, and not on their actual qualities; their incompatibility is perhaps rather apparent than real; it arises on our side and not on theirs."

Mr. George H. Lewes † follows closely Taine's line of argument, but developes it with more system.   He too quotes Tyndall, alludes to DuBois Reymond and makes

---

* On Intelligence, Book III., chap. I.
† Problems of Life and Mind II. pp. 410, 415.

reference to Mill. Lewes holds it to be a severe deduction from proven facts " that the neural process and the feeling are one and the same process viewed under different aspects. Viewed from the physical or objective side, it is a neural process ; viewed from the psychological or subjective side, it is a sentient process."

" It is not wonderful that conceptions so dissimilar as those of Motion and Feeling should seem irreducible to a common term, while the one is regarded as the symbol of a process in the object, and the other as the symbol of a process in the subject. But psychological analysis leads to the conclusion that the objective process and the subjective process are simply the twofold aspects of one and the same fact ; in the one aspect it is the Felt, in the other it is the Feeling."

For the remarkable reasonings by which these assertions are justified, the readers must consult the works quoted. Their novelty renders any but an extended account of them unfair ; and an extended account would be out of place in a general study like this.

Should the analyses of Taine and Lewes prove successful at last, and be accepted by the authorities in speculative philosophy, idealism, as a philosophy, must disappear. The days of metaphysics in the old sense, will be numbered ; the German schools from Kant to Hegel will become obsolete ; Jacobi's doctrine of faith, Fichte's doctrine of the absolute Ego, Schelling's doctrine of intellectual intuition, will be forgotten ; Cousin's influence will be gone ; the fundamental ideas of Transcendental teachers, French, English, American, will be discredited ;

and the beliefs founded on them will fade away. There will, however, be no cause to apprehend the personal, social, moral or spiritual demoralization which the "Sensualist" doctrines of the last century were accused of encouraging. The attitude of the human mind towards the great problems of destiny has so far altered, the problems themselves have so far changed their face, that no shock will be felt in the passage from the philosophy of intuition to that of experience. Questions respecting the origin, order and regulation of the world, the laws of character, the constitution of society, the conditions of welfare, the prospects and relations of the individual, are put in new forms, discussed by new arguments, and answered by new assurances. The words atheism and materialism have passed through so many definitions, the conceptions they stand for have become so completely transformed by the mutations of thought, that the ancient antipathies are not longer excusable; the ancient fears are weak. The sanctities that once were set apart in ideal shrines will be perfectly at home among the demonstrated facts of common life.

If, on the other hand, the school to which Spencer, Fiske and Tyndall belong is right, the science of mind will recover its old dignity, though under new conditions. Nobody has spoken more plainly against the intuitive philosophy, than Mill. No one probably is further from it than Tyndall, though he responds in sentiment to the eloquent affirmations of Martineau, and quotes Emerson enthusiastically, as "a profoundly religious man who is really and entirely undaunted by the discoveries of science, past, present or prospective; one by whom scientific conceptions are continually transmuted into the finer forms and warmer hues of an ideal world." Under the influences of the new psychology, dogmatic idealism will probably be deprived of its sceptre and sway. The claim to intuitive knowledge of definite truths of any order whatsoever will be abandoned, as untenable on scientific or philosophical grounds; but imagination, which, as Emerson says, " respects the cause,"—" the vision of an inspired soul reading arguments and affirmations in all nature of that which it is driven to say; " emotion, which contains all the possibilities of feeling and hope; the moral sentiment, which affirms principles with imperative authority; these remain, and claim their right to create ideal worlds of which the natural world is image and symbol. The Transcendentalism which concedes to all mankind spiritual faculties by virtue whereof divine entities are seen in definite shape—the personal God—the city of the heavenly Jerusalem—will be superseded by the poetic idealism that is the cheer and inspiration of poetic minds, animating them with fine visions, and gladdening them with unfading, though vague, anticipations.

The Transcendental doctrine has been exposed to most deadly assault on the ethical side. The theory of moral intuition, which held that " every man is, according to the cautious statement of James Walker, born with a moral faculty, or the elements of a moral faculty, which, on being developed, creates in him the idea of a right and a wrong in human conduct; which summons him before the tribunal of his own soul for judgment on the rectitude of his purposes; which grows up into an habitual sense of personal responsibility, and thus prepares him, as his views are enlarged, to comprehend the moral government of God, and to feel his own responsibility to God as a moral governor,"—has fallen into general disrepute ; and in its place a persuasion is abroad, that, in the language of Grote, " the universal and essential tendencies of the moral sense, admit of being most satisfactorily deduced from other elementary principles of our nature." It is now a widely accepted belief among conservative thinkers, that " conscience " is not a faculty, or an element, existing here in germ, there in maturity; but is the result of social experience. Moderate Transcendentalists conceded the necessity of *educating* conscience, which still implied the existence of a conscience or moral sense to be educated. It is now contended that conscience itself is a product of education, a deposit left in the crucible of experiment, a habit formed by the usage of mankind. The justification of this view has gone so far, that it seems likely to become the recognized account of this matter; but in course of substantiating this doctrine, a new foundation for ethical feeling and judgment is laid, which is as immovable as the transcendental " facts of consciousness." The moral sentiments are represented as resting on the entire past of the race, on reefs of fact built up by the lives of millions of men, from the bottom of the deep of humanity. The finest moral sensibility caps the peak of the world's effort at self-adjustment, as the white, unsullied snow rests on the summit of the Jungfrau. The intuition is referred to another genesis, but it is equally clear and equally certain. The difference of origin creates no difference of character. Moral distinctions are precisely the same for idealists and sensationalists. Here, at least, the transcendentalist and his adversary can dwell in amity together.

IX.

THE SEER

A DISCERNING German writer, Herman Grimm, closes a volume of fifteen essays, with one on Ralph Waldo Emerson, written in 1861, approved in 1874. The essay is interesting, apart from its literary merit, as giving the impression made by Mr. Emerson on a foreigner to whom his reputation was unknown, and a man of culture to whom books and opinions rarely brought surprise. He saw a volume of the " Essays " lying on the table of an American acquaintance, looked into it, and was surprised that, being tolerably well practised in reading English, he understood next to nothing of the contents. He asked about the author, and, learning that he was highly esteemed in his own country, he opened the book again, read further, and was so much struck by passages here and there, that he borrowed it, carried it home, took down Webster's dictionary, and began reading in earnest. The extraordinary construction of the sentences, the apparent absence of logical continuity, the unexpected turns of thought, the use of original words, embarrassed him at first; but soon he discovered the secret and felt the charm. The man had fresh thoughts, employed a living speech, was a genuine person. The book was bought, read and re-read, " and now every time I take it up, I seem to take it up for the first time."

The power that the richest genius has in Shakspeare, Rafael, Goethe, Beethoven, to reconcile the soul to life, to give joy for heaviness, to dissipate fears, to transfigure care and toil, to convert lead into gold, and lift the veil that conceals the forms of hope, Grimm ascribes in the highest measure to Emerson.

" As I read, all seems old and familiar as if it was my own well-worn thought ; all seems new as if it never occurred to me before. I found myself depending on the book and was provoked with myself for it. How could I be so captured and enthralled ; so fascinated and bewitched ? The writer was but a man like any other ; yet, on taking up the volume again, the spell was renewed—I felt the pure air ; the old weather-beaten motives recovered their tone."

To him Emerson seemed to stand on the ground of simple fact, which he accepted in all sincerity.

" He regards the world in its immediate aspect, with fresh vision ; the thing done or occurring before him opens the way to serene heights. The living have precedence of the dead. Even the living of to-day of the Greeks of yesterday, nobly as the latter thought, moulded, chiselled, sang. For me was the breath of life, for me the rapture of spring, for me love and desire, for me the secret of wisdom and power." * * * " Emerson fills me with courage and confidence. He has read and observed, but he betrays no sign of toil. He presents familiar facts, but he places them in new lights and combinations. From every object the lines run straight out, connecting it with the central point of life. What

I had hardly dared to think, it was so bold, he brings forth as quietly as if it was the most familiar commonplace. He is a perfect swimmer on the ocean of modern existence. He dreads no tempest, for he is sure that calm will follow it ; he does not hate, contradict, or dispute, for he understands men and loves them. I look on with wonder to see how the hurly-burly of modern life subsides, and the elements gently betake themselves to their allotted places. Had I found but a single passage in his writings that was an exception to this rule, I should begin to suspect my judgment, and should say no further word ; but long acquaintance confirms my opinion. As I think of this man, I have understood the devotion of pupils who would share any fate with their master, because his genius banished doubt and imparted life to all things."

Grimm tells us that one day he found Emerson's Essays in the hands of a lady to whom he had recommended them without effect. She had made a thousand excuses ; had declared herself quite satisfied with Goethe, who had all that Emerson could possibly have, and a great deal more ; had expressed doubts whether, even if Emerson were all that his admirers represented, it was worth while to make a study of him. Besides, she had read in the book, and found only commonplace thoughts which had come to herself, and which she considered not of sufficient importance to express. So Emerson was neglected.

" On this occasion she made him the subject of conversation. She had felt that he was something remarkable. She had come upon sentences, many times, that opened the darkest recesses of thought. I listened quietly, but made no response. Not long afterwards she poured out to me her astonished admiration in such earnest and impassioned strain, that she made me feel as if I was the novice and she the apostle."

This experience was repeated again and again, and Grimm had the satisfaction of seeing the indifferent kindle, the adverse turn, the objectors yield. The praise was not universal indeed; there were stubborn dissentients who did not confess the charm, and declared that the enthusiasm was infatuation. Such remained unconverted. It was discovered that Emerson came to his own only, though his own were a large and increasing company.

The reasons of Grimm's admiration have been sufficiently indicated in the above extracts. They are good reasons, but they are not the best. They do not touch the deeper secret of power. That secret lies in the writer's pure and perfect idealism, in his absolute and perpetual faith in thoughts, his supreme confidence in the spiritual laws. He lives in the region of serene ideas; lives there all the day and all the year; not visiting the mount of vision occasionally, but setting up his tabernacle there, and passing the night among the stars that he may be up and dressed for the eternal sunrise. To such a spirit there is no night: "the darkness shineth as the day; the darkness and the light are both alike." There are no cloudy days. Tyndall's expression "in his case Poetry, with the joy of a bacchanal, takes her graver brother science by the hand, and cheers him with immortal laughter"—is singularly infelicitous in phrase, for it is as easy to associate night orgies with the dawn as the bacchanalian spirit with Emerson, who never riots and never laughs, but is radiant with a placid buoyancy that diffuses itself over his countenance and person. Mr. Emerson's characteristic trait is serenity. He is faithful to his own counsel, "Shun the negative side. Never wrong people with your contritions, nor with dismal views of politics or society. Never name sickness; even if you could trust yourself on that perilous topic, beware of unmuzzling a valetudinarian who will soon give you your fill of it." He seems to be perpetually saying "Good Morning."

This is not wholly a result of philosophy; it is rather a gift of nature. He is the descendant of eight generations of Puritan clergymen,—the inheritor of their thoughtfulness and contemplation, their spirit of inward and outward communion. The dogmatism fell away; the peaceful fruits of discipline remained, and flowered beautifully in his richly favored spirit. An elder brother William, whom it was a privilege to know, though lacking the genius of Waldo, was a natural idealist and wise saint. Charles, another brother, who died young and greatly lamented had the saintliness and the genius both. The "Dial" contained contributions from this young man, entitled "Notes from the Journal of a Scholar" that strongly suggest the genius of his eminent brother; a few passages from them may be interesting as throwing light on the secret of Emerson's inspiration.

"This afternoon we read Shakspeare. The verse so sank into me, that as I toiled my way home under the cloud of night, with the gusty music of the storm around and overhead, I doubted that it was all a remembered scene ; that humanity was indeed one, a spirit continually reproduced, accomplishing a vast orbit, whilst individual men are but the points through which it passes.

We each of us furnish to the angel who stands in the sun, a single observation. The reason why Homer is to me like dewy morning, is because I too lived while Troy was, and sailed in the hollow ships of the Grecians to sack the devoted town. The rosy-fingered dawn as it crimsoned the tops of Ida, the broad sea shore covered with tents, the Trojan hosts in their painted armor, and the rushing chariots of Diomed and Idomeneus,—all these I too saw : my ghost animated the frame of some nameless Argive ; and Shakspeare, in King John, does but recall to me myself in the dress of another age, the sport of new accidents. I who am Charles, was sometime Romeo. In Hamlet I pondered and doubted. We forget what we have been, drugged by the sleepy bowl of the Present. But when a lively chord in the soul is struck, when the windows for a moment are unbarred, the long and varied past is recovered. We recognize it all ; we are no more brief, ignoble creatures ; we seize our immortality and bind together the related parts of our secular being."

From the second record of thoughts a passage may be taken, so precisely like paragraphs in the essays that they might have proceeded from the same mind :

" Let us not vail our bonnets to circumstance. If we act so, because we are so ; if we sin from strong bias of temper and constitution, at least we have in ourselves the measure and the curb of our aberration. But if they who are around us sway us ; if we think ourselves incapable of resisting the cords by which fathers and mothers and a host of unsuitable expectations and

duties, falsely so called, seek to bind us,—into what help-
less discord shall we not fall."

" I hate whatever is imitative in states of mind as
well as in action. The moment I say to myself, ' I
ought to feel thus and so,' life loses its sweetness, the
soul her vigor and truth. I can only recover my genuine self by stopping short, refraining from every effort
to shape my thought after a form, and giving it boundless freedom and horizon. Then, after oscillation more
or less protracted, as the mind has been more or less
forcibly pushed from its place, I fall again into my orbit
and recognize myself, and find with gratitude that something there is in the spirit which changes not, neither is
weary, but ever returns into itself, and partakes of the
eternity of God."

Idealism is native to this temperament, the proper expression of its feeling. Emerson was preordained an
idealist ; he is one of the eternal men, bearing about
him the atmosphere of immortal youth. He is now
seventy-three years old, having been born in Boston
May 25th, 1803 ; but his last volume, " Letters and Social Aims," shows the freshness of his first essays. The
opening chapter, " Poetry and Imagination," has the
emphasis and soaring confidence of undimmed years ;
and the closing one, " Immortality," sustains an un-
wearied flight among the agitations of this most hotly-
debated of beliefs. The address before the Phi Beta
Kappa Society at Cambridge, in 1867, equals in moral
grandeur and earnestness of appeal, in faithfulness to
ideas and trust in principles, the addresses that made so
famous the prime of his career. There is absolutely no
abatement of heart or hope ; if anything, the tone is

richer and more assured than ever it was. During the season of his popularity as a lyceum lecturer, the necessity of making his discourse attractive and entertaining, brought into the foreground the play of his wit, and forced the graver qualities of his mind into partial concealment; but in later years, in the solitude of his study, the undertone of high purpose is heard again, in solemn reverberations, reminding us that the unseen realities are present still ; that no opening into the eternal has ever been closed.

" Shall we study the mathematics of the sphere," he says to the Cambridge scholars, " and not its causal essence also ? Nature is a fable, whose moral blazes through it. There is no use in Copernicus, if the robust periodicity of the solar system does not show its equal perfection in the mental sphere—the periodicity, the compensating errors, the grand reactions. I shall never believe that centrifugence and centripetence balance, unless mind heats and meliorates, as well as the surface and soil of the globe."

" On this power, this all-dissolving unity, the emphasis of heaven and earth is laid. Nature is brute, but as this soul quickens it ; nature always the effect, mind the flowing cause. Mind carries the law ; history is the slow and atomic unfolding."

" All vigor is contagious, and when we see creation, we also begin to create. Depth of character, height of genius, can only find nourishment in this soil. The miracles of genius always rest on profound convictions which refuse to be analyzed. Enthusiasm is the leaping lightning, not to be measured by the horse-power of the understanding. Hope never spreads her golden wings but on unfathomable seas."

" We wish to put the ideal rules into practice, to offer liberty instead of chains, and see whether liberty will not disclose its proper checks ; believing that a free press will prove safer than the censorship ; to ordain free trade, and believe that it will not bankrupt us; universal suffrage, believing that it will not carry us to mobs or back to kings again."

" Every inch of the mountains is scarred by unimaginable convulsions, yet the new day is purple with the bloom of youth and love. Look out into the July night, and see the broad belt of silver flame which flashes up the half of heaven, fresh and delicate as the bonfires of the meadow flies. Yet the powers of numbers cannot compute its enormous age—lasting as time and space—embosomed in time and space. And time and space, what are they ? Our first problems, which we ponder all our lives through, and leave where we found them ; whose outrunning immensity, the old Greeks believed, astonished the gods themselves ; of whose dizzy vastitudes, all the worlds of God are a mere dot on the margin ; impossible to deny, impossible to believe. Yet the moral element in man' counterpoises this dismaying immensity and bereaves it of terror."

Emerson has been called the prince of Transcendentalists. It is nearer the truth to call him the prince of idealists. A Transcendentalist, in the technical sense of the term, it cannot be clearly affirmed that he was. Certainly he cannot be reckoned a disciple of Kant, or Jacobi, or Fichte, or Schelling. He calls no man master ; he receives no teaching on authority. It is not certain that he ever made a study of the Transcendental philosophy in the works of its chief exposition. In his lecture on " The Transcendentalist," delivered in 1842, he conveys the impression that it is idealism—active and protesting—an excited reaction against formalism, tradition, and conventionalism in every sphere. As such, he describes it with great vividness and beauty. But as such merely, it was not apprehended by metaphysicians like James Walker, theologians like Parker or preachers like William Henry Channing.

Emerson does not claim for the soul a special faculty, like faith or intuition, by which truths of the spiritual order are perceived, as objects are perceived by the senses. He contends for no doctrines, whether of God or the hereafter, or the moral law, on the credit of such interior revelation. He neither dogmatizes nor defines. On the contrary, his chief anxiety seems to be to avoid committing himself to opinions ; to keep all questions open ; to close no avenue in any direction to the free ingress and egress of the mind. He gives no description of God that will class him as theist or pantheist ; no definition of immortality that justifies his readers in imputing to him any form of the popular belief in regard to it. Does he believe in personal immortality ? It is impertinent to ask. He will not be questioned ; not because he doubts, but because his beliefs are so rich, various and many-sided, that he is unwilling, by laying emphasis on any one, to do an apparent injustice to others. He will be held to no definitions ; he will be reduced to no final statements. The mind must have free range. Critics complain of the tantalizing fragmentariness of his writing ; it is evidence of the shyness and modesty of his mind. He dwells in principles, and will not be cabined in beliefs. He needs the full expanse of

the Eternal Reason.   In the chapter on Worship—" Con·
duct of Life," p. 288, he writes thus :

"Of immortality, the soul, when well employed, is
incurious ; it is so well, that it is sure it will be well ; it
asks no questions of the Supreme Power ; 'tis a higher
thing to confide, that if it is best we should live, we
shall live—it is higher to have this conviction than to
have the lease of indefinite centuries, and millenniums
and æons.   Higher than the question of our duration, is
the question of our deserving.   Immortality will come
to such as are fit for it, and he who would be a great
soul in future, must be a great soul now.   It is a doctrine too great to rest on any legend, that is, on any
man's experience but onr own.   It must be proved, if
at all, from our own activity and designs, which imply
an interminable future for their play."

The discourse on Immortality, which closes the volume, " Letters and Social Aims," moves on with steady
power,   towards   the   conclusion of belief.   Emerson
really seems about to commit himself ; he argues and
affirms, with extraordinary positiveness.   Of skepticism,
on the subject, he says :

" I admit that you shall find a good deal of skepticism in the streets and hotels, and places of coarse
amusement.   But that is only to say that the practical
faculties are faster developed than the spiritual.   Where
there is depravity there is a slaughter-house style of
thinking.   One argument of future life is the recoil of
the mind in such company—our pain at every skeptical
statement."

His enumeration of " the few simple elements of the
natural faith," is as clear and cogent as was ever made.

He urges the delight in permanence and stability, in immense spaces and reaches of time. "Every thing is prospective, and man is to live hereafter." He urges that:

"The implanting of a desire indicates that the gratification of that desire is in the constitution of the creature that feels it; the wish for food; the wish for motion; the wish for sleep, for society, for knowledge, are not random whims, but grounded in the structure of the creature, and meant to be satisfied by food; by motion; by sleep; by society; by knowledge. If there is the desire to live, and in larger sphere, with more knowledge and power, it is because life and knowledge and power are good for us, and we are the natural depositaries of these gifts."

He ranks as a hint of endless being the novelty which perpetually attends life:

"The soul does not age with the body." "Every really able man, in whatever direction he work—a man of large affairs—an inventor, a statesman, an orator, a poet, a painter—if you talk sincerely with him, considers his work, however much admired, as far short of what it should be. What is this 'Better,' this flying ideal but the perpetual promise of his Creator?'[2]

The prophecy of the intellect is enunciated in stirring tones:

"All our intellectual action, not promises but bestows a feeling of absolute existence. We are taken out of time, and breathe a purer air. I know not whence we draw the assurance of prolonged life: of a life which shoots that gulf we call death, and takes hold of what is

real and abiding, by so many claims as from our intel‧
lectual history." "As soon as thought is exercised,
this belief is inevitable ; as soon as virtue glows, this
belief confirms itself. It is a kind of summary or
completion of man."

This reads very much like encouragement to the pop‧
ular persuasion, yet it comes far short of it ; indeed, does
not, at any point touch it. The immortality is claimed
for the moral and spiritual by whom thought is exercised,
in whom virtue glows—for none beside—and for these,
the individual conscious existence is not asserted. In
the midst of the high argument occur sentences like
these :

"I confess that everything connected with our person‧
ality fails. Nature never spares the individual. We are
always balked of a complete success. No prosperity is
promised to *that*. We have our indemnity only in the
success of that to which we belong. *That* is immortal,
and we only through that." "Future state is an illu‧
sion for the ever present state. It is not length of life,
but depth of life. It is not duration, but a taking of the
soul out of time, as all high action of the mind does ;
when we are living in the sentiments we ask no questions
about time. The spiritual world takes place—that which
is always the same."

Goethe is quoted to the same purpose :

"It is to a thinking being quite impossible to think
himself non-existent, ceasing to think and live ; so far
does every one carry in himself the proof of immortality,
and quite spontaneously. But so soon as the man will
be objective and go out of himself, so soon as he dog‧
matically will grasp a personal duration to bolster up in

cockney fashion that inward assurance, he is lost in contradiction."

It is thought worth while to dwell so long on this point, because it furnishes a perfect illustration of Emerson's intellectual attitude towards beliefs, its entire sincerity, disinterestedness and modesty. The serenity of his faith makes it impossible for him to be a controversialist. He never gave a sweeter or more convincing proof of this than in the sermon he preached on the Communion Supper, which terminated his connection with his Boston parish, and with it his relations to the Christian ministry, after a short service of less than four years. The rite in question was held sacred by his sect, as a personal memorial of Jesus perpetuated according to his own request. To neglect it was still regarded as a reproach ; to dispute its authority was considered contumacious ; to declare it obsolete and useless, an impediment to spiritual progress, a hindrance to Christian growth, was to excite violent animosities, and call down angry rebuke. Yet this is what Mr. Emerson deliberately did. That the question of retaining a minister who declined to bless and distribute the bread and wine, was debated at all, was proof of the extraordinary hold he had on his people. Through the crisis he remained unruffled, calm and gracious as in the sunniest days. On the evening when the church were considering his final proposition, with such result as he clearly foresaw, he sat with a brother clergyman talking pleasantly on literature and general topics, never letting fall a hint of the impending judgment, until, as he rose to leave, he said gently, "this is probably the last time we shall meet as brethren in the same calling," added a few words in explanation of the remark, and passed into the street.

The sermon alluded to was a model of lucid, orderly and simple statement, so plain that the young men and women of the congregation could understand it ; so deep and elevated that experienced believers were fed ; learned enough, without a taint of pedantry ; bold, without a suggestion of audacity ; reasonable, without critical sharpness or affectation of mental superiority ; rising into natural eloquence in passages that contained pure thought, but for the most part flowing in unartificial sentences that exactly expressed the speaker's meaning and no more.   By Mr. Emerson's kind permission, the discourse is printed in the last chapter of this volume.   The farewell letter to the parish is also printed here.

BOSTON, 22d December, 1832.

To the Second Church and Society :

CHRISTIAN FRIENDS :—Since the formal resignation of my official relation to you in my communication to the proprietors in September, I had waited anxiously for an opportunity of addressing you once more from the pulpit, though it were only to say, let us part in peace and in the love of God.   The state of my health has prevented, and continues to prevent me from so doing. I am now advised to seek the benefit of a sea voyage. I cannot go away without a brief parting word to friends who have shown me so much kindness, and to whom 1 have felt myself so dearly bound.

Our connection has been very short; I had only begun my work. It is now brought to a sudden close; and I look back, I own, with a painful sense of weakness, to the little service I have been able to render, after so much expectation on my part,—to the checkered space of time, which domestic affliction and personal infirmities have made yet shorter and more unprofitable.

As long as he remains in the same place, every man flatters himself, however keen may be his sense of his failures and unworthiness, that he shall yet accomplish much; that the future shall make amends for the past; that his very errors shall prove his instructors,—and what limit is there to hope? But a separation from our place, the close of a particular career of duty, shuts the book, bereaves us of this hope, and leaves us only to lament how little has been done.

Yet, my friends, our faith in the great truths of the New Testament makes the change of places and circumstances of less account to us, by fixing our attention upon that which is unalterable. I find great consolation in the thought that the resignation of my present relations makes so little change to myself. I am no longer your minister, but am not the less engaged, I hope, to the love and service of the same eternal cause, the advancement, namely, of the Kingdom of God in the hearts of men. The tie that binds each of us to that cause is not created by our connexion, and cannot be hurt by our separation. To me, as one disciple, is the ministry of truth, as far as I can discern and declare it, committed ; and I desire to live nowhere and no longer than that grace of God is imparted to me—the liberty to seek and the liberty to utter it.

And, more than this, I rejoice to believe that my ceasing to exercise the pastoral office among you does not make any real change in our spiritual relation to each other. Whatever is most desirable and excellent therein, remains to us. For, truly speaking, whoever provokes me to a good act or thought, has given me a pledge of his fidelity to virtue,—he has come under bonds to adhere to that cause to which we are jointly attached. And so I say to all you who have been my counsellors and coöperators in our Christian walk, that I am wont to see in your faces the seals and certificates of our mutual obligations. If we have conspired from week to week in the sympathy and expression of devout sentiments ; if we have received together the unspeakable gift of God's truth ; if we have studied together the sense of any divine word ; or striven together in any charity ; or conferred together for the relief or instruction of any brother ; if together we have laid down the dead in a pious hope ; or held up the babe into the baptism of Christianity ; above all, if we have shared in any habitual acknowledgment of that benignant God, whose omnipresence raises and glorifies the meanest offices and the lowest ability, and opens heaven in every heart that worships him,—then indeed are we united, we are mutually debtors to each other of faith and hope, engaged to persist and confirm each other's hearts in obedience to the Gospel.   We shall not feel that the nominal changes and little separations of this world can release us from the strong cordage of this spiritual bond. And I entreat you to consider how truly blessed will have been our connexion, if in this manner, the memory of it shall serve to bind each one of us more strictly to the practice of our several duties.

It remains to thank you for the goodness you have uniformly extended towards me, for your forgiveness of many defects, and your patient and even partial acceptance of every endeavor to serve. you; for the liberal provision you have ever made for my maintenance; and for a thousand acts of kindness which have comforted and assisted me.

To the proprietors I owe a particular acknowledgment, for their recent generous vote for the continuance of my salary, and hereby ask their leave to relinquish this emolument at the end of the present month.

And now, brethren and friends, having returned into your hands the trust you have honored me with,—the charge of public and private instruction in this religious society—I pray God, that, whatever seed of truth and virtue we have sown and watered together, may bear fruit unto eternal life.   I commend you to the Divine Providence. May He grant you, in your ancient sanctuary the service of able and faithful teachers.   May He multiply to your families and to your persons, every genuine blessing; and whatever discipline may be appointed to you in this world, may the blessed hope of the resurrection, which He has planted in the constitution of the human soul, and confirmed and manifested by Jesus Christ, be made good to you beyond the grave.   In this faith and hope I bid you farewell.

Your affectionate servant,

RALPH WALDO EMERSON.

Mr. Emerson's place is among poetic, not among philosophic minds.   He belongs to the order of imaginative men.   The imagination is his organ.   His reading, which is very extensive in range, has covered this department more completely than any.   He is at home with the seers, Swedenborg, Plotinus, Plato, the books of the Hindus, the Greek mythology, Plutarch, Chaucer, Shakspeare, Henry More, Hafiz ; the books called sacred by the religious world ; " books of natural science, especially those written by the ancients,—geography, botany, agriculture, explorations of the sea, of meteors, of astronomy ;" he recommends " the deep books." Montaigne has been a favorite author on account of his sincerity.   He thinks Hindu books the best gymnastics for the mind.

His estimate of the function of the poetic faculty is given in his latest volume.

" Poetry is the perpetual endeavor to express the spirit of the thing ; to pass the brute body, and search the life and reason which causes it to exist ; to see that the object is always flowing away, whilst the spirit or necessity which causes it subsists." " The poet contemplates the central identity ; sees it undulate and roll this way and that, with divine flowings, through remotest things ; and following it, can detect essential resemblances in natures never before compared." " Poetry is faith. To the poet the world is virgin soil ; all is practicable ; the men are ready for virtue ; it is always time to do right. He is the true recommencer, or Adam in the garden again." " He is the healthy, the wise, the fundamental, the manly man, seer of the secret ; against all the appearance, he sees and reports the truth, namely, that the soul generates matter. And poetry is the only verity, the expression of a sound mind, speaking after the ideal, not after the apparent." " Whilst common sense looks at things or visible nature as real and final facts, poetry, or the imagination which dictates it, is a second sight, looking through these and using them as types or words for thoughts which they signify."

By the poet, Emerson is careful to say that he means the potential or ideal man, not found now in any one person.

The upshot of it all is that soul is supreme. Not *the* soul, as if that term designated a constituent part of each man's nature.

" All goes to show that the soul is not an organ, but animates and exercises all the organs ; is not a function, like the power of memory, of calculation, of comparison, but uses these as hands and feet ; is not a faculty, but a light ; is not the intellect or the will, but the master of the intellect and the will ; is the background of our being, in which they lie—an immensity not possessed, and that cannot be possessed. From within or from behind, a light shines through us upon things, and makes us aware that we are nothing, but the light is all. A man is the façade of a temple, wherein all wisdom and all good abide."

We stand now at the centre of Emerson's philosophy. His thoughts are few and pregnant ; capable of infinite expansion, illustration and application. They crop out on almost every page of his characteristic writings ; are iterated and reiterated in every form of speech ; and put into gems of expression that may be worn on any part of the person. His prose and his poetry are aglow with them. They make his essays oracular, and his verse prophetic. By virtue of them his best books belong to the sacred literature of the race ; by virtue of them, but for the lack of artistic finish of rhythm and rhyme, he would be the chief of American poets.

The first article in Mr. Emerson's faith is the primacy of Mind. That Mind is supreme, eternal, absolute, one, manifold, subtle, living, immanent in all things, permanent, flowing, self-manifesting ; that the universe is the result of mind, that nature is the symbol of mind ; that finite minds live and act through concurrence with infinite mind. This idea recurs with such frequency that, but for Emerson's wealth of observation, reading, wit, mental variety and buoyancy, his talent for illustration, gift at describing details, it would weary the reader. As it is, we delight to follow the guide through the labyrinth of his expositions, and gaze on the wonderful phantasmagoria that he exhibits.

His second article is the connection of the individual intellect with the primal mind, and its ability to draw thence wisdom, will, virtue, prudence, heroism, all active and passive qualities. This belief, as being the more practical, has even more exuberant expression than the other :

" The relations of the soul to the divine spirit are so pure that it is profane to seek to interpose helps. Whenever a mind is simple, and receives a divine wisdom, all things pass away—means, teachers, texts, temples fall ; it lives now, and absorbs past and future into the present hour."

" Let man learn the revelation of all nature and all thought to his heart ; this, namely : that the highest dwells with him ; that the sources of nature are in his own mind, if the sentiment of duty is there."

" Ineffable is the union of man and God in every act of the soul ; the simplest person who, in his integrity, worships God, becomes God ; yet for ever and ever the influx of this better and universal self is new and unsearchable."

" We are wiser than we know. If we will not interfere with our thought, but will act entirely, or see how the thing stands in God, we know the particular thing, and every thing, and every man. For the Maker of all things and all persons stands behind us, and casts His dread omniscience through us over things."

" The only mode of obtaining an answer to the questions of the senses, is to forego all low curiosity, and, accepting the tide of being which floats us into the secret of nature, work and live, work and live, and all unawares the advancing soul has built and forged for itself a new condition, and the question and the answer are one."

" We are all discerners of spirits. That diagnosis lies aloft in our life or unconscious power."

" We live in succession, in division, in parts, in particles. Meantime, within man is the soul of the whole ; the wise silence ; the universal beauty, to which every part and particle is equally related ; the eternal ONE. And this deep power in which we exist, and whose beatitude is all accessible to us, is not only self-sufficing and perfect in every hour, but the act of seeing and the thing seen, the seer and the spectacle, the subject and the object, are one."

" All the forms are fugitive,
  But the substances survive ;
  Ever fresh the broad creation—
  A divine improvisation,
  From the heart of God proceeds,
  A single will, a million deeds.
  Once slept the world an egg of stone,
  And pulse and sound, and light was none ;
  And God said ' Throb,' and there was motion,
  And the vast mass became vast ocean.
  Onward and on, the eternal Pan,
  Who layeth the world's incessant plan,
  Halteth never in one shape,
  But forever doth escape,
  Like wave or flame, into new forms
  Of gem and air, of plants and worms.
  I that to-day am a pine,
  Yesterday was a bundle of grass.
  He is free and libertine,
  Pouring of his power, the wine
  To every age—to every race ;
  Unto every race and age
  He emptieth the beverage ;
  Unto each and unto all—
  Maker and original.
  The world is the ring of his spells,
  And the play of his miracles.
  As he giveth to all to drink,
  Thus or thus they are, and think.
  He giveth little, or giveth much,
  To make them several, or such.
  With one drop sheds form and feature ;
  With the second a special nature ;
  The third adds heat's indulgent spark ;
  The fourth gives light, which eats the dark ;

In the fifth drop himself he flings,
And conscious Law is King of kings.
Pleaseth him, the Eternal Child
To play his sweet will—glad and wild.
As the bee through the garden ranges,
From world to world the godhead changes ;
As the sheep go feeding in the waste,
From form to form he maketh haste.
This vault, which glows immense with light,
Is the inn, where he lodges for a night.
What recks such Traveller, if the bowers
Which bloom and fade, like meadow flowers—
A bunch of fragrant lilies be,
Or the stars of eternity ?
Alike to him, the better, the worse—
The glowing angel, the outcast corse.
Thou meetest him by centuries,
And lo ! he passes like the breeze ;
Thou seek'st in globe and galaxy,
He hides in pure transparency ;
Thou askest in fountains, and in fires,
He is the essence that inquires.
He is the axis of the star ;
He is the sparkle of the spar ;
He is the heart of every creature ;
He is the meaning of each feature ;
And his mind is the sky,
Than all it holds, more deep, more high."

Mr. Emerson is never concerned to defend himself
against the charge of pantheism, or the warning to beware lest he unsettle the foundations of morality, anni-
hilate the freedom of the will, abolish the distinction
between right and wrong, and reduce personality to a

mask. He makes no apology ; he never explains; he trusts to affirmation, pure and simple. By dint of affirming all the facts that appear, he makes his contribution to the problem of solving all, and by laying incessant emphasis on the cardinal virtues of humility, fideli ty, sincerity, obedience, aspiration, simple acquiescence in the will of the supreme power, he not only guards himself against vulgar misconception, but sustains the mind at an elevation that makes the highest hill-tops of the accepted morality disappear in the dead level of the plain.

The primary thoughts of his philosophy, if such it may be termed, Emerson takes with him wherever he goes. Does he study history, history is the autobiography of the Eternal Mind. The key is in the sentence that begins the Essay on History :

" There is one mind common to all individual men. Every man is an inlet to the same, and to all of the same. He that is once admitted to the right of reason is made a freeman of the whole estate. What Plato has thought, he may think ; what a saint has felt, he may feel ; what at any time has befallen any man, he can understand. Who hath access to this universal mind, is a party to all that is or can be done, for that is the only and sovereign agent." " This human mind wrote history, and this must read it. The sphinx must solve her own riddle. If the whole of history is in one man, it is all to be explained from individual experience. There is a relation between the hours of our life and the centuries of time. Of the universal mind each individual man is one more incarnation. All its properties consist in him. Each new fact in his private experience flashes a light on what great bodies of men have done, and the crises of his life refer to national crises." In the " Progress of Culture " the same sentiment recurs.

" What is the use of telegraphy ? What of newspapers ? To know in each social crisis how men feel in Kansas, in California, the wise man waits for no mails, reads no telegrams. He asks his own heart. If they are made as he is, if they breathe the same air, eat of the same wheat, have wives and children, he knows that their joy or resentment rises to the same point as his own. The inviolate soul is in perpetual telegraphic communication with the Source of events, has earlier information, a private despatch, which relieves him of the terror which presses on the rest of the community."

" We are always coming up with the emphatic facts of history in our private experience, and verifying them here. All history becomes subjective ; in other words, there is properly no history ; only biography. Every mind must know the whole lesson for itself,— must go over the whole ground. What it does not see, what it does not live, it does not know."

In the appreciation of scientific facts the same method avails. Tyndall commends Emerson as " a poet and a profoundly religious man, who is really and entirely undaunted by the discoveries of science, past, present, or prospective." The praise seems to imply some misconception of Emerson's position. Tyndall intimates that Emerson is undaunted where others fear. But this is not so. No man deserves commendation for not dreading precisely what he desires. Emerson, by his principle, is delivered from the alarm of the religious man who has a creed to defend, and from the defiance of the scientific man who has creeds to assail. To him Nature is but the symbol of spirit; this the scientific men, by their discoveries, are continually proving. The faster they disclose facts, and the more accurately, the more brilliantly do they illustrate the lessons of the perfect wisdom. For the scientific *method* he professes no deep respect; for the scientific *assumptions* none whatever. He begins at the opposite end. They start with matter, he starts with mind. They feel their way up, he feels his way down. They observe phenomena, he watches thoughts. They fancy themselves to be gradually pushing away as illusions the so-called entities of the soul; he dwells serenely with those entities, rejoicing to see men paying jubilant honor to what they mean to overturn. The facts they bring in, chemical, physiological, biological, Huxley's facts, Helmholtz's, Darwin's, Tyndall's, Spencer's, the ugly facts which the theologians dispute, he accepts with eager hands, and uses to demonstrate the force and harmony of the spiritual laws.

"Science," he says, "was false by being unpoetical. It assumed to explain a reptile or mollusk, and isolated it,—which is hunting for life in graveyards; reptile or mollusk, or man or angel, only exists in system, in relation. The metaphysician, the poet, only sees each animal form as an inevitable step in the path of the creating mind." "The savans are chatty and vain; but hold them hard to principle and definition, and they become mute and near-sighted. What is motion? What is beauty? What is matter? What is life? What is force? Push them hard and they will not be loquacious. They will come to Plato, Proclus and Swedenborg. The invisible and imponderable is the sole fact." "The atomic theory is only an interior process *produced*, as geometers say, or the effect of a foregone metaphysical theory. Swedenborg saw gravity to be only an external of the irresistible attractions of affection and faith. Mountains and oceans we think we understand. Yes, so long as they are contented to be such, and are safe with the geologist ; but when they are melted in Promethean alembics and come out men ; and then melted again, come out woods, without any abatement, but with an exaltation of power ! "

Emerson is faithful in applying his principle to social institutions and laws. His faith in ideal justice and love never blenches. In every emergency, political, civil, national, he has been true to his regenerating idea ; true as a recreator from the inside, rather than as a reformer of the outside world. A profounder, more consistent, more uncompromising radical does not exist; a less heated, ruffled or anxious one cannot be thought of. He scarcely ever suggested measures, rarely joined in public assemblies, did not feel at home among politicians or agitators. But his thought never swerved from the line of perfect rectitude, his sympathies were always human. His heart was in the anti-slavery movement from the beginning. He was abroad in its stormy days, his steadfast bearing and cheerful countenance carrying hope whenever he appeared. His name stood with that of his wife in the list of signers to the call for the first National Woman's Rights Convention, in 1850. The Massachusetts Historical Society, the American Society of Arts and Sciences have honored themselves by electing him a member; the Alumni of Harvard

University joyfully made him an overseer; he was proposed as rector of the University of Glasgow. Such confidence did the great idealist inspire, that he has been even called to the duty of Examiner at West Point Military Academy. His name is spoken in no company with other than respect, and his influence is felt in places where it is not acknowledged, and would be officially disavowed.

Mr. A. B. Alcott, a townsman of Mr. Emerson, and a close acquaintance, in his " Concord Days " says pleasant things of his friend, just and discerning things, as well as pleasant.

" Consider," he says, " how largely our letters have been enriched by his contributions. Consider, too, the change his views have wrought in our methods of thinking ; how he has won over the bigot, the unbeliever, at least to tolerance and moderation, if not acknowledgment, by his circumspection and candor of statement." " A poet, speaking to individuals as few others can speak, and to persons in their privileged moments, he is heard as none others are. 'Tis every thing to have a true believer in the world, dealing with men and matters as if they were divine in idea and real in fact, meeting persons and events at a glance, directly, not at a millionth remove, and so passing fair and fresh into life and literature." " His compositions affect us, not as logic linked in syllogisms, but as voluntaries rather, as preludes, in which one is not tied to any design of air, but may vary his key or not at pleasure, as if improvised without any particular scope of argument ; each period, paragraph, being a perfect note in itself, however it may chance chime with its accompaniments in the piece, as a waltz of wandering stars, a dance of Hesperus with Orion."

After this, one is surprised to hear Mr. Alcott say, " I know of but one subtraction from the pleasure the reading of his books—shall I say his conversation ?—gives me ; his pains to be impersonal or discreet, as if he feared any the least intrusion of himself were an offence offered to self-respect, the courtesy due to intercourse and authorship." To others this exquisite reserve, this delicate withdrawal behind his thought, has seemed not only one of Emerson's peculiar charms, but one of his most subtle powers. Personal magnetism is very delightful for the moment. The exhibition of attractive personal traits is interesting in the lecture room ; sometimes in the parlor. The public, large or small, enjoy confidences. But in an age of personalities, voluntary and involuntary, the man who keeps his individual affairs in the background, tells nothing of his private history, holds in his own breast his petty concerns and opinions, and lets thoughts flow through him, as light streams through plate glass, is more than attractive—is noble, is venerable. To his impersonality in his books and addresses, Emerson owes perhaps a large measure of his extraordinary influence. You may search his volumes in vain for a trace of egotism. In the lecture room, he seems to be so completely under the spell of his idea, so wholly abstracted from his audience, that he is as one who waits for the thoughts to come, and drops them out one by one, in a species of soliloquy or trance. He is a bodiless idea. When he speaks or writes, the power is that of pure mind. The incidental, accidental, occasional, does not intrude. No abatement on the score of personal antipathy needs to be made. The thought is allowed to present and commend itself. Hence, when so many thoughts are forgotten, buried beneath affectation and verbiage, his gain in brilliancy and value as time goes on; and in an age of ephemeral literature his books find new readers, his mind exerts wider sway. That his philosophy can be recommended as a sound rule to live by for ordinary practitioners may be questioned. It is better as inspiration than as prescription. For maxims it were wiser to go to Bentham, Mill or Bain. The plodders had best keep to the beaten road. But for them who need an atmosphere for wings, who require the impulse of great motives, the lift of upbearing aspirations— for the imaginative, the passionate, the susceptible, who can achieve nothing unless they attempt the impossible— Emerson is the master. A single thrill sent from his heart to ours is worth more to the heart that feels it, than all the schedules of motive the utilitarian can offer.

X.

THE MYSTIC

IF among the representatives of spiritual philosophy the first place belongs to Mr. Emerson, the second must be assigned to Mr. Amos Bronson Alcott,—older than Mr. Emerson by four years (he was born in 1799), a contemporary in thought, a companion, for years a fellow townsman, and, if that were possible, more purely and exclusively a devotee of spiritual ideas. Mr. Alcott may justly be called a mystic—one of the very small class of persons who accept without qualification, and constantly teach the doctrine of the soul's primacy and pre-eminence. He is not a learned man, in the ordinary sense of the term; not a man of versatile mind or various tastes; not a man of general information in worldly or even literary affairs; not a man of extensive commerce with books. Though a reader, and a constant and faithful one, his reading has been limited to books of poetry—chiefly of the meditative and interior sort—and works of spiritual philosophy. Plato, Plotinus, Proclus, Jamblichus, Pythagoras, Boehme, Swedenborg, Fludd, Pordage, Henry More, Law, Crashaw, Selden, are the names oftener than any on his pages and lips. He early made acquaintance with Bunyan's " Pilgrim's Progress," and never ceased to hold it exceedingly precious, at one period making it a rule to read the volume once a year. His books are his friends; his regard for them seems to be personal; he enjoys their society with the feeling that he gives as well as receives. He loves them in part because they love him; consequently, in all his quoting of them, his own mind comes in as introducer and voucher as it were. His indebtedness to them is expressed with the cordiality of an intimate, rather than with the gratitude of a disciple. His own mind is so wakeful and thoughtful, so quick and ready to take the initiative, that it is hard to say in what respect even his favorite and familiar authors have enriched him. What was not originally his own, is so entirely made his own by sympathetic absorption, that the contribution which others have made is not to be distinguished from his native stores. Few men seem less dependent on literature than he.

Mr. Alcott is a thinker, interior, solitary, deeply conversant with the secrets of his own mind, like thinkers of his order, clear, earnest, but not otherwise than monotonous from the reiteration of his primitive ideas. We have called him a mystic. Bearing in mind the derivations of the word—μυειν—to brood, to meditate, to shut one's self up in the recesses of consciousness, to sink into the depths of one's own being for the purpose of exploring the world which that being contains; of discovering how deep and boundless it is, of meeting in its retreats the form of the Infinite Being who walks there in the evening, and makes his voice audible in

the mysterious whispers that breathe over its plains,—
it well describes him. He is a philosopher of that
school; instead of seeking wisdom by intellectual processes, using induction and deduction, and creeping
step by step towards his goal,—he appeals at once to
the testimony of consciousness, claims immediate insight, and instead of hazarding a doctrine which he has
argued, announces a truth which he has seen; he studies
the mystery of being in its inward disclosures, contemplates ultimate laws and fundamental data in his own
soul.

While Mr. Emerson's idealism was nourished—so far as
it was supplied with nourishment from foreign sources
—by the genius of India, Mr. Alcott's was fed by the
speculation of Greece. Kant was not his master, neither
was Fichte nor Schelling, but Pythagoras rather; Pythagoras more than Plato, with whom, notwithstanding
his great admiration, he is less intimately allied. He
talks about Plato, he talks Pythagoras. Of the latter
he says:

"Of the great educators of antiquity, I esteem
Pythagoras the most eminent and successful; everything
of his doctrine and discipline comes commended by its
elegance and humanity, and justifies the name he bore
of the golden-souled Samian, and founder of Greek cul-
tnre. He seems to have stood in providential nearness
to human sensibility, as if his were a maternal relation
as well, and he owned the minds whom he nurtured and
educated. The first of philosophers, taking the name
for its modesty of pretension, he justified his claim to
it in the attainments and services of his followers; his
school having given us Socrates, Plato, Pericles, Plu-

tarch, Plotinus, and others of almost equal fame, founders of states and cultures. . . . He was rever-
enced by the multitude as one under the influence of
divine inspiration. He abstained from all intoxicating
drinks, and from animal food, confining himself to a
chaste nutriment; hence his sleep was short and undisturbed; his soul vigilant and pure; his body in
state of perfect and invariable health. He was free
from the superstitions of his time, and pervaded with a
deep sense of duty towards God, and veneration for his
divine attributes and immanency in things. He fixed
his mind so intently on the attainment of wisdom,
that systems and mysteries inaccessible to others were
opened to him by his magic genius and sincerity of
purpose. The great principle with which he started,
that of being a seeker rather than a possessor of truth,
seemed ever to urge him forward with a diligence and
activity unprecedented in the history of the past, and
perhaps unequalled since. He visited every man who
could claim any degree of fame for wisdom or learning;
whilst the rules of antiquity and the simplest operations
of nature seemed to yield to his researches; and we
moderns are using his eyes in many departments of activity into which pure thought enters, being indebted to
him for important discoveries alike in science and metaphysics."

It is evident that the New England sage made the
Greek philosopher his model in other respects than the
adoption of his philosophical method implied. The
rules of personal conduct and behavior, of social intercourse, and civil association, were studiously practised
on by the American disciple, who seemed never to forget the dignified and gracious figure whose fame charmed
him.

Mr Alcott's philosophical ideas are not many, but they are profound and significant.

" The Dialectic, or Method of the Mind,"—he says in " Concord Days," under the head of Ideal Culture,— " constitutes the basis of all culture. Without a thorough discipline in this, our schools and universities give but a showy and superficial training. The knowledge of mind is the beginning of all knowledge ; without this, a theology is baseless, the knowledge of God impossible. Modern education has not dealt with these deeper questions of life and being. It has the future in which to prove its power of conducting a cultus answering to the discipline of the Greek thinkers, Pythagoras, Plato, Aristotle."

" As yet we deal with mind with far less certainty than with matter ; the realm of intellect having been less explored than the world of the senses, and both are treated conjecturally rather than absolutely. When we come to perceive that intuition is the primary postulate of all intelligence, most questions now perplexing and obscure will become transparent ; the lower imperfect methods then take rank where they belong, and are available. The soul leads the senses ; the reason the understanding ; imagination the memory ; instinct and intuition include and prompt the Personality entire."

" The categories of imagination are the poet's tools ; those of the reason, the implements of the naturalist. The dialectic philosopher is master of them both. The tools to those only who can handle them skilfully. All others but gash themselves and their subject at best. Ask not a man of understanding to solve a problem in metaphysics. He has neither wit, weight, nor scales for the task. But a man of reason or of imagination solves readily the problems of understanding, the moment these are fairly stated. Ideas are solvents of all mysteries, whether in matter or in mind."

" Having drank of immortality all night, the genius

enters eagerly upon the day's task, impatient of any impertinences jogging the full glass. . . . Sleep and see; wake, and report the nocturnal spectacle. Sleep, like travel, enriches, refreshes, by varying the day's perspective, showing us the night side of the globe we traverse day by day. We make transits too swift for our wakeful senses to follow; pass from solar to lunar consciousness in a twinkling; lapse from forehead and face to occupy our lower parts, and recover, as far as permitted, the keys of genesis and of the fore worlds. 'All truth,' says Porphyry, 'is latent;' but this the soul sometimes beholds, when she is a little liberated by sleep from the employments of the body, and sometimes she extends her sight, but never perfectly reaches the objects of her vision."

" The good alone dream divinely. Our dreams are characteristic of our waking thoughts and states; we are never out of character; never quite another, even when fancy seeks to metamorphose us entirely. The Person is One in all the manifold phases of the Many, through which we transmigrate, and we find ourself perpetually, because we cannot lose ourself personally in the mazes of the many. 'Tis the one soul in manifold shapes. Ever the old friend of the mirror in other face, old and new, yet one in endless revolution and metamorphosis, suggesting a common relationship of forms at their base, with divergent types as these range wider and farther from their central archetype, including all concrete forms in nature, each returning into other, and departing therefrom in endless revolution."

" What is the bad but lapse from good,—the good blindfolded?"

" One's foes are of his own household. If his house is haunted, it is by himself only. Our choices are our Saviors or Satans."

" The celestial man is composed more largely of light and ether. The demoniac man of fire and vapor. The animal man of embers and dust."

" The sacraments, symbolically considered, are

Baptism, or purification by water;
Continence, or chastity in personal indulgences;
Fasting, or temperance in outward delights;
Prayer, or aspiring aims;
Labor, or prayer in act or pursuits.

These are the regimen of inspiration and thought."

The following, from the chapter entitled " Genesis and Lapse," in " Concord Days," extends Mr. Alcott's principle to a deep problem in speculative truth. He quotes Coleridge thus:

" The great maxim in legislation, intellectual or physical, is *subordinate*, not *exclude*. Nature, in her ascent, leaves nothing behind; but at each step subordinates and glorifies,—mass, crystal, organ, sensation, sentience, reflection."

Then he proceeds:

" Taken in reverse order of descent, spirit puts itself before; at each step protrudes faculty in feature, function, organ, limb, subordinating to glorify also,—person, volition, thought, sensibility, sense, body,—animating thus and rounding creation to soul and sense alike. The naturalist cannot urge too strongly the claims of physical, nor the plea of the idealist be too vigorously pressed for metaphysical studies. One body in one soul. Nature and spirit are inseparable, and are best studied as a unit. Nature ends where spirit begins. The idealist's point of view is the obverse of the naturalist's, and each must accost his side with a first love before use has worn off the bloom, and seduced their vision. . . .

" Whether man be the successor or predecessor of his inferiors in nature, is to be determined by exploring faithfully the realms of matter and of spirit alike, and complementing the former in the latter. Whether surveyed in order, descending or ascending, in genesis or process, from the side of the idealist or of the materialist, the keystone of the arch in either case is an ideal, underpropped by nature or upheld by mind."

" Man, the sum total of animals, transcends all in being a Person, a responsible creature. Man is man, in virtue of being a Person, a self-determining will, held ac countable to a spiritual Ideal. To affirm that brute creatures are endowed with freedom and choice, the sense of responsibility, were to exalt them into a spiritual existence and personality ; whereas, it is plain enough that they are not above deliberation and choice, but below it, under the sway of Fate, as men are when running counter to reason and conscience. The will bridges the chasm between man and brute, and frees the fated creature he were else. Solitary, not himself, the victim of appetite, inmate of the den, is man, till freed from individualism, and delivered into his free Personality."

The next extract is from the Chapter on Ideals :

" Enthusiasm is essential to the successful attainment of any high endeavor ; without which incentive, one is not sure of his equality to the humblest undertakings even. And he attempts little worth living for, if he expects completing his task in an ordinary lifetime. This translation is for the continuance of his work here begun ; but for whose completion, time and opportunity were all too narrow and brief. Himself is the success or failure. Step by step one climbs the pinnacles of excellence ; life itself is but the stretch for that mountain of holiness. Opening here with humanity, 'tis the aiming at divinity in ever-ascending circles of aspiration and endeavor. Who ceases to aspire, dies. Our pursuits are our prayers, our ideals our gods."

In the journals of Theodore Parker, Mr. Alcott is represented as taking an active part in the thinking and talking of the period immediately preceding the establishment of the " Dial," and as expressing audacious opinions ; among others, this—which suggests Hegel, though it might have reached Mr. Alcott from a different quarter—that the Almighty progressively unfolds himself towards His own perfection ; and this, that the hideous things in nature are reflections of man's animalism ; that the world being the product of all men, man is responsible for its evil condition ; a doctrine similar to the Augustinian doctrine of the Fall, hinted at also in the Book of Genesis. It was the doctrine of Jacob Boehme, one of Mr. Alcott's seers, that as the inevitable consequence of sin, the operation of the Seven Qualities in Lucifer's dominion became perverted and corrupted. The fiery principle, · instead of creating the heavenly glory, produced wrath and torment. The astringent quality, that should give stability and coherence, became hard and stubborn. The sweet was changed to bitter ; the bitter to raging fury. This earth--- once a province of the heavenly world—was broken up into a chaos of wrath and darkness, roaring with the din of conflicting elements. Eden became a waste ; its innocence departed, its friendly creatures began to bite and tear one another, and man became an exile and a bondsman to the elements he once controlled.

In 1837 Mr. Alcott—not Mr. Emerson—was the reputed leader of the Transcendentalists, none being more active than he in diffusing the ideas of the Spiritual Philosophy, and none being so uncompromising in his interpretations of them. He was generally present at the meetings of the informal Club which, under different names, held meetings at the private houses of members, from 1836 to 1850. Mr. Ripley had consultations with him in regard to the proposed community which was later established at Brook Farm. When Mr. Garrison founded the American Anti-Slavery Society, Mr. Alcott joined that cause, and was faithful to it till the end. With the movement for the emancipation and elevation of women, he was a sympathizer. He was one of the reformers who met at Chardon Street Chapel, in 1840, to discuss plans of universal reform—Garrison, Edmund Quincy, Henry C. Wright, Theodore Parker, William H. Channing, Christopher Greene, Maria Chapman and Abby Kelly being of the number. In those days he was intimate with Emerson, Ripley, Hedge, Brownson, Clarke, Bartol, Stetson, and well known as a leader in speculative thought. His period of Pythagorean discipline had already begun. In 1835 he put away the use of animal food. Declining to join either the Brook Farm community, or that of Adin Ballou, at Milford, he undertook to do his part towards the solution of the " labor and culture problem," by supporting himself by manual labor in Concord, working during the summer in field and garden, and in winter chopping wood in the village woodlands, all the time keeping his mind intent on high thoughts. To conventional people he was an object of ridicule, not unmingled with contempt, as an improvident visionary. But Dr. Channing held him in admiration.

"Mr. Alcott," he wrote to a friend, "little suspects how my heart goes out to him. One of my dearest ideas and hopes is the union of *labor* and *culture*. I wish to see labor honored and united with the free development of the intellect and heart. Mr. Alcott, hiring himself out for day labor, and at the same time living in a region of high thought, is perhaps the most interesting object in our commonwealth. I do not care much for Orpheus, in "The Dial," but Orpheus at the plough is after my own heart. There he teaches a grand lesson, more than most of us teach by the pen."

The Orpheus in "The Dial" perplexed others beside Dr. Channing, and amused nearly all he perplexed—all whom he did not exasperate and enrage. The "Orphic Sayings"—Mr. Alcott's contribution to the magazine —attracted the attention of the critics, who made them an excuse for assailing with ridicule, the entire transcendental party. "Identity halts in diversity." "The poles of things are not integrated." "Love globes, wisdom orbs, all things." "Love is the Genius of Spirit." "Alway are the divine Gemini intertwined,"— the very school-boys repeated these dark sayings, with a tone that consigned the "Dial" and its oracles to the insane asylum. Yet the thought was intelligible, and even simple. In ordinary prose it would have sounded like common-place. It was the mystic phrase, and the perpetual reiteration of absolute principles that made the propositions seem obscure. The extracts from these "Sayings," given in a previous chapter, are remarkable for crystalline clearness of conception, as well as of expression. The writer's aim evidently was to deliver what he had to utter, in language of exact outline, and with the utmost economy of words. A singular sincerity characterized his mind and his life; he formed his beliefs on ideal laws, and based his conduct on them. In conduct and bearing, as in thought, he was a disciple of the philosopher of Samos. Fascinated by his vision of an ideal society, and determined to commence with a scheme of his own, he resolutely began by withdrawing from civil society as constituted, declined to pay the tax imposed by the authorities, and was lodged in Concord jail, where he would have stayed, had not his friend, Samuel Hoar, father of Judge Hoar, paid the tax for him, against his wish, and procured his immediate release. This was in 1843. The next spring found him inspecting lands suitable for a community. The next summer saw him, with some English friends, domesticated on the "Wyman Farm," at Harvard, a piece of ninety acres, bordering the Nashua river, with an old house on it. "Fruitlands"—for so the community was named—did not justify its name. A single summer and autumn dissipated the hopes planted there, and with them the faith that the world could be refashioned by artificial arrangements of circumstances.

The surprising thing was, that such a man should ever have fallen into the notion that it could; he was an idealist; his faith was in the soul—not in organization of any sort; he was a regenerator, not a reformer. All the good work he had done was of the regenerative kind, through an awakening of the spiritual powers of individuals. His mission was to educate—to draw out souls, whether of children or adults. Faith in the soul was his inspiration and his guide. He early accepted the office of teacher, made it the calling of his life, and in the exercise of it, kept in mind this faith in the soul as the highest of qualifications. To understand his enthusiasm, it is only necessary to apprehend his idea. In the chapter on Childhood, in "Concord Days," that idea is thus conveyed :

" To conceive a child's acquirements as originating in nature, dating from his birth into his body, seems an atheism that only a shallow metaphysical theology could entertain in a time of such marvellous natural knowledge as ours. ' I shall never persuade myself,' says Synesius, ' to believe my soul to be of like age with my body.' And yet we are wont to date our birth, as that of the babes we christen, from the body's advent, so duteously inscribed in our family registers, as if time and space could chronicle the periods of the immortal mind, and mark its longevity by our chronometers. Only a God could inspire a child with the intimations seen in its first pulse-plays ; the sprightly attainments of a single day's doings afford the liveliest proofs of an omniscient Deity, revealing His attributes in the motions of the little one ! . . . . Were the skill for touching its tender sensibilities, calling forth its budding gifts, equal to the charms the child has for us, what noble characters would graduate from our families—the community receiving its members accomplished in the personal graces, the state its patriots, the church its saints, all glorifying the race."

The process of education was spiritual, therefore, to entice the indwelling deity forth by sympathy. The first experiment made with set purpose, with definite idea and calculated method, was tried in Cheshire, Connecticut, in 1825. So original was it in design and execution, and so remarkable in results, that the fame of it went abroad. Rev. Samuel J. May, minister in Brooklyn, Conn., a zealous friend of common-school education, being, along with the school committee, convinced that the schools throughout the State needed improvement, prepared a printed circular calling attention to the subject, and propounding questions so framed as to draw out full and precise information from every town. Among the letters received in answer to the circular was one from Dr. Wm. A. Alcott, a " philosopher and philanthropist," author of the " House I Live In," and other books on physical and moral training, calling particular attention to this remarkable school, kept on a very original plan, by his kinsman :

" His account," says Mr. May, " excited so much my curiosity to know more of the American Pestalozzi, as he has since been called, that I wrote immediately to Mr. A. B. Alcott, begging him to send me a detailed statement of his principles and methods of teaching and of training children. In due time came to me a full account of the school of Cheshire, which revealed such a depth of insight into the nature of man ; such a true sympathy with children ; such profound appreciation of the work of education ; and withal, so philosophically arranged and exquisitely written, that I at once felt assured the man must be a genius, and that I must know him more intimately ; so I wrote, inviting him urgently, to visit me. I also sent the account of his school to Mr. William Russell, in Boston, then editing the first Journal of Education ever published in our country.

Mr. Russell thought as highly of the article as I. did, and gave it to the public in his next October number."

" Mr. Alcott accepted my invitation ; he came and passed a week with me before the close of the summer. I have never, but in one other instance, been so immediately taken possession of by any man I have ever met in life. He seemed to me like a born sage and saint. He was radical in all matters of reform ; went to the root of all things, especially the subjects of education, mental and moral culture. If his biography shall ever be written by one who can appreciate him, and es- pecially if his voluminous writings shall be properly published, it will be known how unique he was in wisdom and purity."

The chief peculiarity of the Cheshire School was the effort made there to rouse and elevate individual minds. Single desks were substituted for the long forms in common use ; blackboards were introduced, and slates which put the pupils on their mettle ; a library was instituted of carefully selected books, the reading whereof was diligently supervised and directed ; hopes were appealed to instead of fears ; gentleness took the place of severity ; the affections and moral sentiments were addressed, to give full action to the heart and conscience, the physical being replaced by the spiritual scourge ; light gymnastic exercises were introduced ; evening entertainments gladdened the school room after working hours ; even the youngest scholars were encouraged to clear their minds by keeping diaries. In these and other ways, especially by the enthusiasm and dignity of the master, knowledge was made attractive, and the teacher's office was made venerable.

The plan, albeit nearly the same with that practised by Pestalozzi in Switzerland, was original with Mr. Alcott, the product of his peculiar philosophical ideas. Had those ideas been less deep and lofty, the method might have commended itself to all as it did to Mr. May; but, had they been less deep and lofty, it would not have been tried at all. A profound faith in the soul suggested it, and certainly a profound faith was required to sustain it. But faith in the soul was no more popular then than it is now, implying, as it did, radical convictions on all sorts of questions, and familiar assumption of the truth of the opinions. Such a teacher is not permitted to be conventional. Mr. Alcott showed himself the disciple of Pythagoras in that he was the worshipper of ideal truth and purity, the uncompromising servant of the spiritual laws. When this was fairly understood, as it was in two years, the experiment was terminated.

The idea, which made the teacher suspected by the school committee boards, was recognized and applauded by the finest spirits in New England, New York and Pennsylvania. The reformers hailed the reformer; the spiritualists welcomed the spiritualist. In Hartford, Drs. Gallaudet and Barnard; in Boston, Dr. Channing and Mr. Garrison, the Mays, Quincys, Phillipses, and other families of character and courage; in Philadelphia, Dr. Furness, Matthew Cary, Robert Vaux, and the radical Friends took him up. Mr. Emerson saluted him with high expectation, in the words addressed by Burke to John Howard:

"Your plan is original, and as full of genius as of humanity; so do not let it sleep or stop a day."

The project of a school on the new plan was started in Boston; Margaret Fuller, Elizabeth Peabody, Miss Hoar, Mrs. Nath'l Hawthorne being among the most deeply interested. It was kept in the Masonic Temple during the year 1834. The account of this experiment has been so fully given by Miss Peabody, the original scribe, in a volume entitled "Record of a School," placed within easy reach by a Boston publisher, only two years ago, and largely read, that to describe it here would be impertinent. In her new preface, Miss Peabody, who of late years has become an enthusiastic advocate of Frœbel's method, which approaches the mind from the outside, while Mr. Alcott approaches it from the inside, frankly declares that she has

"Come to doubt the details of his method of procedure, and to believe that Frœbel's method of cultivating children through artistic production in the childish sphere of affection and fancy is a healthier and more effective way than self inspection, for at least those years of a child's life before the age of seven."

While thus honestly declaring her abandonment of Mr. Alcott's plan, she affirms her belief

"That his school was a marked benefit to every child with whom he came into communication. . . ."
"What I witnessed in his school room threw for me a new light into the profoundest mysteries that have been consecrated by the Christian symbols; and the study of

childhood made there I would not exchange for anything else I have experienced in life."

The Boston school was made more closely conformable to the spiritual idea than any previous ones. The intellectual tone of the society he frequented, the sympathy of his transcendental friends, the standing of his pupils, the expectation of exacting lookers on, encouraged the philosopher to give free rein to his theory. The principle of vicarious punishment—the innocent bearing pain for the guilty—the master for the pupil—was adopted as likely to enlist the sentiment of honor and noble shame in the cause of good behavior. A portion of the time was set apart for direct address by way of question and answer, to the higher faculties of the scholars. Mr. Alcott gave a series of "Conversations on the Gospels," with most interesting and surprising results. These too were reported, and are very suggestive and astonishing reading.

But even in Boston, the teacher's faith in the soul found an unresponsive public. The "Conversations on the Gospels" were furiously attacked in the newspapers. The conservative spirit was aroused; the sectarian feeling was shocked; and the school, which began with thirty pupils, and rose to forty, fell away to ten; the receipts, which in the first year were $1,794, in the fourth (1837), were but $549, and at last only $343. In April, 1839, the furniture, library and apparatus of the school were sold to pay debts. The culture, refinement, liberality, philosophic aspiration of Boston, led by such men as James Freeman Clarke, Frederick H. Hedge, Chandler Robbins, George Russell, and by such women as Margaret Fuller, Miss Peabody, Miss Martineau, and the mothers of boys who have since done credit to their names, were not sufficient to protect the institution from failure, or the teacher from insult and obloquy. Prejudice, and prejudice alone, defeated the scheme.

But the idea and the apostle survived. Miss Harriet Martineau, who knew Mr. Alcott well in 1837, spoke of him on her return home to James Pierrepont Greaves, an ardent English disciple of Pestalozzi. Mr. Greaves gave the name "Alcott House," to a school near London, which he had founded on the Pestalozzian method; he even meditated a visit to America, for the express purpose of making the acquaintance of the New England sage, and would have done so but for illness, which terminated in death. A long letter from him to Mr. Alcott, was printed in the "Dial" of April, 1843, a portion whereof it is interesting to read, because it throws light on the cardinal ideas of this school of thinkers. Mr. Alcott's reply to the letter is not before us, but it was probably, in the main, sympathetic. The letter is dated London, 16th December, 1837 :

DEAR SIR,—Believing the Spirit has so far established its nature in you, as to make you willing to co-operate with itself in Love operations, I am induced, without apology, to address you as a friend and companion in the hidden path of Love's most powerful revelations. "The Record of a School" having fallen into my hands, through Miss Harriet Martineau, I have perused it with deep interest; and the object of my present address to

you (occasioned by this work) is to obtain a more intimate acquaintance with one, in our Sister Land, who is so
divinely and universally developed. Permit me, therefore, dear sir, in simple affection, to put a few questions
to you, which, if answered, will give me possession of that
information respecting you and your work, which I think
will be useful to present and to future generations of men.
Also a mutual service may be rendered to ourselves,
by assisting to evolve our own being more completely,
thereby making us more efficient instruments for Love's
use, in carrying forward the work which it has begun
within us. The Unity himself must have his divine
purpose to accomplish in and by us, or he would not
have prepared us as far as he has. I am, therefore,
willing to withhold nothing, but to receive and transmit
all he is pleased to make me *be*, and thus, at length, to
become an harmonious being. This he can readily work
in the accomplishment of his primitive purposes. Should
you think that a personal intercourse of a few weeks
would facilitate the universal work, I would willingly undertake the voyage to America for that purpose. There
is so decided and general a similarity in the sentiments
and natures addressed in the account of your teaching,
that a contact of spirits so alike developed would, no
doubt, prove productive of still further development.
Your school appears to work deeper than any we have
in England, and its inner essential character interests me.
If an American bookseller will send over any of your
books to his correspondents here, I shall be happy to
receive and pay for them.

In the year 1817 some strong interior visitations came
over me, which withdrew me from the world in a considerable degree, and I was enabled to yield myself up to Love's
own manner of acting, regardless of all consequences.
Soon after this time, I met with an account of the Spirit's
work in and by the late venerable Pestalozzi, which so
interested me that I proceeded at once to visit him in
Switzerland, and remained with him in holy fellowship

four years. After that I was working with considerable success amongst the various students in that country, when the prejudices of the self-made wise and powerful men became jealous of my influence, and I was advised to return to England, which I did ; and have been working in various ways of usefulness ever since, from the deep centre to the circumference ; and am now engaged in writing my conscientious experiences as well as I can represent them in words, and in teaching all such as come within my sphere of action. Receptive beings, however, have as yet been but limited, and those who permanently *retain*, have been still less ; yet, at present, there appears a greater degree of awakening to the central love-sensibility than before. I see many more symptoms of the harvest-time approaching in this country, There is, at present, no obvious appearance of the Love-seed beginning to germinate.

.   .   .   .

.   .   .   .

The child has two orders of faculties which are to be educated, essential and semi-essential ; or in other words, roots and branches.

Radical faculties belong to the interior world, and the branchial to the exterior.

To *produce* a central effect on the child, the radical faculties must be first developed; to *represent* this effect, the branchial faculties must be developed.

The radical faculties belong entirely to Love ; the branchial to knowledge and industry.

It is imperative upon us to follow the determination of the radical faculties, and to modify the branchial always in obedience to the radical.

It is the child, or the Love-Spirit in the child, that we

must obey, and not suffer the Parents or any one else to divert us from it.

Good is not to be determined by man's wishes, but Good must originate and determine the wish.

The Preceptor must watch attentively for every new exhibition of the child's radical faculties, and obey them as divine laws.

We must in every movement consider that it is the Infinite perfecting the finite.

All that is unnecessary in the external must be kept from the child.

The Preceptor's duty is, as far as possible, to remove every hindrance out of the child's way.

The closer he keeps the child to the Spirit, the less it will want of us, or anyone else.

The child has an inward, sacred, and unchangeable nature ; which nature is the Temple of Love.   This nature only demands what it will give, if properly attended to, viz.: Unfettered Liberty.

The Love Germs can alone germinate with Love. Light and Life are but conditions of Love.   Divine capacities are made by love alone.

Love education is primarily a passive one ; and, secondarily, an active one.   To educate the radical faculties is altogether a new idea with Teachers at present.

The parental end must be made much more prominent than it has been.

The conceptive powers want much more purification than the perceptive ; and it is only as we purify the conceptive that we shall get the perceptive clear.

It is the essential conceptive powers that tinge all the consequences of the exterior conceptive powers.

We have double conceptions, and double perceptions; we are throughout double beings; and claim the universal morality, as well as the personal.

. We must now educate the universal moral faculties, as before we have only educated the personal moral faculties.

It is in the universal moral faculties that the laws reside; until these laws are developed, we remain lawless beings

The personal moral faculties cannot stand without the aid of the universal moral faculties, any more than the branches can grow without the roots.

Education, to be decidedly religious, should reach man's universal faculties, those faculties which contain the laws that connect man with his maker.

These reflections seem to me to be worthy of consideration. Should any of them strike you as worth while to make an observation upon, I shall be happy to hear it. Suggestions are always valuable, as they offer to the mind the liberty of free activity. The work we are engaged in is too extensive and important, to lose any opportunity of gaining information.

The earlier I receive your reply, the better.

I am, dear Sir, yours faithfully,

J. P. GREAVES.

In 1842, Mr. Alcott visited England with the aim to confer with the philanthropists and educators there, to exchange views, collect information, and gather hints on the subject of literary and social methods. Mr. Greaves was dead; but the living friends of the "First Philosophy" received him with hearty respect and joy, introduced him to men of literary and philanthropic eminence, and made his arrival the occasion of meetings for conversation on the religious, social and ethical questions of the day. The meetings were held mostly at an institution managed on his own methods and called by his own name, the school of Mr. Wright at Alcott House, Ham, Surrey. Strange people were some of those he met, Communists, Alists (deriving their name from Alah—the Hebrew name for God), Syncretic Associationists, Pestalozzians, friends and advocates of self-supporting institutions, experimental Normal Schools, Hydropathic and Philosophical Associations, Health Unions, Philansteries, Utopias of every description, new social arrangements between the sexes, new devices for making marriage what it should be.

The London *Morning Chronicle*, of July 5th, contained the following advertisement:

" Public Invitation.—An open meeting of the friends to human progress will be held to-morrow, July 6th, at Mr. Wright's, Alcott House School, Ham Common, near Richmond, Surrey, for the purpose of considering and adopting means for the promotion of the great end, when all who are interested in human destiny are earnestly urged to attend. The chair taken at three o'clock, and again at seven, by A. Bronson Alcott, Esq., now on a visit from America. Omnibuses travel to and fro, and the Richmond steamboat reaches at a convenient hour."

The call brought together some sixteen or twenty persons, from various distances ; one a hundred miles ; another a hundred and fifty. "We did not find it easy to propose a question sufficiently comprehensive to unfold the whole of the fact with which our bosoms labored," writes a private correspondent of the "Dial."

"We aimed at nothing less than to speak of the instauration of spirit, and its incarnation in a beautiful form. When a word failed in extent of meaning, we loaded the word with new meaning. The word did not confine our experience, but from our own being we gave significance to the word. Into one body we infused many lives, and it shone as the image of divine or angelic, or human thought. For a word is a Proteus, that means to a man what the man is."

The "Dial" of October, 1842, prints an abstract of the proceedings, which are interesting, as illustrations of the phases that the Spiritual Philosophy assumed, but would occupy more space here than their significance warrants. Three papers were presented, on Formation, Transition, Reformation. The views, it is needless to say, were of the extreme school. The essayist on the first theme advanced the doctrine that evil commenced in birth ; that the unpardonable sin was an unholy birth ; that birth "must be surrendered to the spirit." The second essayist maintained that property was held on the tenure of might and immemorial custom ; that "pure love, which is ever communicative, never yet conceded to any being the right of appropriation." "We ignore human governments, creeds and institutions ; we deny the right of any man to dictate laws for

our regulation, or duties for our performance ; and declare our allegiance only to Universal Love, the all-
embracing Justice."

The reader of the paper on Reformation pursued the
same train of thought; he demanded amendment of
monetary arrangements, the penal code, education, the
church, the law of primogeniture, and divorce ; challenged reliance on commercial prosperity and popular
representation ; denied the right of man to inflict pain
on man ; asserted that the question of generation pre-
ceded that of education ; that the reign of love was
supreme over that of opinion ; insisted on "the restoration of all things to their primitive Owner, and hence
the abrogation of property—either individual or collective ;" and on " the divine sanction, instead of the civil
and ecclesiastical authority, for marriage." It was his
idea, that " aspirations are the pledge of their own fulfilment,"—that " beneath the actual which a man is,
there is always covered a possible to tempt him forward "
—that " beneath sense lie reason and understanding ;
beneath them both, humility ; and beneath all, God "—
that " to be God-like we must pass through the grades
of progress." " Even now the God-life is enfolded in
us ; even now the streams of eternity course freely in
our central heart; if impelled by the spirit to intermin-
gle with the arrangements of polities of the world, in
order to improve them, we shall discover the high point
from which we begin, by the God-thought in our inter-
ference ; our act must be divine ; we seem to do, God
does ; God empowers legislators, and ennobles them for

their fidelity ; let them, however, be apostles, not apostles' representatives ; men of God, not men of men ; personal elevation is our credentials ; personal reform is that which is practicable, and without it our efforts on behalf of others are dreams only."

No remarks from Mr. Alcott are recorded. That the meetings satisfied and cheered him may be inferred from the circumsta... that, immediately after his return from England, he undertook to inaugurate the ideal social state at Fruitlands—with what success we know.

In 1859, Mr. Alcott had another and larger opportunity to exercise his wisdom as an educator of youth. He was chosen superintendent of the schools of Concord ; a position that called out the finest qualities of his mind, and put to immediate use the results of his long experience, but relieved him from the business arrangements for which he had never displayed an aptitude. The three brief but remarkable reports that he made on the condition and needs of the schools, increase one's respect for the workings of the spiritual philosophy in this field of effort. If the suggestions offered in those reports were to any considerable extent adopted, if the noble and gracious spirit of them was felt, the schools of Concord should be model schools of their class.

" The school is the primary interest of the community. Every parent naturally desires a better education for his children than he received himself, and spends liberally of his substance for this pleasure ; wisely hoping to make up his deficiencies in that way, and to complement himself in their better attainments ; esteeming these the richest estate he can leave, and the fairest ornaments of his family name."

" Especially have I wished to introduce the young to the study of their minds, the love of thinking ; often giving examples of lessons in analysis and classification of their faculties. I think I may say that these exercises have given much pleasure, and have been found profitable alike to the teacher and the children. In most instances, I have closed my visits by reading some interesting story or parable. These have never failed of gaining attention, and in most cases, prompt responses. I consider these readings and colloquies as among the most profitable and instructive of the superintendent's labors."

Pilgrim's Progress, Krummacher's Parables, Æsop's Fables, Faery Queen, the stories of Plutarch and Shakspeare, were his favorites.

" The graceful exercise of singing has been introduced into some of the schools. It should prevail in all of them. It softens the manners, cultivates the voice, and purifies the taste of the children. It promotes harmony and good feelings. The old masters thought much of it as a discipline. ' Let us sing ' has the welcome sound of ' Let us play,'—and is perhaps the child's prettiest translation of ' Let us pray,'—admitting him soonest to the intimacy he seeks."

" Conversations on words, paraphrases and translations of sentences, are the natural methods of opening the study of language. A child should never be suffered to lose sight of the prime fact that he is studying the realities of nature and of the mind through the picture books of language. Any teaching falling short of this is hollow and a wrong done to the mind."

" For composition, let a boy keep his diary, write his letters, try his hand at defining from a dictionary and paraphrasing, and he will find ways of expressing himself simply as boys and men did before grammars were invented."

"Teaching is a personal influence for the most part, and operating as a spirit unsuspected at the moment. I have wished to divine the secret source of success attained by any, and do justice to this; it seemed most becoming to regard any blemishes as of secondary account in the light of the acknowledged deserts. We require of each what she has to give, no more. Does the teacher awaken thought, strengthen the mind, kindle the affections, call the conscience, the common sense into lively and controlling activity, so promoting the love of study, the practice of the virtues; habits that shall accompany the children outwards into life? The memory is thus best cared for, the end of study answered; the debt of teacher to parents, of parents to teacher discharged, and so the State's bounty best bestowed."

"A little gymnasticon, a system of gestures for the body might be organized skilfully and become part of the daily exercises in our schools. Graceful steps, pretty musical airs, in accompaniment of songs—suiting the sentiment to the motions, the emotions, ideas of the child—would be conducive to health of body and mind alike. We shall adopt dancing presently as a natural training for the manners and morals of the young."

"Conversation is the mind's mouth-piece, its best spokesman; the leader elect and prompter in teaching; practised daily, it should be added to the list of school studies; an art in itself, let it be used as such, and ranked as an accomplishment second to none that nature or culture can give. Certainly the best we can do is to teach ourselves and children how to talk. Let conversation displace much that passes current under the name of recitation; mostly sound and parrotry, a repeating by rote not by heart, unmeaning sounds from the memory and no more. 'Take my mind a moment,' says the teacher, 'and see how things look through that prism,' and the pupil sees prospects never seen before or surmised by him in that lively perspective. So taught the masters ; Plato, Plutarch, Pythagoras, Pestalozzi ; so Christianity was first published from lovely lips ; so every one teaches deserving the name of teacher or interpreter. Illustration always and apt ; life calling forth life ; the giving of life and a partaking. Nothing should be interposed between the mind and its subject matter— cold sense is impertinent ; learning is insufficient—only life alone ; life like a torch lighting the head at the heart."

" Next to thinking for themselves, the best service any teacher can render his scholars is to show them how to use books. The wise teacher is the key for opening the mind to the books he places before it."

" Stories are the idyls of childhood. They cast about it the romance it loves and lives in, rendering the commonest circumstances and things inviting and beautiful. Parables, poems, histories, anecdotes, are prime aids in teaching ; the readiest means of influence and inspiration ; the liveliest substitutes for flagging spirits, fatigued wits."

" A little atlas of the body mythologically shown from the artist's points of view, the plates displaying the person to the eye, in a set of draped figures, is a book much wanted for first lines in drawing. A child's piety is seen in its regards for its body and the concern it shows in its carriage and keeping. Of all forms the human form is most marvellous ; and the modest reverence for its shadings intimates the proper mode of studying it rightly and religiously as a pantheon of powers. The prime training best opens here as an idealism, the soul fashioning her image in the form she animates, and so scrutinizing piously without plucking the forbidden fruits."

" There is a want of suitable aids to the studies of these mysteries. The best books I know are poor enough. In the want of a better, we name for the study of matter in its connection with the mind, including the proper considerations regarding health and temperance, Graham's 'Laws of Life,' a rather dull but earnest book ;

and for smaller classes and beginners Dr. Alcott's ' House I Live In.' Miss Catherine Beecher's book for studies in Physiology and Calisthenics, is a practical treatise, and should be in all schools. Sir John Sinclair's ' Code of Health ' contains a republication of the Wisdom of the Ancients, on these subjects, and is a book for all persons and times."

" Perhaps we are correcting the old affection for flogging at some risk of spoiling the boys of this generation. Girls have always known how to cover with shame any insult of that sort, but the power of persuasion comes slow as a promptitude to supersede its necessity. Who deals with a child, deals with a piece of divinity obeying laws as innate as those he transgresses, and which he must treat tenderly, lest he put spiritual interests in jeopardy. Punishment must be just, else it cannot be accepted as good, and least of all by the wicked and weak."

" The accomplished teacher combines in himself the art of teaching and of ruling ; power over the intellect and the will, inspiration and persuasiveness. And this implies a double consciousness in its possessor that carries forward the teaching and ruling together ; noting what transpires in motive as in act ; the gift that in seeing controls. It is the sway of presence and of mien ; a conversion of the will to his wishes, without which other gifts are of little avail."

" Be sure the liveliest dispensations, the holiest, are his (the unruly boy's)—his as cordially as ours, and sought for as kindly. We must meet him where he is. Best to follow his bent if bent beautifully ; else bending him gently, not fractiously, lest we snap or stiffen a stubbornness too stiff already. Gentleness now ; the fair eye, the conquering glances straight and sure ; the strong hand, if you must, till he fall penitent at the feet of Persuasion ; the stroke of grace before the smiting of the birch ; for only so is the conquest complete, and the victory the Lord's. If she is good enough she may strike strong and frequent, till thanks come for it ; but who is she, much less he, that dares do it more than once, nor repents in sorrow and shame for the strokes given ?   Only ' the shining ones' may do it for good.''

" Our teachers open their schools with readings from the New Testament, and this reading is in some of the schools, and would, but for a diffident piety, be followed in all, by devotions and the singing of some suitable morning hymn.   The spoken prayers and praises are not enjoined by our rules ; and we think we show therein that tender courtesy to the faiths of the heart that true piety loves and cannot overstep.   An earnest and sweet disposition is the spring from which children love to taste, and best always if insinuated softly in mild per-suasions, and so leading to the practice of the loves and graces that soften and save.   A course of readings from the Picture Testament might favor the best ends of spiritual culture.   A child should be approached with reverence, as a recipient of the spirit from above.   The best of books claims the best of persons and the gracious moments to make its meanings clear ; else the reading and listening are but a sound, a pretence, and of no account. I have wished these books were opened with the awe belonging to the eminent Personalities portrayed therein, thinking them best read when the glow of sentiment kindles the meaning into life in the morning hour—the teacher opening her school by opening their leaves."

The following earnest words respecting the duties of the State in regard to the education of its children, may fitly close these fragmentary extracts, which give but the scantiest notions of the richness of suggestion in these reports :

" It is difficult to reach the sources of ignorance and consequent crime in a community like ours, calling itself free, and boasting of its right to do what it will.   But freedom is a social not less than an individual concern, and the end of the State is to protect it. The first object of a free people is the preservation of their liberties. It becomes, then, their first duty to assume the training of all the children in the principles of right knowledge and virtue, as the only safeguard of their liberties. We cannot afford to wait at such hazards. The simplest humanities are also the least costly, and the nearest home. We should begin there. The State is stabbed at the hearth-side and here liberty and honor are first sold. It is injured by family neglect, and should protect itself in securing its children's virtue against their parents' vices; for, by so doing, can it alone redeem its pledges to humanity and its citizens' liberties. A virtuous education is the greatest alms it can bestow on any of its children."

Meetings for conversation with the parents of the scholars were a device of Mr. Alcott for bringing the subject of education home to those whose concern in it should be the deepest.

His faith was from the first in conversation, rather than in lecturing or in preaching. Preaching assumed too much in the single mind, paid less than due respect to the minds of the hearers, and gave no opportunity for the instant exchange of thoughts. Lecturing was intellectual and even less sympathetic. By conversation the best was drawn out and the best imparted. All were put on an equality; all were encouraged, none oppressed.

"Truth," Mr. Alcott declares "is spherical, and seen differently according to the culture, temperament and disposition of those who survey it from their individual standpoint. Of two or more sides, none can be absolutely right, and conversation fails if it find not the central truth from which all radiate; debate is angular, conversation circular and radiant of the underlying unity. Who speaks, deeply excludes all possibility of controversy. His affirmation is self-sufficient ; his assumption final, absolute. Thus holding himself above the arena of dispute he gracefully settles a question by speaking so home to the core of the matter as to under mine the premise upon which an issue had been taken. For whoso speaks to the personality dives beneath the grounds of difference, and deals face to face with prin ciples and ideas."

" Good discourse sinks differences and seeks agreements. It avoids argument, by finding a common basis of agreement ; and thus escapes controversy by rendering it superfluous. Pertinent to the platform, debate is out of place in the parlor. Persuasion is the better weapon in this glittering game."

" Conversation presupposes a common sympathy in the subject, a great equality in the speakers ; absence of egotism, a tender criticism of what is spoken. Good discourse wins from the bashful and discreet what they have to speak, but would not, without this provocation. The forbidding faces are Fates to overbear and blemish true fellowship. We give what we are, not necessarily what we know ; nothing more, nothing less, and only to our kind ; those playing best their parts who have the nimblest wits, taking out the egotism, the nonsense, putting wisdom, information in their place."

Mr. Alcott therefore forsook the platform, seldom entered the pulpit, adopted the parlor, and made it what its name imports, the talking place. Collecting a company of ladies and gentlemen, larger or smaller, as nearly as possible of similar tastes and culture, he started a topic of general interest and broad scope—usually one of social concern with deep roots and wide branches,—and began his soliloquy in a calm and easy strain, throwing out suggestions as he went on, and enticing thoughts from the various minds present. If none responded or accompanied, the discourse proceeded evenly till the measure of an hour was filled. If the company was awake, and sympathetic, the soliloquy became conversation and an evening full of instruction and entertainment followed. When circumstances favored—the room, decorations, atmosphere, mingling of elements—the season was delightful. The unfailing serenity of the leader, his wealth of mental resource, his hospitality of thought, his wit, his extraordinary felicity of language, his delicacy of touch, ready appreciation of different views, and singular grace in turning opinions towards the light, made it clear to all present that to this especial calling he was chosen. For years Mr. Alcott's conversations have been a recognized institution in Eastern and Western cities. Every winter he takes the field, and goes through the Northern and North Western States, with his scheme of topics. The best minds collect about him, and centres of influence are established that act as permanent distributors of culture. The noble idealism never pales or falters. Neither politics, science, financial convulsion, or civil war, disturb the calm serenity of the soul that is sure that mind is its own place, and that infinite and absolute mind is supreme above all.

XI.

THE CRITIC

MARGARET FULLER—she was called Ossoli long after
the time we are concerned with, in a foreign land and
amid foreign associations—Margaret Fuller. died July
16th, 1850. In 1852 her Memoirs were published in
Boston, written by Ralph Waldo Emerson, James Freeman Clarke, and William Henry Channing : each giving
an individual and personal account of her. These three
gentlemen—all remarkable for intellectual capacity,
sympathetic appreciation, and literary skill—undertook
their task in the spirit of loving admiration, and exe-
cuted it with extraordinary frankness, courage and delicacy. No more unique or satisfactory book of biography was ever made. They had known Margaret personally and well ; were intimately acquainted with her
mind, and deeply interested in her character. They
had access to all the necessary materials. The whole
life—inward and outward—was open to them, and they
described it with no more reserve than good taste imposed. Those who are interested to know what sort
of a person she was, are referred to that book, from

which the biographical materials for this little sketch have, in the main, been taken. Her place here is due to her association with the leaders of the Transcendental movement, and to the peculiar part she played in it.

Strictly speaking, she was not a Transcendentalist, though Mr. Channing declares her to have been "in spirit and thought pre-eminently a transcendentalist;" and Mr. Alcott wrote that she adopted "the spiritual philosophy, and had the subtlest perception of its bearings." She was enthusiastic rather than philosophical, and poetic more than systematic. Emerson's judgment is that—

"Left to herself, and in her correspondence, she was much the victim of Lord Bacon's *idols of the cave*, or self-deceived by her own phantasms. . . . . Her letters are tainted with a mysticism which, to me, appears so much an affair of constitution, that it claims no more respect than the charity or patriotism of a man who has dined well and feels better for it. In our noble Margaret, her personal feeling colors all her judgment of persons, of books of pictures, and even of the laws of the world. . . . . Whole sheets of warm, florid writing are here, in which the eye is caught by 'sapphire,' 'heliotrope,' 'dragon,' 'aloes,' 'Magna Dea,' 'limboes,' 'stars,' and 'purgatory'—but one can connect all this or any part of it with no universal experience.

"In short, Margaret often loses herself in sentimentalism; that dangerous vertigo nature, in her case, adopted, and was to make respectable. . . . . Her integrity was perfect, and she was led and followed by love; and was really bent on truth, but too indulgent to the meteors of her fancy."

She said of herself :

" When I was in Cambridge I got Fichte and Jacobi ;
I was much interrupted, but some time and earnest
thought I devoted ; Fichte I could not understand at
all, though the treatise which I read was one intended
to be popular, and which he says must compel to conviction. Jacobi I could understand in details, but not
in system. It seemed to me that his mind must have
been moulded by some other mind, with which I ought
to be acquainted, in order to know him well—perhaps
Spinoza's. Since I came home I have been consulting
Buhle's and Tennemann's histories of philosophy, and
dipping into Brown, Stewart, and that class of books."

This was in 1832, before the transcendental movement
began. At the same period, writing to a friend on the
subject of religious faith—a subject intimately allied with
philosophy—she said :

" I have not formed an opinion ; I have determined
not to form settled opinions at present ; loving or feeble
natures need a positive religion—a visible refuge, a protection—as much in the passionate season of youth as
in those stages nearer to the grave. But mine is not
such. My pride is superior to any feelings I have yet
experienced ; my affection is strong admiration, not the
necessity of giving or receiving assistance or sympathy.
When disappointed, I do not not ask or wish consolation ;
I wish to know and feel my pain, to investigate its nature and its source ; I will not have my thoughts di-
verted or my feelings soothed ; 'tis therefore that my
young life is so singularly barren of illusions. I know I
feel the time must come when this proud and impatient
heart shall be stilled, and turn from the ardors of search
and action to lean on something above. But shall I say
it ?—the thought of that calmer era is to me a thought
of deepest sadness ; so remote from my present being

is that future existence, which still the mind may conceive ; I believe in eternal progression ; I believe in a God, a beauty and perfection, to which I am to strive all my life for assimilation. From these two articles of belief I draw the rules by which I strive to regulate my life ; but though I reverence all religions as necessary to the happiness of man, I am yet ignorant of the religion of revelation. Tangible promises, well-defined hopes, are things of which I do not *now* feel the need. At present, my soul is intent on this life, and I think of religion as its rule ; and in my opinion this is the natural and proper course from youth to age."

The tone of this extract is negatively transcendental ; that is, it implies that the writer did not belong to the opposite school, in any sense ; and that her mind was in condition to accept the cardinal truths of a philosophy, the special doctrines whereof she did not apprehend or feel interested in. Had she entertained a philosophical creed, it would have been the creed of Schelling, more likely than any other.

Margaret Fuller was a critic, and a critic rather from natural gift than from trained perception. Her genius was her guide. Persons and things came to her for judgment, and judgment they received. Searching and frank, but hearty and loving, she judged from the inside. To her, so her biographers tell, with unanimous voice, " the secrets of all hearts were revealed." In private intercourse, in letters, in parlor conversations on books, pictures, statues, architecture, she was ever the judge. The most unlike minds and characters receive their dues with entire impartiality ; Goethe, Lessing, Novalis, Jean Paul, were each in kind honored. The last is "infinitely variegated, and certainly most exquisitely colored, but fatigues attention; his philosophy and religion seem to be of the sighing sort." She is steeped to the lips in enjoyment by Southey, whom she was inclined to place next to Wordsworth. Coleridge, Heine, Carlyle, Herschel, attract her mind. She ponders before Michael Angelo's sibyls; displays a singular penetration in her analysis of them, and makes them all interpreters of the genius of woman. The soul of Greek art, as contrasted with Christian, is disclosed to her with a clear perception; the Greek mythology gave up to her its secret; emblems, symbols, dark parables, enigmas, mysteries, laid aside their vails. A friend said of her: "She proceeds in her search after the unity of things, the divine harmony, not by exclusion but by comprehension; and so no poorest, saddest spirit but she will lead to hope and faith. I have thought, sometimes, that her acceptance of evil was *too* great; that her theory of the good to be educed proved too much; but I understand her now better than I did." Atkinson, the "mesmeric atheist," struck her as "a fine instinctive nature, with a head for Leonardo to paint," who "seems bound by no tie, yet looks as if he had relatives in every place." Mazzini impressed her as one "in whom holiness has purified, but somewhat dwarfed the man." Carlyle "is arrogant and overbearing; but in his arrogance there is no bitterness, no self-love. It is the heroic arrogance of some old Scandinavian conqueror; it is his nature, and the untamable energy that has given him power to crush the dragon." Dr. Wilkinson, the Swedenborgian, is "a sane, strong, well-exercised mind ; but in the last degree unpoetical in its structure ; very simple, natural, and good ; excellent to see, though one cannot go far with him." Rachel, Fourier, Rousseau—she has a piercing glance for them all ; a word of warm admiration, all the more weighty for being qualified by criticism.

It was probably this keen penetration, this capacity to appreciate all kinds, this inclusiveness of sympathy, that prompted the selection of Margaret Fuller as chief editor of the " Dial," the organ of transcendental thought. Thus she regarded the enterprise :

" What others can do—whether all that has been said is the mere restlessness of discontent, or there are thoughts really struggling for utterance,—will be tested now. A perfectly free organ is to be offered for the expression of individual thought and character. There are no party measures to be carried, no particular standards to be set up ; a fair, calm tone, a recognition of universal principles, will, I hope, pervade the essays in every form. I trust there will be a spirit neither of dogmatism nor compromise, and that this journal will aim, not at leading public opinion, but at stimulating each man to judge for himself, and to think more deeply and more nobly, by letting him see how some minds are kept alive by a wise self-trust. We must not be sanguine at the amount of talent which will be brought to bear on this publication. All concerned are rather indifferent, and there is no great promise for the present. We cannot show high culture, and I doubt about vigorous thought. But we shall manifest free action as far as it goes, and a high aim. It were much if a periodical could be kept open, not to accomplish any outward object, but merely to afford an avenue for what of liberal and calm thought might be originated among us, by the wants of individual minds."

"Mr. Emerson best knows what he wants; but he has already said it in various ways. Yet this experiment is well worth trying; hearts beat so high, they must be full of something, and here is a way to breathe it out quite freely. It is for dear New England that I want this review. For myself, if I had wished to write a few pages now and then, there were ways and means enough of disposing of them.' But in truth I have not much to say; for since I have had leisure to look at myself, I find that, so far from being an original genius, I have not yet learned to think to any depth, and that the utmost I have done in life has been to form my character to a certain consistency, cultivate my tastes, and learn to tell the truth with a little better grace than I did at first. For this the world will not care much, so I shall hazard a few critical remarks only, or an unpretending chalk sketch now and then till I have learned to do something. There will be beautiful poesies; about prose we know not yet so well. We shall be the means of publishing the little Charles Emerson left as a mark of his noble course, and, though it lies in fragments, all who read will be gainers."

That these modest anticipations were justified and more, need not be said. The "beautiful poesies" came, and so did the various, eloquent, well-considered prose. The people who expected the whole gospel of Trans-cendentalism may have been disappointed; for the editor gave the magazine more of a literary than philos-ophical or reformatory tone. That she looked for from others, and was more than willing to welcome. She had a discerning eye for the evils of the time, and a sincere respect for the men and women who were disposed to counteract them. Another extract from her correspondence at this time—1840— taken, like the former, from the second volume of the memoirs, leaves no doubt on this point. After speaking of "the tendency of circumstances," since the separation from England, "to make our people superficial, irreverent, and more anxious to get a living than to live mentally and morally," she continues :

"New England is now old enough, some there have leisure enough to look at all this, and the consequence is a violent reaction, in a small minority, against a mode of culture that rears such fruits. They see that political freedom does not necessarily produce liberality of mind, nor freedom in church institutions, vital religion ; and, seeing that these changes cannot be wrought from without inwards, they are trying to quicken the soul, that they may work from within outwards. Disgusted with the vulgarity of a commercial aristocracy, they become radicals ; disgusted with the materialistic working of "rational" religion they become mystics. They quarrel with all that is because it is not spiritual enough. They would, perhaps, be patient, if they thought this the mere sensuality of childhood in our nation, which it might outgrow ; but they think that they see the evil widening, deepening, not only debasing the life, but corrupting the thought of our people ; and they feel that if they know not well what should be done, yet that the duty of every good man is to utter a protest against what is done amiss. Is this protest undiscriminating ? Are these opinions crude ? Do these proceedings threaten to sap the bulwarks on which men at present depend ? I confess it all, yet I see in these men promise of a better wisdom than in their opponents. Their hope for man is grounded on his destiny as an immortal soul, and not as a mere comfort-loving inhabitant of earth, or as a subscriber to the social contract. It was not meant that the soul should cultivate the earth, but that the earth should educate and maintain the soul. Man is not made for society, but society is made for man. No institution can be good which does not tend to improve the individual. In these principles I have confidence so profound, that I am not afraid to trust those who hold them, despite their partial views, imperfectly developed characters, and frequent want of practical sagacity. I believe, if they have opportunity to state and discuss their opinions, they will gradually sift them, ascertain their grounds and aims with clearness, and do the work this country needs. I hope for them as for the 'leaven that is hidden in the bushel of meal till all be leavened.' The leaven is not good by itself, neither is the meal; let them combine, and we shall yet have bread."

"Utopia it is impossible to build up; at least, my hopes for the race on this one planet are more limited than those of most of my friends; I accept the limitations of human nature, and believe a wise acknowledgment of them one of the best conditions of progress; yet every noble scheme, every poetic manifestation, prophesies to man his eventual destiny; and were not man ever more sanguine than facts at the moment justify, he would remain torpid, or be sunk in sensuality. It is on this ground that I sympathize with what is called the 'Transcendental Party,' and that I feel their aim to be the true one. They acknowledge in the nature of man an arbiter for his deeds—a standard transcending sense and time—and are, in my view, the true utilitarians. They are but at the beginning of their course, and will, I hope, learn to make use of the past, as well as to aspire for the future, and to be true in the present moment."

Margaret Fuller's power lay in her faith in this spiritual capacity. The confidence began with herself,

and was extended to all others, without exception. Mr.
Channing says :

" Margaret cherished a trust in her powers, a confidence in her destiny, and an ideal of her being, place
and influence, so lofty as to be extravagant. In the
morning hour and mountain air of aspiration, her
shadow moved before her, of gigantic size, upon the
snow-white vapor."

Mr. Clarke says :

" Margaret's life *had an aim*, and she was, therefore,
essentially a moral person, and not merely an overflow-
ing genius, in whom impulse gives birth to impulse,
deed to deed. This aim was distinctly apprehended
and steadily pursued by her from first to last. It was a
high, noble one, wholly religious, almost Christian. It
gave dignity to her whole career, and made it heroic.

" This aim, from first to last, was SELF-CULTURE. If
she was ever ambitious of knowledge and talent, as a
means of excelling others, and gaining fame, position,
admiration—this vanity had passed before I knew her,
and was replaced by the profound desire for a full
development of her whole nature, by means of a full
experience of life."

Speaking of her demands on others, her three biographers agree that they were based on the expectation
in them of spiritual excellence :

" One thing only she demanded of all her friends—
that they should have some ' extraordinary generous
seeking ;' that they should not be satisfied with the
common routine of life—that they should aspire to something higher, better, holier, than they had now attained.
Where this element of aspiration existed, she demanded

no originality of intellect, no greatness of soul. If these were found, well; but she could love, tenderly and truly, where they were not.

"She never formed a friendship until she had seen and known this germ of good, and afterwards judged conduct by this. To this germ of good, to this highest law of each individual, she held them true.

"Some of her friends were young, gay, and beautiful; some old, sick, or studious; some were children of the world, others pale scholars; some were witty, others slightly dull; but all, in order to be Margaret's friends, must be capable of seeking something—capable of some aspiration for the better. And how did she glorify life to all! All that was tame and common vanishing away in the picturesque light thrown over the most familiar things by her rapid fancy, her brilliant wit, her sharp insight, her creative imagination, by the inexhaustible resources of her knowledge, and the copious rhetoric, which found words and images always apt and always ready."

"Margaret saw in each of her friends the secret interior capability, which might be hereafter developed into some special beauty or power. By means of this penetrating, this prophetic insight, she gave each to himself, acted on each to draw out his best nature; gave him an ideal, out of which he could draw strength and liberty, hour by hour. Thus her influence was ever ennobling, and each felt that in her society he was truer, wiser, better, and yet more free and happy than elsewhere. The 'dry light,' which Lord Bacon loved, she never knew: her light was life, was love, was warm with sympathy and a boundless energy of affection and hope. Though her love flattered and charmed her friends, it did not spoil them, for they knew her perfect truth; they knew that she loved them, not for what she imagined, but for what she saw, though she saw it only in the germ. But as the Greeks beheld a Persephone and Athene in the passing stranger, and ennobled humanity into ideal beauty, Margaret saw all her friends thus idealized ; she was a balloon of sufficient power to take us all up with her into the serene depth of heaven, where she loved to float, far above the low details of earthly life ; earth lay beneath us as a lovely picture—its sounds came up mellowed into music."

" Margaret was, to persons younger than herself, a Makaria and Natalia. She was wisdom and intellectual beauty, filling life with a charm and glory ' known to neither sea nor land.' To those of her own age, she was sibyl and seer,—a prophetess, revealing the future, pointing the path, opening their eyes to the great aims only worthy of pursuit in life. To those older than herself, she was like the Euphorion in Goethe's drama, child of Faust and Helen,—a wonderful union of exuberance and judgment, born of romantic fulness and classic limitation. They saw with surprise her clear good sense, balancing her flow of sentiment and ardent courage. They saw her comprehension of both sides of every question, and gave her their confidence, as to one of equal age, because of so ripe a judgment."

" An interview with her was a joyous event ; worthy men and women who had conversed with her, could not forget her, but worked bravely on in the remembrance that this heroic approver had recognized their aims. She spoke so earnestly, that the depth of the sentiment prevailed, and not the accidental expression, which might chance to be common. Thus I learned the other day, that in a copy of Mrs. Jameson's ' Italian Painters,' against a passage describing Coreggio as a true servant of God in his art, above sordid ambition, devoted to truth, ' one of those superior beings of whom there are so few ;' Margaret wrote on the margin : ' And yet all might be such.' The book lay long on the table of the owner, in Florence, and chanced to be read there by an artist of much talent. ' These words ' said he, months afterwards, ' struck out a new strength in me. They revived resolutions long fallen away, and made me set my face like a flint.' "

" ' Yes, my life is strange ;' she said, ' thine is strange.

We are, we shall be, in this life, mutilated beings, but there is in my bosom a faith, that I shall see the reason ; a glory, that I can endure to be so imperfect ; and a feeling, ever elastic, that fate and time shall have the shame and the blame, if I am mutilated. I will do all I can,—and if one cannot succeed, there is a beauty in martyrdom.' "

" ' Would not genius be common as light if men trusted their higher selves ? ' "

" She won the confidence and affection of those who attracted her, by unbounded sympathy and trust. She probably knew the cherished secrets of more hearts than any one else, because she freely imparted her own. With a full share both of intellectual and of family pride, she preëminently recognized and responded to the essential brotherhood of all human kind, and needed but to know that a fellow being required her counsel or assistance, to render her not merely willing, but eager to impart it. Loving ease, luxury, and the world's good opinion, she stood ready to renounce them all, at the call of pity or of duty. I think no one, not radically averse to the whole system of domestic servitude, would have treated servants, of whatever class, with such uniform and thoughtful consideration—a regard which wholly merged their factitious condition in their antecedent and permanent humanity. I think few servants ever lived weeks with her, who were not dignified and lastingly benefited by her influence and her counsels. They might be at first repelled, by what seemed her too stately manner and exacting disposition, but they soon learned to esteem and love her.

" I have known few women, and scarcely another maiden, who had the heart and the courage to speak with such frank compassion, in mixed circles, of the most degraded and outcast portion of the sex. The contemplation of their treatment, especially by the guilty authors of their ruin, moved her to a calm and mournful indignation, which she did not attempt to suppress nor control. Others were willing to pity and de·

plore; Margaret was more inclined to vindicate and to redeem.

" ' In the chamber of death,' she wrote, ' I prayed in very early years : " Give me truth ; cheat me by no illusion." O, the granting of this prayer is sometimes terrible to me! I walk over burning ploughshares, and they sear my feet ; yet nothing but truth will do ; no love will serve that is not eternal, and as large as the universe ; no philanthropy, in executing whose behests I myself become unhealthy ; no creative genius which bursts asunder my life, to leave it a poor black chrysalid behind ; and yet this last is too true of me.' "

Margaret Fuller did justice to the character of Fourier, admired his enthusiasm, honored his devotion, acknowledged the terrible nature of the evils he gave the study of a life-time to correct, and paid an unstinting tribute to the disinterested motives that impelled him ; but with his scheme for refashioning society she had no sympathy. William H. Channing was an intimate friend, whose sincerity had her deepest respect, whose enthusiasm won her cordial admiration ; she listened to his brilliant expositions of socialism, but was not persuaded. Practical difficulties always appeared, and she never could believe that any rearrangement of circumstances would effect the regeneration of mankind. She was acquainted from the first with the experiment of Brook Farm ; knew the founders of it ; watched with genuine solicitude the inauguration of the scheme and its fortunes ; talked over the principles and details of it with the leading spirits ; visited the community ; examined for herself the working of the plan ; gave her talent to the entertainment and edification of the associates ; discerned with clear eye the distinctions between this experiment and those of European origin ; but still questioned the practical wisdom of the institution, and declined to join the fraternity, even on the most flattering terms, for the reason that, interested as she was in the experiment, it was, in her judgment, too purely an experiment to be personally and practically sanctioned by one who had no more faith in its fundamental principles than she.

She was not to be thrown off from her essential position, the primacy and all sufficiency of the soul. No misery or guilt daunted her, no impatience at slowness tempted her to resort to artificial methods of cure. Her visit to Sing Sing, and her intercourse with the abandoned women there was exceedingly interesting in this view.

" ' They listened with earnest attention, and many were moved to tears. I never felt such sympathy with an audience as when, at the words " Men and Brethren," that sea of faces, marked with the scars of every ill, were upturned, and the shell of brutality burst apart at the touch of love. I knew that at least heavenly truth would not be kept out by self complacence and dependence on good appearances. . . . These women were among the so-called worst, and all from the lowest haunts of vice. Yet nothing could have been more decorous than their conduct, while it was also frank ; and they showed a sensibility and sense of propriety which would not have disgraced any society.' "

" She did not hesitate to avow that, on meeting some of these abused, unhappy sisters, she had been surprised to find them scarcely fallen morally below the ordinary standard of womanhood,—realizing and loathing their debasement; anxious to escape it; and only repelled by the sad consciousness that for them sympathy and society remained only so long as they should persist in the ways of pollution."

Margaret Fuller's loyalty to principles was proof against bad taste ; which is saying a good deal, for many a reformer is of opinion that blunders are worse than crimes, and that vulgarity is more offensive than wickedness. She found the Fourierites in Europe terribly wearisome, and yet did not forget that they served the great future which neither they nor she would live to see. At home she could not endure the Abolitionists—"they were so tedious, often so narrow, always so rabid and exaggerated in their tone. But, after all, they had a high motive, something eternal in their desire and life; and if it was not the only thing worth thinking of, it was really something worth living and dying for, to free a great nation from such a blot, such a plague." In Europe she was disgusted at hearing Americans urging the same arguments against the freedom of the Italians that they urged at home against the emancipation of the blacks ; the same arguments in favor of the spoliation of Poland that they used at home in favor of the conquest of Mexico. With her, principles were independent of time and place. She always believed in liberty as a condition of enlightenment, and in enlightenment as a condition of progress. This practical faith in the intellectual and moral nature is the key to all her work. Every chamber that opened she entered and occupied, fearless of ghosts and goblins. The chambers that opened not she was content to leave unopened altogether.

On the table where the writer pens this poor tribute to a most remarkable woman, are the bulky volumes of her unpublished letters and diaries, revealing some things too personal for the public eye, but nothing in the least incongruous with the best things recorded by her biographers and suggested here ; and how much they tell that illustrates and confirms the moral nobleness and sweetness of her nature. They contain a psychometric examination from two letters, given after the manner familiar to those interested in such things, by one of the chief of these spiritual vaticinators. We shall not transcribe it, for it is long and indistinct. The indistinctness is the one interesting feature of the sketch. The sensitive reporter confessed herself put out by the singular commingling of moods and dispositions, and seemed to be describing several persons in one. But through them all the same general impression was clear ; the impression of a fascinating, lovable, earnest and lofty spirit, which, whether sad or gay, intellectual or sentimental, bore itself like a queenly woman.

When the news of her death reached Boston, one of Boston's eminent men in letters and public affairs quietly remarked : " it is just as well so." He was thinking of the agitation she might cause by her brilliant conversations and her lightning pen, if she brought back from her Italian heroisms the high spirit of liberty. The times were growing dark in America. The Slave Power was drawing its lines closer about the citadel of freedom.

The brave voices were few and fewer ; the conservatives were glad when one was hushed by death. The movement she had encouraged was waning. The high enthusiasm was smouldering in breasts that anticipated the battle which came ten years later. The period of poetic aspiration and joy was ended, and the priestess, had she survived, would have found a deserted shrine.

No accessible portrait of Margaret Fuller exists, that worthily presents her. Thomas Hicks painted a likeness, of cabinet size, in Rome, which her friends approved. The daguerreotype was too painfully literal to be just ; the sun having no sentiment or imagination in his eye. She was not beautiful in youth, nor was she one of those who gain beauty with years. Her physical attractions were of the kind that time impairs soon, and though she died at forty, her personal charm was gone. Intellect gave her what beauty she had, and they saw it who saw her intellect at play. Her image, therefore, is best preserved in the memory of her friends. They cannot put it on exhibition.

XII.

THE PREACHER.

TRANSCENDENTALISM is usually spoken of as a philosophy. It is more justly regarded as a gospel. As a philosophy it is abstract and difficult—purely metaphysical in character, resting on no basis of observed and scientifically-proven fact, but on the so-called data of consciousness, which cannot be accurately defined, distinctly verified, or generally recommended. It must be, therefore, inexact and inconclusive; so far from uniform in its structure, that it may rather be considered several systems than one. As a gospel, it possesses all the qualities desirable for effect. It is worth remarking that its chief disciples have been clergymen. In Germany, Schleiermacher—if we may count him a Transcendentalist; he was the author of the doctrine, that the essence of religion consisted in the *sense of dependence*, which figured largely in the sermons of New England divines—was a clergyman; Fichte assumed the prophetic tone; the German professors associated religious teaching with the duties of their chairs. In England, Coleridge was a preacher by practice, and, part of his life, by profession; Carlyle was never anything else, his essays and even his histories being sermons in disguise, and disguise of the most transparent sort. In New England, Emerson began his career as a Unitarian minister; so did Walker; so did Ripley; so did W. H. Channing; so did J. S. Dwight; so did C. P. Cranch. Dr. Channing, a Transcendentalist without knowing it, was the greatest preacher of his generation. Brownson was a preacher of all orders in succession; Bartol preaches still; Clarke preaches still. Of the younger men, Johnson, Longfellow, Wasson, Higginson, are, or were, Unitarian clergymen. Alcott is a preacher without a pulpit. The order of mind that was attracted to the ministry was attracted to the Transcendental ideas.

The explanation is easy; Transcendentalism possessed all the chief qualifications for a gospel. Its cardinal "facts" were few and manageable. Its data were secluded in the recesses of consciousness, out of the reach of scientific investigation, remote from the gaze of vulgar skepticism; esoteric, having about them the charm of a sacred privacy, on which common sense and the critical understanding might not intrude. Its oracles proceeded from a shrine, and were delivered by a priest or priestess, who came forth from an interior holy of holies to utter them, and thus were invested with the air of authority which belongs to exclusive and privileged truths, that revealed themselves to minds of a contemplative cast. It dealt entirely with "divine things," "eternal realities;" supersensible forms of thought; problems that lay out of the reach of observation, such as the essential cause, spiritual laws, the life after death, the essence of the good, the beautiful, the true; the ideal possibilities of the soul; its organ was intuition; its method was introspection: its brightness was inspiration. It possessed the character of indefiniteness and mystery, full of sentiment and suggestion, that fascinates the imagination, and lends itself so easily to acts of contemplation and worship. The German Mystics were in spirit Transcendentalists. The analogies are close between Boehme and Schelling; between Eckardt and Fichte; Frederick Schlegel had much in common with Boehme; Coleridge acknowledged his debt to him and to other Mystics; even Hegel ran in line with them on some of his high roads. Minds as opposite as Alcott and Parker met in communion here—Alcott going to the Mystics for inspiration; Parker resorting to them for rest. The Mystics were men of feeling; the Transcendentalists were men of thought: but thought and feeling sought the same object in the same region. Piety was a feature of Transcendentalism; it loved devout hymns, music, the glowing language of aspiration, the moods of awe and humility, emblems, symbols, expressions of inarticulate emotion, silence, contemplation, breathings after communion with the Infinite. The poetry of Transcendentalism is religious, with scarcely an exception; the most beautiful hymns in our sacred collections, the only deeply impressive hymns, are by transcendental writers.

This was the aspect of Transcendentalism that fascinated Theodore Parker. His intellect was constructed on the English model. His acute observation; his passion for external facts; his faith in statistics; his hun-

ger for information on all external topics of history and
politics ; his capacity for retaining details of miscellaneous knowledge ; his logical method of reasoning ; his
ability to handle masses of raw mental material, to distribute and classify ;—all indicate intellectual power of the
English rather than of the German type. It was his custom to speak slightingly of the " Bridgewater Treatises "
and works of a similar class, in which the processes of
inductive argument are employed to establish truths of
the " Pure Reason ;" but he easily fell into the same
habit, and pushed the inductive method as far as it
would go. His discourses on Providence, the Economy
of Pain and Misery, Atheism, Theism, in the volume
entitled " Theism, Atheism, and The Popular Theology,"
are quite in the style of the " Bridgewater Treatises."
Parker was, in many respects, the opposite of a Mystic ;
he was a realist of the most concrete description, entirely
at home among sensible things, a good administrator, a
safe investor of moneys, a wise counsellor in practical
affairs. But along with this intellectual quality which
he inherited from his father, was an interior, sentimental, devotional quality, derived from his mother. The
two were never wholly blended ; often they were wide
apart, occupying different spheres, and engaged in different offices ; sometimes they were in apparent opposition. Neither could subdue or overshadow the other ;
neither could keep the other long in abeyance. As a
rule, the dominion was divided between them : the practical understanding assumed control of all matters pertaining to this world ; the higher reason claimed su·

premacy in all matters of faith. But for the tendency to poetic idealism, which came to him from his mother, Parker might, from the constitution of his mind, have belonged to an opposite school. A passage in the letter from Santa Cruz, entitled "Theodore Parker's Experience as a Minister," is curious, as showing how the two tendencies of his mind overlapped; he is speaking of the two methods of developing the contents "of the instinctive intuitions of the divine, the just, and the immortal,"—the inductive and the deductive. After a few words respecting the inductive method of gathering facts from the history of mankind, he speaks thus of the deductive : "Next, from the primitive facts of consciousness given by the power of instinctive intuition, I endeavored to deduce the true notion of God, of justice, and futurity." Then, forgetting that the power of instinctive intuition must be self-authenticating—cannot, at any rate, be authenticated by miscellaneous facts in the religious history of mankind—he continues :

"To learn what I could about the spiritual faculties of man, I not only studied the sacred books of various nations, the poets and philosophers who professedly treat thereof, but also such as deal with sleep-walking, dreams, visions, prophecies, second-sight, oracles, ecstasies, witchcraft, magic-wonders, the appearance of devils, ghosts, and the like. Besides, I studied other works which lie out from the regular highway of theology ; the spurious books attributed to famous Jews and Christians ; Pseudepigraphy of the Old Testament, and the Apocrypha of the New ; with the strange fantasies of the Neoplatonists and Gnostics."

Very important reading all this for one who studied

to qualify himself to instruct his fellow men in the natural history of the world's religions ; but not so valuable as illustrating the " instinctive intuitions of human nature." Kant, Fichte, Schelling, Hegel, Boehme, Eckardt, never worked by that method, which may properly be called the method of Sensationalism applied to Transcendentalism. Parker, on the religious side, was a pure Transcendentalist without guile, accepting the transcendental ideas with no shadow of qualification ; stating them with the concrete sharpness of scientific propositions, and applying them with the exactness of mathematical principles. He took them as he found them in the writings of the great German thinkers ; shaped them as he, better than any body else, could shape thought in form of words,—as he shaped the formula of republican government—" government of the people, by the people, for the people "—from the looser statement of Daniel Webster,—and laid them down as corner-stones of a new theological structure. The materials were furnished by Schleiermacher, Spinoza, Jacobi, Schelling ; the architectural skill was his own. Consciousness he did not undertake to analyze ; the " facts of consciousness " he took on others' verification ; their spiritual import he perceived, developed and applied. Transcendentalism put into his hands the implements he was in special need of.

It is not easy to determine the precise period at which Parker fully accepted, with all its consequences, the transcendental philosophy. He was not a Transcendentalist—not distinctly and avowedly one—at the time of his ordination, in 1837 ; he clearly was in 1840, the date of the Levi Blodgett letter, which contains the most thorough-going statement of the transcendental idea to be found in any single tractate. The probability is, that he always was one in sentiment, and became more and more consciously one in thought, as he found it necessary to shift his position in order to save his faith. So long as the beliefs he cherished seemed to be satisfactorily supported on the old grounds, he was content ; but as the old grounds, one after another, gave way, the beliefs were transferred to the keeping of new principles. Then the sentiments of his youth hardened into ideas ; the delicate creatures that lived and gleamed beneath the waters of faith's tropical ocean, became reefs of white stone, that lifted their broad surface above the level of the sea, and offered immovable support to human habitations.

Parker was, more than anything, a preacher ;—preacher more than theologian, philosopher or scholar. Whatever else he was, contributed to his greatness in this. He had a profuse gift of language ; expression was a necessity to him ; his thoughts came swiftly, and clothed in attractive garments ; he had wit, and he had humor ; laughter and tears were equally at his command. His resources of illustration, drawn from history, literature, biography, nature, were simply inexhaustible ; the fruits of enormous reading were at the immediate disposal of a memory that never lost a trifle of the stores committed to it. The religious emotions were as genuine with him as they were quick, and as deep as they were glowing :

the human sympathies were wide as the widest, and tender as the tenderest. He had the power of persuasion and of rebuke, a withering sarcasm, a winning compassion. His indignation at wrong was not so qualified by sentimental regard for the wrong doer that invective was wasted on lifeless abstractions, nor was his judgment of evil doers so austere that wickedness escaped by being made incredible. It cannot be said of anybody that he has been able to discriminate nicely, in hours of moral feeling, between wrong doers and wrong deeds; that cannot be done in the present state of psychological science. We simply do not know what the limits of personal responsibility are; how much power is entrusted to the will; how much allowance is to be made for temperament and circumstance; at what point the individual is detached from the mass of mankind, and constituted an accountable person. Parker was guilty, as others are, of personal injustice in holding individuals answerable for sins of their generation, and for vices transmitted with their blood; conscience and charity were occasionally at issue with him; but if righteousness was betrayed into intemperance of zeal, peace made haste to offer its kiss of sorrow, and unaffected tears damped down the flames of wrath when they threatened to consume the innocent. This two-fold power of blasting and of blessing, was vastly effective both on large audiences and on small. The personal integrity which no one ever doubted, the courage which was evident to even hasty observers, the mental independence which justified the boldness of its position by an indefatigable

purpose to discover truth, were prime qualifications for
the office he filled. The very disadvantages,—an un-
heroic presence, an uninspired countenance, an unmelo-
dious and unpliable voice, the necessity of interposing
glasses between his clear blue eyes and his audience,
and thus veiling the heavens that lay behind them,—
helped him by putting out of mind all thought of meretricious attempts at influence, and compelling recognition
of the intellectual and moral force which could so easily
dispense with what most orators consider invaluable
aids.

All that Parker had went into his preaching; the
wealth of his library, the treasures of his heart, the
sweetness of his closet meditations, the solemnity of his
lonely musings. But it was not this that gave him his
great power as a preacher. That, we are persuaded, was
due in chief part to the earnestness of his faith in the
transcendental philosophy. How cordially he entertained that faith, what to him it signified in politics,
ethics, religion, may be learned by any who will take
pains to read a lecture by him on Transcendentalism,
recently published by the Free Religious Association.
That he ascribed the popular interest in his preaching to his philosophical ideas will not perhaps be
accepted as evidence on the point, for men are apt
to be mistaken in regard to the sources of their
power; but it is interesting as a testimony to his own
belief, to know that he did so. In a sermon preached
on November 14th, 1852, the occasion being his leaving
the Melodeon for the Music Hall, he presents first the

current modes of accounting for his success, and then his own.

"The first reason assigned for the audience coming together was this : they came from vain curiosity, having itching ears to hear ' what this babbler sayeth.'

"Then it was said, men came here because I taught utter irreligion, blank immorality ; that I had no love of God, no fear of God, no love of man ; and that you thought, if you could get rid of your conscience and soul, and trample immortality under foot, and were satisfied there was no God, you should have a very nice time of it here and hereafter.

"Then it was declared that I was a shrewd, practical man, perfectly well ' posted up' in every thing that took place ; knew how to make investments and get very large returns,—unluckily it has not been for myself that this has been true. And it was said that I collected large headed, practical men to hear me, and that you were a ' boisterous assembly.'

"Then, that I was a learned man and gave learned discourses on ecclesiastical history or political history,— things which have not been found very attractive in the churches hitherto.

"Again, that I was a philosopher, with a wise head, and taught men theological metaphysics ; and so a large company of men seemed all at once smitten with a panic for metaphysics and abstract preaching. It was never so before.

"Next it was reported that I was a witty man, and shot nicely feathered arrows very deftly into the mark ; and that men came to attend the sharp shooting of a wit.

"Then there was a seventh thing,—that I was an eloquent man ; and I remember certain diatribes against the folly of filling churches with eloquence.

"Then again, it was charged against me that I was a philanthropist, and taught the love of men, but did not teach at all the love of God ; and that men really loved to love one another, and so came.

" Then it was thought that I was a sentimentalist, and tickled the ears of ' weak women,' who came to delight themselves and be filled full of poetry and love.

" The real thing they did not seem to hit; that I preached an idea of God, of man and of religion, which commended itself to the nature of mankind."

The great preacher is always an idealist, and according to the fervor of his idealism is he great. This was the source of Channing's power; it was the charm of Emerson's. In reply to a friend who questioned her as to the nature of the benefits conferred on her by Mr. Emerson's preaching, Margaret Fuller wrote :

" His influence has been more beneficial to me than that of any American, and from him I first learned what is meant by an inward life. Many other springs have since fed the stream of living waters, but he first opened the fountain. That the ' mind is its own place ' was a dead phrase to me till he cast light upon my mind. Several of his sermons stand apart in memory, like landmarks of my spiritual history. It would take a volume to tell what this one influence did for me."

Mr. Parker's ministry had three periods, in each of which the ideal element was the attraction. The first was the period of quiet influence in West Roxbury, where the stream of his spiritual life flowed peacefully through green pastures, and enriched simple hearts with its unintermitted current. Accounts agree that at this time there was a soul of sweetness in his preaching, that was a good deal more than the body of its thought. The second was the period at the Boston Melodeon, the first of his experience before the crowd of a metropolis.

This was the controversial epoch, and, from the nature of the case, was largely polemical and negative as towards the popular theology. But even then the strain of spiritual faith was heard above the din of battle, and souls that were averse to polemics were fed by the enthusiasm that came from the inner heights of aspiration. The last period was that of the Music Hall—the famous period. Then the faith was defined and formulated; the corner-stones were hewn and set; the fundamental positions were announced with the fidelity of iteration that was customary with the " painful preachers of the Word" in churches where people were duly stretched upon the Five Points of Calvin. The three cardinal attestations of the universal human consciousness—

> The Absolute God,
> The Moral Law,
> The Immortal Life,

were asseverated with all the earnestness of the man, and declared to be the constituent elements of the Rock of Ages.

Standing on this tripod, Parker spoke as one having authority; he judged other creeds—Orthodox, Unitarian, Scientific—with the confidence of one who felt that he had inspiration on his side. It was difficult for him to understand how, without his faith, others could be happy. The believers in tradition seemed to him people who walked near precipices, leaning on broken reeds; the unbelievers were people who walked near the same precipices, with bandaged eyes.

"If to-morrow I am to perish utterly, then I shall only take counsel for to-day, and ask for qualities which last no longer. My fathers will be to me only as the ground out of which my bread-corn is grown; dead, they are like the rotten mould of earth, their memory of small concern to me. Posterity—I shall care nothing for the future generations of mankind. I am one atom in the trunk of a tree, and care nothing for the roots below or the branches above; I shall sow such seed as will bear harvest to-day; I shall know no higher law; passion enacts my statutes to-day; to-morrow ambition revises the statutes, and these are my sole legislators; morality will vanish, expediency take its place; heroism will be gone, and instead of it there will be the brute valor of the he-wolf, the brute-cunning of the she-fox, the rapacity of the vulture, and the headlong daring of the wild bull; but the cool, calm courage which, for truth's sake, and for love's sake, looks death firmly in the face, and then wheels into line, ready to be slain— that will be a thing no longer heard of."

"The atheist sits down beside the coffin of his only child—a rose-bud daughter, whose heart death slowly ate away; the pale lilies of the valley which droop with fragrance above that lifeless heart, are flowers of mockery to him, their beauty is a cheat; they give not back his child, for whom the sepulchral monster opens his remorseless jaws. The hopeless father looks down on the face of his girl, silent—not sleeping, cold—dead. . . . He looks beyond—the poor sad man—it is only solid darkness he looks on; no rainbow beautifies that cloud; there is thunder in it, not light; night is behind—without a star."

This is the way the Protestant Christians spoke of him; the "Evangelicals" spoke thus of the Unitarians; the believers in miraculous revelations spoke thus of the rationalists. They that are sure always speak so of those who, in their judgment, have no right to be sure at all.

Yet Parker had a hospitable mind, and his hospitality was due also to his faith. The spiritual philosophy which maintained the identity in all men of consciousness, and the eternal validity of its promises, which no error or petulance could discredit, was indulgent to the unfortunates who had not the satisfaction of its assurance. It pitied, but did not reproach them. They were children of God no less for being ignorant of their dignity. It was impossible for Parker to believe that rational beings could be utterly insensible to the essential facts of their own nature. Their error, misconception, misconstruction, to whatever cause due, could be no more than incidental. Skepticism might make wild work of definitions, but ultimate facts it could never disturb ; these would thrust themselves up at last, as inevitably as the rocky substratum of the globe presents itself in the green field. In a thanksgiving sermon he thanked God that atheism could freely deliver its creed and prove that it was folly. He was persuaded that the disbelievers believed better than they knew ; in their paroxysms of denial, he saw the blind struggles of faith ; he gave the enemies of religion credit for qualities that made their hostility look like a heroic protest against the outrages inflicted in the name of religion upon religion itself.

" It is a fact of history, that in old time, from Epicurus to Seneca, some of the ablest heads and best hearts of Greece and Rome sought to destroy the idea of immortality. This was the reason: they saw it was a torment to mankind; that the popular notion of immortality was too bad to be true; and so they took pains to break down the Heathen Mythology, though with it they destroyed the notion of immortal life. They did a great service to mankind in ridding us from this yoke of fear.

" Many a philosopher has seemed without religion, even to a careful observer—sometimes has passed for an atheist. Some of them have to themselves seemed without any religion, and have denied that there was any God; but all the while their nature was truer than their will; their instinct kept their personal wholeness better than they were aware. These men loved absolute truth, not for its uses, but for itself; they laid down their lives for it, rather than violate the integrity of their intellect. They had the intellectual love of God, though they knew it not, though they denied it.

" I have known philanthropists who undervalued piety; they liked it not—they said it was moonshine, not broad day; it gave flashes of lightning, all of which would not make light. . . . Yet underneath their philanthropy there lay the absolute and disinterested love of other men. They knew only the special form, not the universal substance thereof.

" Men of science, as a class, do not war on the truths, the goodness and the piety that are taught as religion, only on the errors, the evil, the impiety which bear its name. Science is the natural ally of religion. Shall we try and separate what God has joined? We injure both by the attempt. The philosophers of this age have a profound love of truth, and show great industry and boldness in search thereof. In the name of truth they pluck down the strongholds of error—venerable and old.

" All the attacks made on religion itself by men of science, from Celsus to Feuerbach, have not done so much to bring religion into contempt as a single persecution for witchcraft, or a Bartholomew massacre made in the name of God."

Parker had human sympathies strong and deep, and could never have been indifferent to the pains and misery of his fellow creatures; yet these sympathies owed their persistency, their endurance, and their indomitable sweetness, to the spiritual faith which he professed. He had a passionate head-strong nature; he knew the charm of pleasant looks, congenial companions, elegant and luxurious circumstances. His love of leisure was keen; it was the desire of his life to enjoy the scholar's privilege of uninterrupted hours, in the delicious seclusion of the library. With a different philosophy he would have been a very different man. The creed he held made self-indulgence impossible.

" I have always taught," he said—in a sermon before quoted, the last he preached in the Melodeon—" that the religious faculty is the natural ruler in all the commonwealth of man; the importance of religion, and its commanding power in every relation of life. This is what I have continually preached, and some of you will remember that the first sermon I addressed to you was on this theme :—The absolute necessity of religion for safely conducting the life of the individual, and the life of the State. You knew very well I did not begin too soon ; yet I did not then foresee that it would soon be denied in America, in Boston, that there was any law higher than an Act of Congress." The allusion is to the Fugitive Slave Bill then recently enacted, which brought

to a close issue the controversy between the Abolitionists and the Government, and imposed on Mr. Parker
and the rest who felt as he did, duties of watchfulness
and self-denial, that for years put to flight all thoughts
of personal ease.

He continues :

"Woman I have always regarded as the equal of man
—more nicely speaking, the equivalent of man ; superior in some things, inferior in some others ; inferior in
the lower qualities, in bulk of body and bulk of brain ;
superior in the higher and nicer qualities—in the moral
power of conscience, the loving power of affection, the
religious power of the soul ; equal on the whole, and of
course entitled to just the same rights as man ; the same
rights of mind, body and estate ; the same domestic, social, ecclesiastical, and political rights as man, and only
kept from the enjoyment of these by might, not right ;
yet herself destined one day to acquire them all."

The belief in the spiritual eminence of woman was
part of the creed of the Transcendentalist ; it was intimately connected with his reverence for interior, poetic,
emotional natures ; with his preference for feeling above
thought, of spontaneity above will. In the order of
rank, Parker assigned the first place to the "religious
faculty," as he termed it, which gave immediate vision of
spiritual truth ; the second place was given to the affections ; conscience he ranked below these ; and lowest of
all stood the intellect. The rational powers were held
subordinate to the instinctive, or rather the rational and
the instinctive were held to be coincident. The feminine characteristic being affection, which is spontaneous

and the masculine being intellect, which is not, the feminine was set above the masculine—love above light, pity above justice, sympathy above rectitude, compassion above equity. Parker had feminine attributes, and was slightly enamored of them; thought, or tried to think them the glory of his manhood; but the masculine greatly predominated in him. To people in general he seemed to reverse his own order, in practice. Weak, dependent, dreamy men he had no patience with; sentimentalism was his aversion; the moral element alone commanded his absolute respect. Masculine women were equally distasteful; while he admired the genius of Margaret Fuller, his personal attraction toward her seldom brought him into her society. That a man constituted as he was, self-reliant to aggressiveness, inclined to be arbitrary, dogmatical, and imperious, of prodigious force of will and masterly power of conscience, entered as he did into advocacy of the rights of the African and the prerogatives of woman, is evidence of the whole-heartedness with which he adopted the transcendental philosophy. It was, indeed, a faith to him, that ruled his life and appointed his career. It gave him his commission as prophet, reformer, philanthropist. It was the consecrating oil that sanctified him, from the crown of his head to the soles of his feet.

Parker believed in the gospel of Transcendentalism, and was fully persuaded that it was to be the gospel of the future. "The religion I preach," he was accustomed to say, "will be the religion of enlightened men for the next thousand years." He anticipated an earthly immortality for his thought, an extensive circulation of his books, a swift course for his word, among the people. The expectation seemed not unreasonable twenty years ago.

The prediction has not thus far been justified. Parker died in 1860, on the eve of the civil war, which he prognosticated, sixteen years ago. The war fairly ended, efforts were made to revive the prophet's memory and carry out the cherished purpose of his heart. But their ill success has gone far to prove—what needed no evidence—that prophecies may fail, and tongues cease and knowledge pass away. The philosophy that Parker combated and ridiculed and cast scorn at, declared to be self-refuted and self-condemned, has revived under a new name, as the "philosophy of experience," is professed by the ablest thinkers of the day, taught in high places, in the name of science, set forth as the hope of man ; the creeds he pronounced irrational, and fancied to be obsolete still hold nominal sway over the minds of men ; the Christianity of the letter and the form is the only Christianity that is officially acknowledged ; the gospel is an institution still, not a faith ; revivalism has the monopoly of religious enthusiasm ; preaching is giving place to lecturing ; the pulpit has been taken down ; science alone is permitted to speak with authority ;—literature, journalism, politics, trade, attract the young men that once sought the ministry ; the noble preachers of a noble gospel are the few remaining idealists, who have kept the faith of their youth ; they are growing old ; one by one they leave their place, and there are none like them to fill it. Parker was one of the last of the grand preachers who spoke with power, bearing commission from the soul. The commissions which the soul issues are, for the time being, discredited, and discredited they will be, so long as the ideal philosophy is an outcast among men. Should that philosophy revive, the days of great preaching will return with it. Bibles will be read and hymns sung, and sermons delivered to crowds from pulpits. The lyceum and the newspaper will occupy a subordinate position as means of social and moral influence, and the prophets will recover their waning reputation. Until then, the work they did when living must attest their greatness with such as can estimate it at its worth.

XIII

THE MAN OF LETTERS

THE man who was as influential as any in planting the seeds of the transcendental philosophy in good soil, and in showing whither its principles tended, is known now, and has from the first been known, chiefly as a man of letters, a thoughtful observer, a careful student and a serious inquirer after knowledge. George Ripley, one year older than Emerson, was one of the forerunners and prophets of the new dispensation. He was by temperament as well as by training, a scholar, a reader of books, a discerner of opinions, a devotee of ideas. A mind of such clearness and serenity, accurate judgment, fine taste, and rare skill in the use of language, written and spoken, was of great value in introducing, defining and interpreting the vast, vague thoughts that were burning in the minds of speculative men. He was one of the first in America to master the German language; and, his bent of mind being philosophical and theological, he became a medium through which the French and German thought found its way to New England. He was an importer, reader and lender of the new books of the living Continental thinkers. His library contained a rich collection of works in philosophy, theology, hermeneutics, criticism of the Old and New Testaments, and divinity in its different branches of dogmatics and sentiment. He was intimate with N. L. Frothingham and Convers Francis, the admirable scholar, the hospitable and independent thinker, the enthusiastic and humane believer, the centre and generous distributor of copious intellectual gifts to all who came within his reach. Theodore Parker was the intellectual product of these two men, Convers Francis and George Ripley. The former fed his passion for knowledge; the latter, at the period of his life in the divinity school, gave direction to his thought. The books that did most to determine the set of Parker's mind were taken from Mr. Ripley's library. For a considerable time, in Parker's early ministry, they were close and thoroughly congenial friends. They walked and talked together; made long excursions; attended conventions; were members of the same club or coterie; joined in the discussions at which Emerson, Channing, Hedge, Clarke, Alcott took part; and, though parted, in after life, by circumstances which appointed them to different spheres of labor,—one in Boston, the other in New York,—they continued to the end, constant and hearty well wishers. At the close of his life, Parker expressed a hope that Ripley might be his biographer.

Mr. Ripley prepared for the ministry at the Cambridge divinity school; in 1826 accepted a call to be pastor and preacher of the church, organized but eighteen months before, and within two months worshipping in their new meeting-house on Purchase street, Boston. The ordination took place on Wednesday, Nov. 8th, of

the same year. " Under his charge," said his successor,
Rev. J. I. T. Coolidge, in 1848, " the society grew from
very small beginnings to strength and prosperity. As a
preacher, he awakened the deepest interest, and as a
devoted pastor, the warmest affection, which still sur-
vives, deep and strong, in the hearts of those who were
the objects of his counsel and pastoral care. After the
lapse of almost fifteen years, the connection was dis-
solved, for reasons which affected not the least the relations of friendship and mutual respect between the parties. It has been a great satisfaction to me, as I have
passed in and out among you, to hear again and again
the expressions of love and interest with which you remember the ministry of your first servant in this church."
That this was not merely the formal tribute which the
courtesies of the profession exacted, is proved, as well
as such a thing can be proved, by the published correspondence between the pastor and his people, by the
frank declarations of the pastor in his farewell address,
and by a remarkable letter, which discussed in full the
causes that led to the separation of the pastor and his
flock. In this long and candid letter to the church,
Mr. Ripley declared himself a Transcendentalist, and
avowed his sympathy with movements larger than the
Christian Church represented.

The declaration was hardly necessary. Mr. Ripley
was known to be the writer of the review of Martineau's " Rationale of Religious Enquiry," which
raised such heated controversy ; his translation of
Cousin's " Philosophical Miscellanies," with its impor-

tant Introduction, had attracted the attention of literary circles ; a volume of discourses, entitled " Discourses on the Philosophy of Religion," comprising seven sermons delivered in the regular course of his ministry, left no doubt in any mind respecting his position. The controversy with Andrews Norton on " The Latest Form of Infidelity," was carried on in 1840, the year before Mr. Ripley's ministry ended. The calmness of tone that characterized all these writings, the clearness and serenity of statement, the seemingly easy avoidance of extremes, the absence of passion, showed the supremacy of intellect over feeling. Yet of feeling there must have been a good deal. There was a great deal in the community ; there was a great deal among the clergy of his denomination ; that it had found expression within his own society, is betrayed in the farewell sermon ; that his own heart was deeply touched, was confessed by the fact that on the very day after his parting words to his congregation were spoken—on March 29th, 1841— Mr. Ripley took up his new ministry at Brook Farm.

The character of that Association has been described in a previous chapter, with as much minuteness of detail as is necessary, and the purposes of its inaugurators have been sufficiently indicated. The founder of it was not a " doctrinaire," but a philanthropist on ideal principles. With the systems of socialism current in Paris, he was at that period wholly unacquainted. The name of Charles Fourier was unfamiliar to him. He had faith in the soul, and in the soul's prophecy of good ; he saw that the prophecy was unheeded, that society rested on principles which the soul abhorred ; that between the visions of the spiritual philosophy and the bitter realities of vice, misery, sin, in human life, there was an unappeasable conflict; and he was resolved to do what one man might to create a new earth in preparation for a new heaven. He took the Gospel at its word, and went forth to demonstrate the power of its principles, by showing the Beatitudes to be something more substantial than dreams. His costly library, with all its beloved books, was offered for sale at public auction, and the price thereof, with whatever else he possessed, was consecrated to the cause of humanity that he had at heart. He had no children, and few ties of kindred ; but the social position of the clergy was above any secular position in New England at that time ; the prejudices and antipathies of the clerical order were stubborn ; the leaders of opinion in state and church were conservative, to a degree it is difficult for us to believe ; the path of the reformer was strewn with thorns and beset with difficulties most formidable to sensitive spirits. Mr. Emerson had resigned his ministry nine years before, and for the reason too that he was a Transcendentalist, but had retired to the peaceful walks of literature, and had made no actual assault on social institutions. Mr. Ripley associated himself at once with people of no worldly consideration, avowed principles that were voted vulgar in refined circles, and identified himself with an enterprise which the amiable called visionary, and the unamiable wild and revolutionary. But his conviction was clear, and his will was fixed. Sustained by the entire sympathy of a very noble woman, his wife—who was one with him in aspiration, purpose, and endeavor, till the undertaking ended—he put "the world" behind him, sold all, and followed the Master.

Mr. and Mrs. Ripley were the life of the Brook Farm Association. Their unfaltering energy, unfailing cheer, inexhaustible sweetness and gayety, availed to keep up the tone of the institution, to prevent its becoming common-place, and to retain there the persons on whose character the moral and intellectual standard depended. It was due to them that the experiment was tried as long as it was—six years ;—that while it went on, it avoided, as it did, the usual scandal and reproach that bring ruin on schemes of that description; and that, when finally it ended in disaster, it commanded sympathy rather than contempt, and left a sweet memory behind. The originator was the last to leave the place of his toil and vain endeavor ; he left it, having made all necessary provision for the discharge of debts, which only through arduous labors in journalism he was able afterwards to pay.

In Mr. Ripley's mind the Idea was supreme. In 1844 he, with Mr. Dana and Mr. Channing, lectured and spoke on the principles of Association,—the foreign literature on the subject being more familiar to him then,—commended the doctrine of Fourier, and was prepared for a more sympathetic propagandism than he had meditated hitherto. In 1845, the " Harbinger " was started,—a weekly journal, devoted to Social and Political Progress ; published by the Brook Farm Phalanx. The Prospectus, written by Mr. Ripley, made this announcement : "The principles of universal unity taught by Charles Fourier in their application to society, we believe are at the foundation of all genuine social progress ; and it will ever be our aim to discuss and defend those principles without any sectarian bigotry, and in the catholic and comprehensive spirit of their great discoverer." An introductory notice by the same pen, among other things pertaining to the aims and intentions of the paper, contained this passage :

"The interests of Social Reform will be considered as paramount to all others in whatever is admitted into the pages of the "Harbinger." We shall suffer no attachment to literature, no taste for abstract discussion, no love of purely intellectual theories, to seduce us from our devotion to the cause of the oppressed, the down trodden, the insulted and injured masses of our fellow men. Every pulsation of our being vibrates in sympathy with the wrongs of the toiling millions ; and every wise effort for their speedy enfranchisement will find in us resolute and indomitable advocates. If any imagine from the literary tone of the preceding remarks that we are indifferent to the radical movement for the benefit of the masses which is the crowning glory of the nineteenth century, they will soon discover their egregious mistake. To that movement, consecrated by religious principle, sustained by an awful sense of justice, and cheered by the brightest hopes of future good, all our powers, talents, and attainments are devoted. We look for an audience among the refined and educated circles, to which the character of our paper will win its way ; but we shall also be read by the swart and sweaty artisan ; the laborer will find in us another champion ; and many hearts struggling with the secret hope which no weight of care and toil can entirely suppress, will pour on us their benedictions, as we labor for the equal rights of all."

In the four years of its existence, the paper was faithful to this grand and high sounding promise. A powerful company of writers contributed their labor to help forward the plan. The Journal was affluent and sparkling. The literary criticism was the work of able pens ; the musical and art criticism was in the hands of the most competent judges in the country ; the æsthetics were not neglected ; the verse was excellent; but the social questions were of first consideration. These were never treated slightingly, and the treatment of them never deviated from the high standard proposed by the editors. The list of its contributors contained the names of Stephen Pearl Andrews, Albert Brisbane, W. H. Channing, W. E. Channing, Walter Channing, James Freeman Clarke, Geo. H. Calvert, J. J. Cooke, A. J. H. Duganne, C. P. Cranch, Geo. W. Curtis, Charles A. Dana, J. S. Dwight, Horace Greeley, Parke Godwin, F. H. Hedge, T. W. Higginson, M. E. Lazarus, J. R. Lowell, Osborn Macdaniel, Geo. Ripley, S. D. Robbins, L. W. Ryckman, F. G. Shaw, W. W. Story, Henry James, John G. Whittier, J. J. G. Wilkinson—a most remarkable collection of powerful names.

The departments seem not to have been systematically arranged, but the writers sent what they had, the same writer furnishing articles on a variety of topics. Mr. F. G. Shaw published, in successive numbers, an admirable translation of George Sand's " Consuelo," and wrote against the iniquities of the principle of competition in trade. C. A. Dana noticed books, reported movements, criticized men and measures, translated poetry from the German, and sent verses of a mystical and sentimental character of his own. C. P. Cranch contributed poems and criticisms on art and music. J. S. Dwight paid attention to the musical department, but also wrote book reviews and articles on the social problem. W. H. Channing poured out his burning soul in denunciation of social wrong and painted in glowing colors the promise of the future. G. W. Curtis sent poetry and notes on literature and music in New York. T. W. Higginson printed there his " Hymn of Humanity." Messrs. Brisbane, Godwin and Greeley confined themselves to social problems, doing a large part of the heavy work. Mr. Ripley, the Managing Editor, supervised the whole ; wrote much himself on the different aspects of Association ; reported the progress of the cause at home and abroad ; answered the objections that were current in the popular prejudice, and gave to the paper the encouraging tone of his cheery, earnest spirit.

As interpreted by the " Harbinger," the cause of Association was hospitable and humane. The technicalities of special systems were avoided ; dry discussions of theory and method were put aside ; generous sympathy was shown towards philanthropic workers in other fields ; the tone of wailing was never heard, and the anticipations of the future were steadily bright and bold. When reformers of a pronounced type, like the abolitionists, spoke of it slightingly as a " kid glove " journal that was afraid of soiling its fingers with ugly matters like slavery, the Associationists explained that their plan was the more comprehensive; that they struck at the root of every kind of slavery; and that the worst evils would disappear when their beneficent principle should be recognized. That the "Harbinger" should have lived no longer than it did, with such a corps of writers and so great a cause,—the last number is dated February 10, 1849,—may be accounted for by the feeble hold that Socialism had in this country. In Europe the hearts of the working people were in it. It originated among them, expressed their actual sorrows, answered their living questions, promised satisfaction to their wants, and predicted the only future they could imagine as in any way possible. Here it was an imported speculation; the working people were not driven to it for refuge from their misery; they did not ask the questions it proposed to answer, nor did it hold out prospects that gladdened their eyes. The advocates of it were cultivated men, literary and æsthetical, who represented the best the old world had to give, rather than the worst the New World had experienced; and their words met with no response from the multitudes in whose behoof they were spoken. America was exercised then by questions of awful moment. The agitation against slavery had taken hold of the whole country; it was in politics, in journalism, in literature, in the public hall and the parlor. Its issues were immediate and urgent. People had neither heads nor hearts for schemes of comprehensive scope that must be patiently meditated and matured for generations. No talents, no brilliancy, no earnestness even, would engage interest in what seemed visionary, however glorious the vision.   The socialistic enterprises in America were all short lived.   Brook Farm was an idyl; and in the days of epics, the idyl is easily forgotten.

The decease of the " Harbinger " was the end of that phase of Transcendentalism.   The dream of the king-dom of heaven faded.   The apostles were dispersed. Some kept their faith and showed their fidelity in other places and other work.   Three or four went into the Roman Church, and found rest on its ancient bosom. Others found a field for their talents in literature, which they beautified with their genius, and ennobled by their ideas.   Others devoted themselves to journalism.   Of the last was George Ripley.   *The New York Tribune* offered him the post of literary critic on its editorial staff. That position he has occupied for twenty-five years, in a way honorable to himself and to good letters.   It has been in his power to aid the development of litera-ture in America, in many ways, by encouraging young writers; by giving direction to ambitious but immature gifts; by erecting a standard of judgment, high, without being unreasonable, and strict, without being austere. A large acquaintance with books, a cultivated taste, a hospitable appreciation, a hearty love of good literary work, a cordial dislike of bad, a just estimation of the rights and duties of literary men, and the office they should fill in a republican community, have marked his administration of the department assigned to him.   He has held it to be his duty to make intelligent reports of current literature, with enough of criticism to convey his own opinion of its character, without dictating opinions to others. Worthless books received their due, and worthy books received theirs in full measure. The books in which worth and worthlessness were united were discriminatingly handled, the emphasis being laid on the better qualities. Many of the reviews were essays, full of discernment. All showed that respect for mind which might be expected from one so carefully trained.

Mr. Ripley has been true to the ideas with which he set out in his early life. His period of philosophical propagandism being over ; his young enthusiasm having spent itself in experiments which trial proved to be premature, to say the least, if not essentially impracticable; his dreams having faded, when his efforts ended in disappointment, he retired from public view neither dispirited, nor morose. His interest in philosophy continues undiminished; his hope of man, though more subdued, is clear ; his faith in the spiritual basis of religion is serene. Disappointment has not made him bitter, reckless or frivolous. His power of moral indignation at wrong and turpitude is unimpaired, though it no longer breaks out with the former vehemence. A cheerful wisdom gained by thought and experience of sorrow, tempers his judgment of men and measures. His confidence is in culture, in literature, generously interpreted and fostered, in ideas honestly entertained and freely expressed.

The Transcendentalist keeps his essential faith. Generally the Transcendentalists have done this. It was a faith too deeply planted, too nobly illustrated, too fervent and beautiful in youth, to be laid aside in age. James Walker died in the ripeness of it ; Parker died in the strength of it ; others—old and grave men now—live in the joy of it.   The few who have relapsed, have done so, some under pressure of worldly seduction—they having no depth of root—and some under the influence of scientific teaching, which has shaken the foundation of their psychology.   The original disciples, undismayed by the signs of death, still believe in the Master, and live in the hope of his resurrection.

XIV.

MINOR PROPHETS

THE so-called Minor Prophets of the Old Testament owed that designation to the brevity, rather than to the insignificance of their utterances. They were among the most glowing and exalted of the Hebrew bards, less sustained in their flight than their great fellows, but with as much of the ancient fire as any of them. It is proper to say as much as this to justify the application of the title to the men who claim mention now as prominent in the transcendental movement.

William Henry Channing is not quite fairly ranked among minor prophets, even on this explanation, for he has been copious as well as intense. A nephew of the great Doctor Channing—a favorite, nephew, on account of his moral earnestness, and the close sympathy he felt with views that did honor to human nature and glorified the existence of man,—he grew up in the purest atmosphere that New England supplied—the most intellectual, the most quickening. He was born in the same year with Theodore Parker, and but three months earlier, and was native to the same spiritual climate. He was educated at Harvard, and prepared for the ministry at Cambridge Divinity School, where the new ideas were fermenting. He was graduated the year before Parker entered. His name was conspicuous among the agitators of the new faith. He was a contributor to the "Dial." In 1848 he published the Memoirs of his uncle, in three volumes, proving his fitness for the task by the sincerity in which he discharged it. In 1840 he translated Jouffroy's Ethics, in two volumes, for Ripley's "Specimens of Foreign Standard Literature." In 1852 he took part in writing the Memoirs of Margaret Fuller, the second volume being chiefly his work. "The Life and Writings of James H. Perkins," of Cincinnati, a pioneer of rationalism at the West, came more fitly from his pen than from any other. In the "Western Messenger," which he edited for one year; the "Present," and the "Spirit of the Age," short-lived journals, of which he was the soul; in the "Harbinger," to which he was a generous and sympathetic contributor—he exhibited a fine quality of genius. The intensity of his nature, his open-mindedness, frankness, and spiritual sensitiveness, his fervency of aspiration and his outspokenness, made the office of settled pastor and steady routine preacher distasteful to him. He was a prophet who went from place to place, with a message of joy and hope. Meadville, Cincinnati, Nashua, Rochester, Boston, and New York, were scenes of his pastoral service. His preaching was every where attended by the clearest heads and the deepest hearts. In New York his society was composed of free elements altogether, come-outers, reformers, radicals of every description. His command of language, his free delivery, his musical voice, his expressive countenance, his noble air, his extraordinary power of kindling enthusiasm, his affluence and boldness of thought, his high standard of character, made him in his prime an enchanting speaker.

Very early in his career Mr. Channing committed himself to the transcendental philosophy as interpreted by the French School, for he possessed the swiftness of perception, the felicity of exposition, the sensibility to effects, the passion for clean statement and plausible generalization that distinguish the French genius from the German and the English. The introduction to Jouffroy's Ethics contained the principles of the French school of philosophy, which, to judge from his approving tone, he had himself accepted:

That Psychology is the basis of Philosophy.

That the highest problems of Ontology may be solved by inductions from the facts which Psychology ascertains.

That Psychology and the History of Philosophy reciprocally explain each other.

With these ideas firmly fixed in his mind he went forth on a prophetic mission, to which he remained unfalteringly true.

We saw him first at a convention in Boston called by the reformers who demanded the abolition of the gallows. There were several speakers—Edwin H. Chapin, then in the days of his moral enthusiasm, Wendell Phillips, already known as an agitator and an orator— all spoke well from their different grounds, but the image of Channing is the most distinct in mind to-day.

His manner, attitude, speech, are all recalled. The arguments he used abide in memory. He wasted words on no incidental points of detail, but at once took his stand on the principle of the idealist that man is a sacred being, and life a sacred gift, and love the rule of the divine law. Chapin thundered; Phillips criticized and stung; Channing burned with a pure enthusiasm that lifted souls into a celestial air and made all possibilities of justice seem practicable. He did not argue or denounce; he prophesied. There was not a word of scorn or detestation; but there were passages of touching power, describing the influence of gentleness and the response that the hardest hearts would give to it, that shamed the listeners out of their vindictiveness. On the anti-slavery platform his attitude was the same. There was no more persuasive speaker.

In the controversy between the Unitarians of the transcendental and those of the opposite school, Mr. Channing's sympathies were with the former, but he took no very prominent public part in it. He was averse to controversy; questions of sectarian opinion and organization had little interest for him. His mind lived in broad principles and positive ideas; the method he believed in was that of winning minds to the truth by generous appeals, and so planting out error. Against everything like injustice or illiberality, his protest was eager, but he was willing to leave polemics to others; what he said was in the strain of faith in larger and more inclusive beliefs. He had a passion for catholicity, which came partly from his temperament, and partly

from the eclecticism he professed. His word was re-
conciling, like his influence, which was never associated
with partisanship.

Mr. Channing was early attracted to the bearings of
the spiritual philosophy on the problems of society, the
elevation of the working classes, the rescue of humanity
from pauperism and crime. As an interpreter of Christian socialism his activity was incessant. He took part in
the discussions that led to the experiment of Brook
Farm, and was acquainted intimately with the projecting
of it, having himself entire faith in the reorganization of
society on principles of equity. Had circumstances permitted—he was then minister to a church in Cincinnati,
and much occupied with professional duties—he would
have connected himself with the Brook Farm Association.
As it was, he visited it whenever he could, spending several days at a time. In 1844, when the union was formed
with the New York Socialists and the leaders went out to
enlighten and stimulate public sentiment on the subject, Mr. Channing did faithful work as a lecturer. He
was president of the Boston Union of Associationists,
and wrote a book on the Christian Church and Moral
Reform. From the first, being of a speculative, philosophical and experimental turn of mind, he entertained
more systematic views than were common among New
England socialists, but the principle of love was always
more to him than opinions or schemes. His views coin-
cided with Fourier, but his heart was Christian. On the
failure of the associated plans of his friends, and the cessation of interest in Socialism on this side of the Atlantic,

his thoughts turned towards the Christian Church as the providentially appointed means of obtaining what the Utopians had failed of reaching. He was never a Churchman ; never abandoned the views that made him an independent preacher ; but he never lost faith in the ministry ; his hopes turned toward the institutions of religion as having in them the ideal potencies he trusted ; he looked for faith and love in the Gospel, and sought to draw out the lessons of charity that were inculcated by Jesus ; to deliver these from the hands of the formalists and sectarians ; to make peace between parties and churches ; to discover common ground for all believers to stand and labor on—was his aim. Had his faith not been inclusive of all forms of the religious sentiment, he might, in England, where he resided so long, have been a broad-churchman. But Christianity, in his view, was but one of many religions, all essentially divine, and he could not belong to any church less wide than the church universal.

During a portion of the civil war, Mr. Channing was in Washington preaching the gospel of liberty and loyalty, and laboring in the hospitals with unflagging devotion, thankful for an opportunity to put into work the enthusiasm of his passionate soul. Later, he revisited his native country, and showed his interest in the cause of religious freedom and unity.

The name of Channing is conspicuous in the history of American idealism. Another nephew of Dr. Channing, William F. Channing, was a man of original force of mind and character, a bold adventurer in literature and life, of independent ideas, principles and deeds, an abolitionist, a friend of Garrison and Parker, reformer and philosopher. W. E. was author of many volumes, wrote poetry and prose for the "Dial," and, in 1873, a life of Henry Thoreau.

In the list of the Transcendentalists Cyrus Augustus Bartol must not be forgotten, a soaring mind enamored of thoughts on divine things, inextricably caught in the toils of speculation. Acute and brilliant, but wayward; with a quick eye for analogies, fanciful and eccentric, of clear intuitions, glimpses, perceptions astonishingly luminous; but without fixed allegiance to system, and therefore difficult to classify under any school. In the Unitarian controversy, which was a tryer of spirits, it was not always plain to observers in which camp he belonged; not that his fundamental principle was unsteady, but because his curious and critical mind was detained by considerations that others did not see; and his absolute sincerity gave expression to the moods of feeling as they passed over him. Some words in Parker's farewell letter to him seem to imply that at critical junctures they had been on opposite sides, but the difference could scarcely have touched fundamental truths. No man was further from the school of Locke, Paley or Bentham than C. A. Bartol. His Transcendentalism had a cast of its own; it was not made after any pattern; it took its color from an original genius illuminated by various reading of books, and by deep meditation in the privacy of the closet, and the companionship of nature of which he is a child-like worshipper. No wealth of human sympathy prevents his being a solitary. His song is lyrical; his prophecy drops like a voice from the clouds. In the agitations of his time he has had small share; organized and associated effort did not attract him. To many he represents the model Transcendentalist, for he seems a man who lives above the clouds,—not always *above* them, either.

His faith in the soul has never known eclipse. It waxes strong by its wrestling, and becomes jubilant in proportion as nature and life try to stare it out of countenance. Ballast is wings to him.

" Transcendentalism relies on those ideas in the mind which are laws in the life. Pantheism is said to sink man and nature in God; Materialism to sink God and man in nature, and Transcendentalism to sink God and nature in man. But the Transcendentalist at least is belied and put in jail by the definition which is so neat at the expense of truth. He made consciousness, not sense, the ground of truth; and in the present devotion to physical science, and turn of philosophy to build the universe on foundations of matter, we need to vindicate and reassert his promise. Is the soul reared on the primitive rock? or is no rock primitive, but the deposit of spirit—therefore in its lowest form alive, and ever rising into organism to reach the top of the eternal circle again, as in the well one bucket goes down empty and the other rises full? The mistake is to make the everlasting things subjects of argument instead of sight."

" Our soul is older than our organism. It precedes its clothing. It is the cause, not the consequence, of its material elements; else, as materialists understand, it does not exist."

" What is it that accepts misery from the Most High, defends the Providence that inflicts its woes, espouses its chastiser's cause, purges itself in the pit of its misery of all contempt of His commands, and makes its agonies the beams and rafters of the triumph it builds? It is an immortal principle. It is an indestructible essence. It is part and parcel of the Divinity it adores. It can no more die than he can. It needs no more insurance of life than its author does. Prove its title? It is proof itself of all things else. It is substantive, and everything adjective beside. It is the kingdom all things will be added to."

This was published in 1872, and proves that one Transcendentalist has kept his faith.

James Freeman Clarke as little deserves to be ranked among the Minor Prophets as any, for he was one of the earliest Transcendentalists, a contemporary and intimate ally of Parker, a co-worker with Channing, a close friend and correspondent of Miss Fuller, a sympathizer with Alcott in his attempts to spiritualize education, a frequent contributor to the "Dial," the intellectual fellow of the brilliant minds that made the epoch what it was. But his interest was not confined to the school, nor did the technicalities or details of the transcendental movement embarrass him; his catholic mind took in opinions of all shades, and men of all communions. His place is among theologians and divines rather than among philosophers. But, though churchly tastes led him away from the company of thinkers where he intellectually belonged, and an unfailing common sense saved him from the extravagances into which some of them fell, a Transcendentalist he was, and an uncompromising one. The intuitive philosophy was his guide. It gave him his assurance of spiritual truths;

it interpreted for him the gospels and Jesus ; it inspired his endeavors to reconcile beliefs, to promote unity among the discordant sects, to enlighten and redeem mankind.   His mission has been that of a spiritual peace-maker.   But while doing this, he has worked faithfully at particular causes ; was an avowed and earnest aboli-tionist in the anti-slavery days ; was ever a disbeliever in war, an enemy of vindictive and violent legislation, a hearty friend and laborer in the field of woman's elec-tion to the full privileges of culture and citizenship ; a man in whom faith, hope and charity abounded and abound ; a man of intellectual convictions which made a groundwork for his life.

Mr. Clarke is a conspicuous example of the way in which the intuitive philosophy leavened the whole mind. It associated him closely both with radicals and con-servatives ; with the former, because his principle in-volved faith in progress ; with the latter, because it im-plied respect for the progress of past times which insti-tutions preserved.   His conservatism attested the fidel-ity of his radicalism, and both avouched the loyalty of his idealism.   The conservative aspect of Transcenden-talism which was exhibited in the case of Mr. Channing, who never left the Christian Church, was yet more strikingly illustrated by Mr. Clarke.   All his books, but particularly the " Ten Great Religions," show the power of the transcendental idea to render justice to all forms of faith, and give positive interpretations to doc-trines obscure and revolting.   It detects the truth in things erroneous, the good in things evil.

A more remarkable instance of this tendency is Samuel Johnson's volume on the religions of India. None save a Transcendentalist could have succeeded in extracting so much deep spiritual meaning from the symbols and practices of those ancient faiths. The intuitive idea takes its position at the centre, and at once all blazes with glory.

" Man is divinely prescient of his infinity of mind as soon as he begins to meditate and respire."

"That a profound theistic instinct, the intuition of a divine and living whole, is involved in the primitive mental processes we are here studying, I hold to be beyond all question."

" From the first stages of its growth onwards, the spirit weaves its own environment; nature is forever the reflex of its life, and what but an unquenchable aspiration to truth could have made it choose Light as its first and dearest symbol, reaching out a child's hand to touch and clasp it, with the joyous cry, 'Tis mine, mine to create, mine to adore!'"

" Man could not forget that pregnant dawn of revelation, the discovery of his own power to rekindle the life of the universe."

" Man is here dimly aware of the truth that he makes and remakes his own conception of the divine; that the revealing of duty must come in the natural activity of his human powers."

" As far back as we can trace the life of man, we find the river of prayer and praise flowing as naturally as it is flowing now; we cannot find its beginning, because we cannot find the beginning of the soul."

These passages give the key to Mr. Johnson's explanation of the oriental religions, and to his little monograph on " The Worship of Jesus," and to the printed lectures, addresses, essays, sermons, in which subjects of religion, philosophy, political and social reform have been profoundly treated.

Mr. Johnson came forward when the excitement of transcendentalism was passing by; the " Dial" no longer marked the intellectual hours; the Unitarian controversy had spent its violence. It was in part owing to this, but more to the spiritual character of his genius, that his Transcendentalism was free from polemic and dogmatic elements; but it was none the less positive and definite for that—if anything, it was more so. In the divinity school he was an ardent disciple of the intuitive philosophy. On leaving Cambridge he became an independent minister of the most pronounced views, but of most reverent spirit; a " fideist" or faith man, he loved to call himself; his aim and effort was to awaken the spiritual nature, to interpret the spiritual philosophy, and to apply the spiritual laws to all personal, domestic and social concerns. Like all the Transcendentalists, he was a reformer, and an enthusiastic one; interested in liberty and progress, but primarily in intellectual emancipation and the increase of rational ideas. The alteration of the lot was incidental to the regeneration of the person. So absolute is his faith in the soul that he renders poetic justice to its manifestations, seeing indications of its presence where others see none, and glorifying where others are inclined to pity. The ideal side is never turned away from him. He discerned the angel in the native African, the saint in the slave, the devotee in the idolater. During the civil war, his faith in the triumph of justice and the establishment of a pure republic, converted every defeat into a victory ; as in the vision of Ezekiel, the Son of Man was ever visible riding on the monstrous beasts. If at any time his sympathy has seemed withdrawn from any class of social reformers, it has been because the phase of reform they presented held forth no promise of intellectual or moral benefit.

Mr. Johnson illustrates the individualism of the Transcendentalist. While Mr. Channing trusted in social combinations, and Mr. Clarke put his faith in organized religion, he had a clear eye to the integrity of the separate soul. He attended no conventions, joined no societies, worked with no associations, had confidence in no parties, sects, schemes, or combinations, but nursed his solitary thought, delivered his personal message, bore his private witness, and there rested.

Were Mr. Johnson more known, were his thoughts less interior, his genius less retiring, his method less private, his form of statement less close and severe, he would be one of the acknowledged and conspicuous leaders of the ideal philosophy in the United States, as he is one of the most discerning, penetrating, sinewy, and heroic minds of his generation.

A contemporary and intimate friend of Johnson, a Transcendentalist equally positive, but of more mystical type, is Samuel Longfellow. The two are interestingly contrasted, and by contrast, blended. Between them they collected and published a book of hymns—" Hymns of the Spirit "—to which both contributed original pieces, remarkably rich in sentiment, and of singular poetical merit. Johnson's were the more intellectual, Longfellow's the more tender; Johnson's the more aspiring, Longfellow's the more devout; Johnson's the more heroic and passionate, Longfellow's the more mystical and reflective. Like his friend, Longfellow is quiet and retiring—not so scholarly, not so learned, but meditative. His sermons are lyrics; his writings are serene contemplations, not white and cold, but glowing with interior and suppressed radiance. A recluse and solitary he is, too, though sunny and cheerful; a thinker, but not a dry one; of intellectual sympathies, warm and generous; of feeble intellectual antipathies, being rather unconscious of systems that are foreign to him than hostile to them. He enjoys his own intellectual world so much, it is so large, rich, beautiful, and satisfying, that he is content to stay in it, to wander up and down in it, and hold intercourse with its inhabitants; yet he understands his own system well, is master of its ideas, and abundantly competent to defend them, as his essays published in the "Radical" during its short existence, testify. He has published little; ill health has prevented his taking a forward place among reformers and teachers; but where he has ministered, his influence has been deep and pure. Not few are the men and women who ascribe to him their best impulses, and owe him a debt of lasting gratitude for the moral faith and intellectual enthusiasm he awakened in them.

Another remarkable man, of the same school, but of still different temper—a man who would have been greatly distinguished but for the disabilities of sickness—is

David A. Wasson. Though contemporary, he came forward later ; but when he came, it was with a power that gave promise of the finest things. As his latent faith in the intuitive philosophy acquired strength, he broke away from the Orthodoxy in which he had been reared, with an impulse that carried him beyond the lines of every organized body in Christendom, and bore him into the regions of an intellectual faith, where he found satisfaction. He has been a diligent writer, chiefly on Ethical and Philosophical themes, on the border land of theology. His published pamphlets and sermons on religious questions, even the best of them, give scarcely more than an indication of his extraordinary powers. He is a poet too, of fine quality ; not a singer of sentimental songs, nor a spinner of elegant fancies, but a discerner of the spirit of beauty. " All's Well," "Ideals," " The Plover," " At Sea," are worthy of a place in the best collections.

It has been the appointed task of Mr. Wasson to be on the alert against assaults on the intuitive philosophy from the side of material science. Like Transcendentalists generally, he has accepted the principles of his philosophy on the testimony of consciousness and as self-evidencing ; but more than most, he has regarded them as essential to the maintenance of truths of the spiritual order ; and as a believer in those truths, he has been holily jealous of the influence of men like Herbert Spencer, Mill, Bain, and the latest school of experimental psychologists. His doctrine, in its own essence, and as related to the objective or material system, is closely stated in the essay on the "Nature of Religion, contained in the volume, entitled "Freedom and Fellowship in Religion," recently published by the Free Religious Association. It is not easily quotable, but must be read through and attentively. Whoever will take pains to do that, may understand, not merely what Mr. Wasson's position is, but what fine analysis the intuitive philosophy can bring to its defence. A volume of Mr. Wasson's prose essays and poems would be a valuable contribution to the literature of Transcendentalism ; for he is, on the whole, the most capable critic on its side. Unfortunately for the breadth of his fame and the reach of his power, he writes for thinkers, and the multitude will never follow in his train.

The names of the disciples and prophets of Transcendentalism multiply as they are told off. There is T. W. Higginson, the man of letters—whom every body knows —a born Transcendentalist, and an enthusiastic one, from the depth of his moral nature, the quickness of his poetic sensibility, his love of the higher culture. His sympathies early led him to the schools of the ideal philosophy. He edited the works of Epictetus ; speaks glowingly on the "Sympathy of Religions ;" is interested in the pacification of the sects and churches on the basis of spiritual fellowship in truths of universal import ; lectures appreciatingly on Mohammed and Buddha ; holds Spencer in light esteem by the side of Emerson. In the controversial period—which was not ended when he left the Divinity School—he was entirely committed to the party of progress. Hennell's " Christian Theism" lay on his table at Divinity Hall. He was an ally of Parker; an abolitionist; the colonel of a black regiment in the civil war; and from the first has been a champion of woman's claim to fulness of culture and the largest political rights. A clear and powerful mind, that in controversy would make its mark, if controversy were to its taste, as it is not.

Earlier mention should have been made of John Weiss, who wrote philosophical articles thirty years ago, that won encomiums from the most competent judges— a student at Heidelberg, a scholar of Kant, and an admirer of his system. He too has a paper on "Religion and Science," in the volume of "Freedom and Fellowship," which will convince the most skeptical that the days of Transcendentalism are not numbered; a man of insight; poetical, according to Emerson's definition; supremely intellectual, capable of treading, with steady step, the hair lines of thought; a poet too, as verses in the "Radical" bear witness. The Philosophical and Æsthetic Letters and Essays of Schiller were presented to the American public by his hand. He wrote the preface to the American edition of Smith's Memoir of Fichte. The "Boston Quarterly," the "Massachusetts Quarterly," the "Christian Examiner," the "Radical," were illuminated by his brilliant thoughts on subjects of religious philosophy. The volume entitled "American Religion," published in 1871, shows the power of the spiritual philosophy to extract noble meanings from the circumstances of the New World. Weiss treads the border-land between religion and science, recognizing the claims of both, and bringing to their adjustment as fine intellectual scales as any of his contemporaries. His method is peculiar to himself; his is not the exulting mood of Emerson, or the defiant mood of Wasson; it is purely poetic, imaginative. The doctrine of the divine immanence is glorious in his eyes; the faith in personal immortality is taken into the inner citadel of metaphysics, where Parker seldom penetrated.

These men, Weiss and Wasson and Higginson, nursed in the transcendental school, thoroughly imbued with its principles, committed to them, wedded to them by the conflicts they waged in their defence when they were assailed by literalists, dogmatists, and formalists, look out now upon the advancing ranks of the new materialism as the holders of a royal fortress looked out on a host of insurgents; as the king and queen of France looked out on the revolution from the palace at Versailles: the onset of the new era they instinctively dread, feeling that dignity, princeliness, and spiritual worth are at stake. They will fight admirably to the last; but should they be defeated, it is yet possible that the revolution may bring compensations to humanity, which will make good the overthrow of their " diademed towers."

In these sketches of transcendental leaders—as in this study of the transcendental movement,—few have been included but those whom the intuitive philosophy drew away from their former church connections and gathered into a party by themselves—a party of protestants against literalism and formalism. The transcendental philosophy in its main ideas, was held by eminent orthodox divines who accepted it as entirely in accordance with the Christian scheme, and used it in fact as an efficient support for the doctrines of the church. The most eminent divines of New England did this, and were considered entirely orthodox in doing it, their Christian faith gaining warmth and color from the intuitive system. As has already been said, the Trinitarian scheme has close affinities with Platonism. But none of these men called themselves or were called Transcendentalists. The Transcendentalist substituted the principles of his Philosophy and the inferences therefrom for the creed of the church, and became a separatist. With him the soul superseded the church; the revelations of the soul took the place of bible, creed and priesthood. The men that have been named all did this, with the exception of James Freeman Clarke, who adhered to the ministry and the church. But his intimacy with the transcendental leaders, and his cooperation with them in some of their most important works, to say nothing of the unique position his transcendental ideas compelled him to assume, as well in ecclesiastical matters as in social reform, entitle him to mention. Convers Francis—parish minister at Watertown from 1819 till 1842, and Parkman professor of Pulpit Eloquence and the Pastoral Care at Cambridge from 1842 till 1863—though never conspicuous either as preacher or minister, and never recognized as a representative apostle, was influential as a believer in the spiritual philosophy, among young men. To him Theodore Parker acknowledged his debt; to him successive classes of divinity students owed the

stimulus and direction that carried them into the trans
cendental ranks; Johnson, Longfellow, Higginson were
his pupils at Cambridge, and carried thence ideas which
he had shaped if not originated. In many things conservative, disagreeing on some points with Emerson,
whom he revered and loved as a man, regretting much
that seemed sarcastic, arrogant, derisive in Parker's
"Discourse of Religion," he gave his full assent to the
principles of the intuitive philosophy, and used them as
the pillars of Christianity. Had he been as electric and
penetrating as he was truthful and obedient, high-
minded and sincere, hearty and simple, he would have
been a force as well as an influence. In 1836 he foresaw
the rupture between "the Old or English school belonging
to the sensual and empiric philosophy,—and the New or
German school, belonging to the spiritual philosophy,"
and gave all his sympathy to the latter as having the
most of truth. He was the senior member of the
"Transcendental Club," composed of the liberal thinkers who met to discuss literary and spiritual subjects on
the ground of reason and the soul's intuitive perceptions.
With deep interest he followed the course of speculative
and practical reform to the close of his life. Some, of
whom he was not one, engaged in the discussions for a
little while, attended the meetings, and set forth bold
opinions, but retired within their close fellowships as
soon as plans for propagandism or schemes of organization were proposed. Their sympathies were literary
and within the recognized limits of literature; but they
had either too little courage of conviction, or too little

conviction, to depart from accustomed ways or break with existing associations. The number of professed transcendentalists in the restricted sense, was never large, and, after the first excitement, did not greatly increase. There was but one generation of births. The genuine transcendentalists became so in their youth, ripened into full conviction in middle life, and, as a rule, continued so to old age. The desertions from the faith were not many. Half a dozen perhaps became catholics; as many became episcopalians; but by far the greater part maintained their principles and remained serene dissenters, "in the world, but not of it."

Transcendentalism was an episode in the intellectual life of New England; an enthusiasm, a wave of sentiment, a breath of mind that caught up such as were prepared to receive it, elated them, transported them, and passed on,—no man knowing whither it went. Its influence on thought and life was immediate and powerful. Religion felt it, literature, laws, institutions. To the social agitations of forty years ago it was invaluable as an inspiration. The various reforms owed everything to it. New England character received from it an impetus that never will be spent. It made young men see visions and old men dream dreams. There were mounts of Transfiguration in those days, upon which apostles thought they communed visibly with lawgivers and prophets. They could not stay there always, but the memory will never cease to be glorious. Transcendentalism as a special phase of thought and feeling was of necessity transient—having done its work it terminated its existence. But it did its work, and its work was glorious. Even its failures were necessary as showing what could not be accomplished, and its extravagances as defining the boundaries of wise experiment. Its successes amply redeemed them all, and would have redeemed them had they been more glaring and grotesque. Had it bequeathed nothing more than the literature that sprung from it, and the lives of the men and women who had their intellectual roots in it, it would have conferred a lasting benefit on America. The philosophical school has taken refuge in St. Louis, and there comes to surprising life in "The Journal of Speculative Philosophy" conducted by Wm. T. Harris, an accomplished thinker and educator, who keeps alive the interest in German thought in the West. Through him and his little band of helpers the names of Kant, Schelling and Hegel are made illustrious again. Eastern Transcendentalism turns its eyes thitherward, if not with glowing anticipations for the future, still with hearty satisfaction in the present.

XV.

LITERATURE.

A few words on the literary fruits of Transcendentalism will fitly close this history. To gather them all
would be exceedingly difficult, but that is not necessary, and will not be required. The chief results have
already been indicated. The indirect influence may be
left unestimated in detail. Transcendentalism has more
than justified itself in literature. The ten volumes of
Emerson's writings, including the two volumes of
poetry, are a literature by themselves ; a classic literature that loses no charm by age, and which years pre-
pare new multitudes of readers to enjoy.

The writings of Theodore Parker contain much that
entitles them to a permanent place in letters. Could
they be sifted, compressed, strained, the incidental and
personal portion discarded, and the human alone preserved, the remainder would interest, for many years yet,
a numerous class of men. In their present condition they
are too diffuse, as well as too voluminous and miscellaneous to be manageable. The sermon style is unsuited to
literature, and Parker's sermon style was especially so,
from its excessive redundancy. He paid little heed to
the literary laws in his compositions, which were all de-

signed for immediate effect.   Aside from the fatal injury
that the process must do to the intellectual harmony of
the work, there is an objection to abbreviating and
abstracting when an author does not perform the task
for himself, for no other is credited with ability or
judgment to do it for him.   In Parker's case the difficulty
would be more than commonly great, for the reason
that it is not a question of omitting volumes, or even
chapters, but of straining the contents of pages,—
"boiling down" masses of material, till the spiritual
residue alone is left.   There is no likelihood that such a
task will ever be performed, and therefore his writings
must be placed in the rank of occasional literature, valuable for many days, but not precious for generations.

Brownson's writings were astonishingly able, particularly his discussions in the Boston "Quarterly Review;"
but their interest ceased with their occasion.   His philosophical pieces have no value.   They served polemically
an incidental purpose, but having no merit of idea
or construction, they perished.

The papers of Mr. Alcott in "Tablets" and "Concord Days," are thoughtful and quaint, written with a
lucid simplicity that will always possess a charm for a
small class of people ; but they have not the breadth of
humanity that commends writings to the general acceptance ; nor have they the raciness that makes books of
their class spicy and aromatic to the literary epicures
who never tire of Selden or Sir Thomas Browne.

The writings of Margaret Fuller possess a lasting
value, and will continue to be read for their wit and wis·

dom, when those of her more ambitious companions are forgotten. For she treated ever-recurring themes in a living way—vigorous and original, but human. Her taste was educated by study of the Greek classics, and she had the appreciation of form that belongs to the literary order of mind. Her writings are not for those who read as they run, but for those who read for instruction and suggestion. As the number of such increases, it is not unreasonable to expect an increase in her audience. With her, thinking and talking were serious matters. She discussed nothing in a spirit of frivolity; her thoughts came from a penetrating, and not from a merely acute mind ; the trains of reflection that she started are still in motion, from the momentum she gave, and the goal she aimed at is not yet discerned by professed disciples of her own ideas.

The " Dial " is a treasury of literary wealth. There are pieces in it of prose and verse that should not and will not be lost. The character for oddity and extravagance which Transcendentalism bore in its day, and has borne on the strength of tradition ever since, would have to be borne no longer, if the contents of that remarkable magazine could be submitted to the calmer judgment of to-day. Not that the sixteen rich numbers contain a great deal that would be pleasing to the hasty mental habit of this generation, but to the lovers of earnest thinking and eloquent writing they have the flavor of a choice intellectual vintage. It is the misfortune of periodical literature to be ephemeral. The magazine sows, but does not harvest. It brings thoughts suddenly to the light, but buries them in season for the next issue, which must have its turn to live. Volumes that are compiled from magazines have lost their bloom. The chapters have already discharged their virtue, and spent their perfume on the air ; the smell of the " old numbers " clings to the pages, which are not of to-day, but of the day before yesterday. We call for living mind, and fancy that butterflies, because we see them fluttering in the garden, are more alive than the phœnix that has risen unscathed from the ashes of consuming fires.

The thoughts of William Henry Channing, though keen, brilliant, of great potency in their time, and admirable in expression, were addressed to the exigencies of the hour, and absorbed by them. Such as were committed to paper in the " Harbinger," the " Spirit of the Age," and other periodicals, will never be heard of again ; and such as were printed in books passed from memory with the themes he dealt with. His biographical works deserve a place with the prominent contributions of that department.

The poetry of William Ellery Channing has a recognized place in American literature, though much of it has disappeared. Dana's " Household Book of Poetry " contains a single piece of his on " Death," that is characterized by a depth of sentiment and a richness of expression, which his more distinguished contemporary, Mr. Bryant, does not surpass. Mr. Emerson's " Parnassus" contains eight, the last of which, entitled " A Poet's Hope," closes with the wonderful line—

" If my bark sink, 'tis to another sea."

Of Cranch's poems, several have been adopted by collectors,—notably the lines—

> " Thought is deeper than all speech—
> Feeling deeper than all thought;
> Soul to soul can never teach
> What unto itself was taught."

Weiss, Wasson, and Higginson are true artists in letters. The essays of the last named of the three are the best known, partly by reason of their greater popularity of theme ; but Mr. Wasson's discussions on ethical and philosophical subjects are distinguished by their luminous quality. Except for the vein of unhopefulness —partly due to ill health—that pervades them, the chill communicated by the regions he sails by, three or four of them would, without hesitation, be classed among the gems of speculative literature. The best work of Weiss, his lectures on the Greek Ideas for example, stands apart by itself, perhaps unrivalled as an attempt to unveil the glory of the ancient mythology. The interpretation of religious symbols is his province, where, by the power of " sympathetic perception,"—to use Mr. Wasson's fine phrase—he penetrates the secret of mysteries, and brings the soul of dark enigmas to the light ; and his beauty of expression more than restores to the imagination the splendors which the unpoetic interpreter reduces to meretricious fancy.

The influence of Transcendentalism on pulpit literature—if there be such a thing—has probably been sufficiently indicated ; but the privilege of printing a sermon of Mr. Emerson's—the only one ever published, the famous one, that was the occasion of his leaving the ministry and adopting the profession of literature— affords opportunity for a special illustration. The sermon —which is interesting in itself, from the subject, the occasion that called it forth, the insight it gives into Mr. Emerson's mind and character—is interesting as an example of the method and spirit which Transcendentalism introduced into discussions that are usually dry and often angry.

The Kingdom of God is not meat and drink, but righteousness, and peace, and joy in the Holy Ghost.—ROMANS XIV. 17.

IN the history of the Church no subject has been more fruitful of controversy than the Lord's Supper. There never has been any unanimity in the understanding of its nature, nor any uniformity in the mode of celebrating it. Without considering the frivolous questions which have been lately debated as to the posture in which men should partake of it; whether mixed or unmixed wine should be served; whether leavened or unleavened bread should be broken; the questions have been settled differently in every church, who should be admitted to the feast, and how often it should be prepared. In the Catholic Church, infants were at one time permitted and then forbidden to partake; and, since the ninth century, the laity receive the bread only, the cup being reserved to the priesthood. So, as to the time of the solemnity. In the fourth Lateran Council, it was decreed that any believer should communicate at least once in a year—at Easter. Afterwards it was determined that this Sacrament should be received three times in the year—at Easter, Whitsuntide, and Christmas. But more important controversies have arisen respecting its nature. The famous question of the Real Presence was the main controversy between the Church of England and the Church of Rome. The doctrine of the Consubstantiation taught by Luther was denied by Calvin. In the Church of England, Archbishops Laud and Wake maintained that the elements were an Eucharist or sacrifice of Thanksgiving to God; Cudworth and Warburton, that this was not a sacrifice, but a sacrificial feast; and Bishop Hoadley, that it was neither a sacrifice nor a feast after sacrifice, but a simple commemoration. And finally, it is now near two hundred years since the Society of Quakers denied the authority of the rite altogether, and gave good reasons for disusing it.

I allude to these facts only to show that, so far from the supper being a tradition in which men are fully agreed, there has always been the widest room for difference of opinion upon this particular.

Having recently given particular attention to this subject, I was led to the conclusion that Jesus did not intend to establish an institution for perpetual observance when he ate the Passover with his disciples; and, further, to the opinion, that it is not expedient to celebrate it as we do. I shall now endeavor to state distinctly my reasons for these two opinions.

I. The authority of the rite.

An account of the last supper of Christ with his disciples is given by the four Evangelists, Matthew, Mark, Luke, and John.

In St. Matthew's Gospel (Matt. XXVI. 26-30) are recorded the words of Jesus in giving bread and wine on that occasion to his disciples, but no expression occurs intimating that this feast was hereafter to be commemorated.

In St. Mark (Mark XIV. 23) the same words are recorded, and still with no intimation that the occasion was to be remembered.

St. Luke (Luke XXII. 15), after relating the breaking of the bread, has these words : This do in remembrance of me.

In St. John, although other occurrences of the same evening are related, this whole transaction is passed over without notice.

Now observe the facts. Two of the Evangelists, namely, Matthew and John, were of the twelve disciples, and were present on that occasion. Neither of them drops the slightest intimation of any intention on the part of Jesus to set up anything permanent. John, especially, the beloved disciple, who has recorded with minuteness the conversation and the transactions of that memorable evening, has quite omitted such a notice. Neither does it appear to have come to the knowledge of Mark who, though not an eye-witness, relates the other facts. This material fact, that the occasion was to be remembered, is found in Luke alone, who was not present. There is no reason, however, that we know, for rejecting the account of Luke. I doubt not, the expression was used by Jesus. I shall presently consider its meaning. I have only brought these accounts together, that you may judge whether it is likely that a solemn institution, to be continued to the end of time by all mankind, as they should come, nation after nation, within the influence of the Christian religion, would have been established in this slight manner—in a manner so slight, that the intention of commemorating it should not appear, from their narrative, to have caught the ear or dwelt in the mind of the only two among the twelve who wrote down what happened.

Still we must suppose that the expression, "*This do in remembrance of me,*" had come to the ear of Luke from some disciple who was present. What did it really signify? It is a prophetic and an affectionate expression. Jesus is a Jew, sitting with his countrymen, celebrating their national feast. He thinks of his own impending death, and wishes the minds of his disciples to be prepared for it. "When hereafter," he says to them, "you shall keep the Passover, it will have an altered aspect to your eyes. It is now a historical covenant of God with the Jewish nation. Hereafter, it will remind you of a new covenant sealed with my blood. In years to come, as long as your people shall come up to Jerusalem to keep this feast, the connection which has subsisted between us will give a new meaning in your eyes to the national festival, as the anniversary of my death." I see natural feeling and beauty in the use of such language from Jesus, a friend to his friends ; I can readily imagine that he was willing and desirous, when his disciples met, his memory should hallow their intercourse; but I cannot bring myself to believe that in the use of such an expression he looked beyond the living generation, beyond the abolition of the festival he was celebrating, and the scattering of the nation, and meant to impose a memorial feast upon the whole world.

Without presuming to fix precisely the purpose in the mind of Jesus, you will see that many opinions may be entertained of his intention, all consistent with the opinion that he did not design a perpetual ordinance. He may have foreseen that his disciples would meet to remember him, and that with good effect. It may have crossed his mind that this would be easily continued a hundred or a thousand years—as men more easily transmit a form than a virtue—and yet have been altogether out of his purpose to fasten it upon men in all times and all countries.

But though the words, *Do this in remembrance of me*, do not occur in Matthew, Mark, or John, and although it should be granted us that, taken alone, they do not necessarily import so much as is usually thought, yet many persons are apt to imagine that the very striking and personal manner in which this eating and drinking is described, indicates a striking and formal purpose to found a festival. And I admit that this impression might probably be left upon the mind of one who read only the passages under consideration in the New Testament. But this impression is removed by reading any narrative of the mode in which the ancient or the modern Jews have kept the Passover. It is then perceived that the leading circumstances in the Gospels are only a faithful account of that ceremony. Jesus did not celebrate the Passover, and afterwards the Supper, but the Supper *was* the Passover. He did with his disciples exactly what every master of a family in Jerusalem was doing at the same hour with his household. It appears that the Jews ate the lamb and the unleavened bread, and drank wine after a prescribed manner. It was the custom for the master of the feast to break the bread and to bless it, using this formula, which the Talmudists have preserved to us, " Blessed be Thou, O Lord our God, the King of the world, who hast produced this food from the earth,"—and to give it to every one at the table. It was the custom of the master of the family to take the cup which contained the wine, and to bless it, saying, "Blessed be Thou, O Lord, who givest us the fruit of the vine,"—and then to give the cup to all. Among the modern Jews who in their dispersion retain the Passover, a hymn is also sung after this ceremony, specifying the twelve great works done by God for the deliverance of their fathers out of Egypt.

But still it may be asked, why did Jesus make expressions so extraordinary and emphatic as these—"This is my body which is broken for you. Take ; eat. This is my blood which is shed for you. Drink it."—I reply they are not extraordinary expressions from him. They were familiar in his mouth. He always taught by parables and symbols. It was the national way of teaching and was largely used by him. Remember the readiness which he always showed to spiritualize every occurrence. He stooped and wrote on the sand. He admonished his disciples respecting the leaven of the Pharisees. He instructed the woman of Samaria respecting living water. He permitted himself to be anointed, declaring that it was for his interment. He washed the feet of his disciples. These are admitted to be symbolical actions and expressions. Here, in like manner, he calls the bread his body, and bids the disciples eat. He had used the same expression repeatedly before. The reason why St. John does not repeat his words on this occasion, seems to be that he had reported a similar discourse of Jesus to the people of Capernaum more at length already (John VI. 27). He there tells the Jews, "Except ye eat the flesh of the Son of Man and drink His blood, ye have no life in you." And when the Jews on that occasion complained that they did not comprehend what he meant, he added for their better understanding, and as if for our understanding, that we might not think his body was to be actually eaten, that he only meant, *we should live by his commandment*. He closed his discourse with these explanatory expressions: "The flesh profiteth nothing; the *words* that I speak to you, they are spirit and they are life."

Whilst I am upon this topic, I cannot help remarking that it is not a little singular that we should have preserved this rite and insisted upon perpetuating one symbolical act of Christ whilst we have totally neglected all others—particularly one other which had at least an equal claim to our observance. Jesus washed the feet of his disciples and told them that, as he had washed their feet, they ought to wash one another's feet; for he had given them an example, that they should do as he had done to them. I ask any person who believes the

Supper to have been designed by Jesus to be commemorated forever, to go and read the account of it in the other Gospels, and then compare with it the account of this transaction in St. John, and tell me if this be not much more explicitly authorized than the Supper. It only differs in this, that we have found the Supper used in New England and the washing of the feet not. But if we had found it an established rite in our churches, on grounds of mere authority, it would have been impossible to have argued against it. That rite is used by the Church of Rome, and by the Sandemanians. It has been very properly dropped by other Christians. Why? For two reasons: (1) because it was a local custom, and unsuitable in western countries; and (2) because it was typical, and all understand that humility is the thing signified. But the Passover was local too, and does not concern us, and its bread and wine were typical, and do not help us to understand the redemption which they signified.

These views of the original account of the Lord's Supper lead me to esteem it an occasion full of solemn and prophetic interest, but never intended by Jesus to be the foundation of a perpetual institution.

It appears however in Christian history that the disciples had very early taken advantage of these impressive words of Christ to hold religious meetings, where they broke bread and drank wine as symbols.

I look upon this fact as very natural in the circumstances of the church. The disciples lived together; they threw all their property into a common stock;

they were bound together by the memory of Christ, and nothing could be more natural than that this eventful evening should be affectionately remembered by them ; that they, Jews like Jesus, should adopt his expressions and his types, and furthermore, that what was done with peculiar propriety by them, his personal friends, with less propriety should come to be extended to their companions also. In this way religious feasts grew up among the early Christians. They were readily adopted by the Jewish converts who were familiar with religious feasts, and also by the Pagan converts whose idolatrous worship had been made up of sacred festivals, and who very readily abused these to gross riot, as appears from the censures of St. Paul. Many persons consider this fact, the observance of such a memorial feast by the early disciples, decisive of the question whether it ought to be observed by us. For my part I see nothing to wonder at in its originating with them; all that is surprising is that it should exist among us. There was good reason for his personal friends to remember their friend and repeat his words. It was only too probable that among the half converted Pagans and Jews, any rite, any form, would find favor, whilst yet unable to comprehend the spiritual character of Christianity.

The circumstance, however, that St. Paul adopts these views, has seemed to many persons conclusive in favor of the institution. I am of opinion that it is wholly upon the epistle to the Corinthians, and not upon the Gospels, that the ordinance stands. Upon this

matter of St. Paul's view of the Supper, a few impor
tant considerations must be stated.

The end which he has in view, in the eleventh chapter of the first epistle is, not to enjoin upon his friends
to observe the Supper, but to censure their abuse of it.
We quote the passage now-a-days as if it enjoined
attendance upon the Supper; but he wrote it merely to
chide them for drunkenness. To make their enormity
plainer he goes back to the origin of this religious feast
to show what sort of feast that was, out of which this
riot of theirs came, and so relates the transactions of
the Last Supper. "*I have received of the Lord,*" he
says, "*that which I delivered to you.*" By this expression
it is often thought that a miraculous communication is implied; but certainly without good reason, if it is remembered that St. Paul was living in the lifetime of all the
apostles who could give him an account of the transaction; and it is contrary to all reason to suppose that
God should work a miracle to convey information that
could so easily be got by natural means. So that the
import of the expression is that he had received the
story of an eye-witness such as we also possess.

But there is a material circumstance which diminishes
our confidence in the correctness of the Apostle's view;
and that is, the observation that his mind had not
escaped the prevalent error of the primitive church, the
belief, namely, that the second coming of Christ would
shortly occur, until which time, he tells them, this feast
was to be kept. Elsewhere he tells them, that, at that
time the world would be burnt up with fire, and a new

government established, in which the Saints would sit on thrones ; so slow were the disciples during the life, and after 'the ascension of Christ, to receive the idea which we receive, that his second coming was a spiritual kingdom, the dominion of his religion in the hearts of men, to be extended gradually over the whole world.

In this manner we may see clearly enough how this ancient ordinance got its footing among the early Christians, and this single expectation of a speedy reappearance of a temporal Messiah, which kept its influence even over so spiritual a man as St. Paul, would naturally tend to preserve the use of the rite when once established.

We arrive then at this conclusion, *first*, that it does not appear, from a careful examination of the account of the Last Supper in the Evangelists, that it was designed by Jesus to be perpetual ; *secondly*, that it does not appear that the opinion of St. Paul, all things considered, ought to alter our opinion derived from the evangelists.

One general remark before quitting this branch of the subject. We ought to be cautious in taking even the best ascertained opinions and practices of the primitive church, for our own. If it could be satisfactorily shown that they esteemed it authorized and to be transmitted forever, that does not settle the question for us. We know how inveterately they were attached to their Jewish prejudices, and how often even the influence of Christ failed to enlarge their views. On every other subject succeeding times have learned to form a judgment more in accordance with the spirit of Christianity than was the practice of the early ages.

But it is said : " Admit that the rite was not designed to be perpetual. What harm doth it ? Here it stands, generally accepted, under some form, by the Christian world, the undoubted occasion of much good ; is it not better it should remain ? "

II. This is the question of expediency.

I proceed to state a few objections that in my judgment lie against its use in its present form.

1. If the view which I have taken of the history of the institution be correct, then the claim of authority should be dropped in administering it. You say, every time you celebrate the rite, that Jesus enjoined it ; and the whole language you use conveys that impression. But if you read the New Testament as I do, you do not believe he did.

2. It has seemed to me that the use of this ordinance tends to produce confusion in our views of the relation of the soul to God. It is the old objection to the doctrine of the Trinity,—that the true worship was transferred from God to Christ, or that such confusion was introduced into the soul, that an undivided worship was given nowhere. Is not that the effect of the Lord's Supper ? I appeal now to the convictions of communicants—and ask such persons whether they have not been occasionally conscious of a painful confusion of thought between the worship due to God and the commemoration due to Christ. For, the service does not stand upon the basis of a voluntary act, but is imposed by

authority. It is an expression of gratitude to Christ, enjoined by Christ. There is an endeavor to keep Jesus in mind, whilst yet the prayers are addressed to God. I fear it is the effect of this ordinance to clothe Jesus with an authority which he never claimed and which distracts the mind of the worshipper. I know our opinions differ much respecting the nature and offices of Christ, and the degree of veneration to which he is entitled. I am so much a Unitarian as this: that I believe the human mind cannot admit but one God, and that every effort to pay religious homage to more than one being, goes to take away all right ideas. I appeal, brethren, to your individual experience. In the moment when you make the least petition to God, though it be but a silent wish that he may approve you, or add one moment to your life,—do you not, in the very act, necessarily exclude all other beings from your thought? In that act, the soul stands alone with God, and Jesus is no more present to the mind than your brother or your child.

But is not Jesus called in Scripture the Mediator? He is the mediator in that only sense in which possibly any being can mediate between God and man—that is an Instructor of man. He teaches us how to become like God. And a true disciple of Jesus will receive the light he gives most thankfully; but the thanks he offers, and which an exalted being will accept, are not *compliments*—commemorations,—but the use of that instruction.

3. Passing other objections, I come to this, that the

use of the elements, however suitable to the people and
the modes of thought in the East, where it origin-
iated, is foreign and unsuited to affect us.   Whatever
long usage and strong association may have done in
some individuals to deaden this repulsion, I apprehend
that their use is rather tolerated than loved by any of
us.   We are not accustomed to express our thoughts
or emotions by symbolical actions.   Most men find the
bread and wine no aid to devotion and to some, it is a
painful impediment.   To eat bread is one thing ; to love
the precepts of Christ and resolve to obey them is quite
another.

The statement of this objection leads me to say that I
think this difficulty, wherever it is felt, to be entitled to
the greatest weight.   It is alone a sufficient objection to
the ordinance.   It is my own objection.   This mode of
commemorating Christ is not suitable to me.   That is
reason enough why I should abandon it.   If I believed
that it was enjoined by Jesus on his disciples, and that
he even contemplated making permanent this mode of
commemoration, every way agreeable to an eastern mind,
and yet, on trial, it was disagreeable to my own feelings,
I should not adopt it.   I should choose other ways which,
as more effectual upon me, he would approve more.
For I choose that my remembrances of him should be
pleasing, affecting, religious.   I will love him as a glorified friend, after the free way of friendship, and not pay
him a stiff sign of respect, as men do to those whom they
fear.   A passage read from his discourses, a moving
provocation to works like his, any act or meeting which

tends to awaken a pure thought, a flow of love, an original design of virtue, I call a worthy, a true commemoration.

4. Fourthly, the importance ascribed to this particular ordinance is not consistent with the spirit of Christianity. The general object and effect of this ordinance is unexceptionable. It has been, and is, I doubt not, the occasion of indefinite good; but an importance is given by Christians to it which never can belong to any form. My friends, the apostle well assures us that " the kingdom of God is not meat and drink, but righteousness and peace and joy, in the Holy Ghost." I am not so foolish as to declaim against forms. Forms are as essential as bodies; but to exalt particular forms, to adhere to one form a moment after it is out-grown, is unreasonable, and it is alien to the spirit of Christ. If I understand the distinction of Christianity, the reason why it is to be preferred over all other systems and is divine is this, that it is a moral system; that it presents men with truths which are their own reason, and enjoins practices that are their own justification; that if miracles may be said to have been its evidence to the first Christians, they are not its evidence to us, but the doctrines themselves; that every practice is Christian which praises itself, and every practice unchristian which condemns itself. I am not engaged to Christianity by decent forms, or saving ordinances; it is not usage, it is not what I do not understand, that binds me to it—let these be the sandy foundations of falsehoods. What I revere and obey in it is its reality, its boundless charity, its

deep interior life, the rest it gives to my mind, the echo it returns to my thoughts, the perfect accord it makes with my reason through all its representation of God and His Providence ; and the persuasion and courage that come out thence to lead me upward and onward. Freedom is the essence of this faith. It has for its object simply to make men good and wise. Its institutions, then, should be as flexible as the wants of men. That form out of which the life and suitableness have departed, should be as worthless in its eyes as the dead leaves that are falling around us.

And therefore, although for the satisfaction of others, I have labored to show by the history that this rite was not intended to be perpetual ; although I have gone back to weigh the expressions of Paul, I feel that here is the true point of view. In the midst of considerations as to what Paul thought, and why he so thought, I cannot help feeling that it is time misspent to argue to or from his convictions, or those of Luke and John, respecting any form. I seem to lose the substance in seeking the shadow. That for which Paul lived and died so gloriously ; that for which Jesus gave himself to be crucified ; the end that animated the thousand martyrs and heroes who have followed his steps, was to redeem us from a formal religion, and teach us to seek our well-being in the formation of the soul. The whole world was full of idols and ordinances. The Jewish was a religion of forms. The Pagan was a religion of forms ; it was all body—it had no life—and the Almighty God was pleased to qualify and send forth a man to teach men that they must serve him with the heart; that only that life was religious which was thoroughly good; that sacrifice was smoke, and forms were shadows. This man lived and died true to this purpose; and now, with his blessed word and life before us, Christians must contend that it is a matter of vital importance—really a duty, to commemorate him by a certain form, whether that form be agreeable to their understandings or not.

Is not this to make vain the gift of God? Is not this to turn back the hand on the dial? Is not this to make men—to make ourselves—forget that not forms, but duties; not names, but righteousness and love are enjoined; and that in the eye of God there is no other measure of the value of any one form than the measure of its use?

There remain some practical objections to the ordinance into which I shall not now enter. There is one on which I had intended to say a few words; I mean the unfavorable relation in which it places that numerous class of persons who abstain from it merely from disinclination to the rite.

Influenced by these considerations, I have proposed to the brethren of the Church to drop the use of the elements and the claim of authority in the administration of this ordinance, and have suggested a mode in which a meeting for the same purpose might be held free of objection.

My brethren have considered my views with patience and candor, and have recommended unanimously an adherence to the present form. I have, therefore, been compelled to consider whether it becomes me to admin-

ister it. I am clearly of opinion I ought not. This discourse has already been so far extended, that I can only
say that the reason of my determination is shortly this :
—It is my desire, in the office of a Christian minister, to
do nothing which I cannot do with my whole heart.
Having said this, I have said all. I have no hostility
to this institution ; I am only stating my want of sympathy with it. Neither should I ever have obtruded
this opinion upon other people, had I not been called by
my office to administer it. That is the end of my opposition, that I am not interested in it. I am content that
it stand to the end of the world, if it please men and
please heaven, and I shall rejoice in all the good it
produces.

As it is the prevailing opinion and feeling in our religious community, that it is an indispensable part of
the pastoral office to administer this ordinance, I am
about to resign into your hands that office which you
have confided to me. It has many duties for which I
am feebly qualified. It has some which it will always
be my delight to discharge, according to my ability,
wherever I exist. And whilst the recollection of its
claims oppresses me with a sense of my unworthiness, I
am consoled by the hope that no time and no change
can deprive me of the satisfaction of pursuing and exercising its highest functions.

September 9, 1832.

———

The influence of Transcendentalism on general literature can be only indicated in loose terms. Its current

was so strong, that like the Orinoco rushing down between the South American continent and the island of Trinidad, it made a bright green trail upon the dark sea into which it poured, but the vehemence of the flood forbade its diffusion. The influence was chiefly felt on the departments of philosophy and ethics. It created the turbulent literature of reform, the literature born of the "Enthusiasm of Humanity," the waves whereof are still rolling, though not with their original force. The literature of politics was profoundly affected by it; the political radicals, philosophical democrats, anti-slavery whigs or republicans, enthusiasts for American ideas, prophets of America's destiny, being, more or less wittingly, controlled by its ideas. In this department Parker made himself felt, not on the popular mind alone, but on the recognized leaders of opinion East and West. The writings of Sumner and his school owe their vigor to these ideas. In history Bancroft was its great representative, his earliest volumes especially revealing in the richness, depth, and hopefulness of their interpretations of men and measures, the faith in humanity so strongly characteristic of the philosophy he professed.

In poetry the influence is distinctly traceable, though here also it was confined within somewhat narrow limits. Bryant betrays scarcely perceptible marks of it, though he ascribed to Wordsworth a fresh inspiration of love for nature. It is hardly perceptible in Longfellow, whose verse, bubbling from the heart, gently meanders over the meadows and through the villages, gladdening daily existence with its music. Neither Bryant nor Longfellow had the intellectual passion that Transcendentalism roused. The earlier pieces of Lowell, the anti-slavery lyrics and poems of sentiment, were inspired by it. Whittier was wholly under its sway. The delicious sonnets of Jones Very were oozings from its spring. Julia Ward Howe's "Passion Flowers," though published as late as 1854, burn and throb with feeling that had its source in these heights.

The writers of elegant literature, essays, romances, tales, owed to Transcendentalism but a trifling debt, not worth acknowledging. They were out of range. It was their task to entertain people of leisure, and they derived their impulse from the pleasure their writings gave them or others. It was not to be expected that authors like Irving, Paulding, Cooper, would feel an interest in ideas so grave and earnest, or would catch a suggestion from them. But Lydia Maria Child, whose "Letters from New York"—1841, 1843—were models in their kind; whose stories for young people have not been surpassed by those of any writer, except Andersen; whose more labored works have a quality that entitles them to a high place among the products of mind, is a devotee of the transcendental faith. A very remarkable book in the department of fiction was Sylvester Judd's "Margaret; a tale of the Real and the Ideal; Blight and Bloom." It contained the material for half a dozen ordinary novels; was full of imagination, aromatic, poetical, picturesque, tender, and in the dress of fiction set forth the whole gospel of Transcendentalism in religion, politics, reform, social ethics, personal character, professional and private life.

As has been already remarked, the transcendental faith found expression in magazines and newspapers, which it called into existence, and which no longer survive. Its elaborate compositions were, from the nature of the case, few; its intellectual occupancy was too brief for the creation of a permanent literature. Had Transcendentalism been chiefly remarkable as a literary curiosity, the neglect of the smallest scrap of paper it caused to be marked with ink would be culpable. As it was, primarily and to the end, an intellectual episode, turning on a few cardinal ideas, it is best studied in the writings and lives of its disciples. They knew better than any body what they wanted; they were best acquainted with their own ideas, and should be permitted to speak for themselves. Earnest men and women no doubt they were; better educated men and women did not live in America; they were well born, well nurtured, well endowed. Their generation produced no warmer hearts, no purer spirits, no more ardent consciences, no more devoted wills. Their philosophy may be unsound, but it produced noble characters and humane lives. The philosophy that takes its place may rest on more scientific foundations; it will not more completely justify its existence or honor its day.

INDEX

DA⁺

90